HE DID NOT CONQUER

HE DID NOT CONQUER

Benjamin Franklin's Failure to Annex Canada

MADELAINE DROHAN

DUNDURN PRESS

Publisher: Meghan Macdonald | Acquiring editor: Kathryn Lane | Editor: Jess Shulman
Cover designer: Laura Boyle
Cover image: Portrait of Benjamin Franklin: Joseph Siffrein Duplessis; Map: "The United States of America laid down from the best authorities, agreeable to the Peace of 1783," John Wallis. Both images public domain.
Stamps on page 216: © Canada Post Corporation, 2021. Reproduced with Permission.

Library and Archives Canada Cataloguing in Publication

Title: He did not conquer : Benjamin Franklin's failure to annex Canada / Madelaine Drohan.
Other titles: Benjamin Franklin's failure to annex Canada
Names: Drohan, Madelaine, author
Description: Includes bibliographical references and index.
Identifiers: Canadiana (print) 20250155559 | Canadiana (ebook) 20250155613 | ISBN 9781459754188 (softcover) | ISBN 9781459754195 (PDF) | ISBN 9781459754201 (EPUB)
Subjects: LCSH: Franklin, Benjamin, 1706-1790. | LCSH: Canada—History—1775-1783.
Classification: LCC FC161 .D76 2025 | DDC 971.02—dc23

We acknowledge the support of the Canada Council for the Arts and the Ontario Arts Council for our publishing program. We also acknowledge the financial support of the Government of Ontario, through the Ontario Book Publishing Tax Credit and Ontario Creates, and the Government of Canada.

Printed and bound in Canada.

Dundurn Press
1382 Queen Street East
Toronto, Ontario, Canada M4L 1C9
dundurn.com, @dundurnpress

To David

Contents

A Note About Terminology and Map Sources

Alleghenies and Appalachians

These two names were used interchangeably in this period to describe the mountains that separated the thirteen colonies from the contested interior territories occupied by Indigenous Peoples and claimed by competing European powers. I use "Appalachian Mountains," except when the words "Allegheny" or "Alleghenies" appear in quotes.

Canada

The name "Canada" was used throughout this period. The area was also called "New France" under the French regime and the "Province of Quebec" under the British. The Royal Proclamation of 1763 set clear boundaries for the Province of Quebec, but the exact borders of Canada remained hazy. The name "Canada" first appeared on a printed map engraved in 1560 by Paolo Forlani in Venice. It appeared on maps throughout the eighteenth century, sometimes placed below the Great Lakes but most frequently above it, usually near Montreal, Trois-Rivières, and Quebec City. There were wide differences between French and British mapmakers about where the borders should be drawn. There were similar disagreements about the location of Louisiana and the western borders of the thirteen colonies. The maps used in this book illustrate these divergences and note whether it is a French or British view being depicted. I use the word "Canada" to describe this expanding and contracting territory. It does not include Newfoundland, Nova Scotia, and St. John's Island (Prince Edward Island), which were separate colonies.

Canadians and Americans

I use the words "Canadians" and "Americans" to describe the European colonists in North America because that is what they called themselves. For most of the period covered, this was a statement of geographic fact, not a cultural concept. Saying you were Canadian or American did not have the same patriotic implications that it does today. Nationalism was not born until the Americans created what Benedict Anderson, an Irish political scientist and historian, called "an imagined political community" that was both limited and sovereign. People could and did have multiple identities, describing themselves as being British, American, and from a particular colony all at the same time. Canadians were almost entirely French speaking and Roman Catholic throughout this period. After the British conquest in 1760, more English speakers from the thirteen colonies and Britain arrived, but they remained a small minority in Canada during the period covered by the book. After the conquest, I differentiate between French Canadians, English Canadians, and British authorities when appropriate. For Indigenous Peoples, see the entry below.

Currency

There is no accurate way to translate the currencies used in Franklin's time to exact modern equivalents. The colonists used whatever hard currency came to hand, including British pounds and Spanish dollars. They also used paper script. I have left them in their original amounts.

England and Britain

Great Britain was not created until the English and Scottish Parliaments passed the Acts of Union in 1707. Afterward, "England" and "Britain" were often used interchangeably. I use "England" and "Britain" and "English" and "British" in the appropriate time periods, unless the words are in quotes.

Gender-Specific Words

I have kept gender-specific words in the text for reasons of historical accuracy. For example, Franklin referred to himself as a tradesman and not a tradesperson.

Indigenous Peoples

In letters and documents from this time, Indigenous Peoples are referred to as "Indians," "savages," or worse, and their exact affiliation was infrequently given. When these derogatory terms appear in exact quotes, I have left them. Elsewhere, I use "Indigenous Peoples" or give the specific name of the group if it is available from the text. I have opted for this because the term "First Nations," which is widely used in Canada, is not commonly used in the United States. One of the two groups most frequently mentioned is the Six Nations (Seneca, Cayuga, Onondaga, Oneida, Mohawk, and Tuscarora). They mostly lived in what is now upper New York State and were largely allied with the British. They were sometimes referred to as Iroquois or the Iroquois Confederacy. They call themselves the Haudenosaunee Confederacy. Many moved to Canada after the revolution. The other main group is the Algonquian, a broad cultural and linguistic grouping whose members included the Algonquin, Mississauga, Ojibwe, Cree, Abenaki, Mi'kmaq, Wolastoqiyik, Innu, Niitsítapi, and others. They mostly lived in what is now Ontario and Quebec and were partners in the fur trade with the French. They call themselves Anishinabek. Members of both groups sometimes shifted their alliance from France to Britain or the reverse.

Maps

The maps in this book are based on original maps from the period. The old maps often contained errors in geography and scale. Transposing the originals onto more precise modern maps involved some guesswork, especially in drawing the borders. The borders in this book should be regarded as estimates. References for the source maps are listed in the Map Credits. The modern maps were created by Julie Witmer of Julie Witmer Custom Map Design.

Spelling and Capitalization

The eighteenth century was a bit of a free-for-all for spelling and capitalization. The same word could be spelled three different ways in the same letter. Capitals were put in for emphasis, wherever the writer pleased. I have left the original spelling and capitalization in direct quotes because it gives a distinct flavour to the writings from that time.

Introduction

BENJAMIN FRANKLIN WAS SICK IN BODY AND IN MIND WHEN HE FLED Montreal early in the morning of May 11, 1776. He had arrived less than a fortnight earlier, along with the richest man in the American colonies and a fellow delegate from the continental congress. The three were under instructions to salvage an increasingly shambolic American invasion of Canada that had begun with so much promise in 1775. Troops from the thirteen colonies had quickly taken Montreal and Trois-Rivières. If they could take Quebec City, where the British colonial governor was holed up, they would complete the conquest. But Franklin had been in Montreal only a week when British warships appeared on the St. Lawrence River, sparking the panicked retreat of the American troops who had besieged Quebec City through the harsh, northern winter. They abandoned cannon, muskets, and wounded comrades in their rushed escape. News that at least one British warship was continuing upriver to Montreal caused a chaotic departure from that city by its American occupiers. Franklin, seventy years old and suffering from boils, gout, and an illness he called scurf or scurviness, was bundled into a boat for the short crossing to the south shore of the St. Lawrence River and a long journey home. Accompanying him were the disappointed wives of two supporters of the Americans, one of whom kept shrewishly reminding him that he had failed utterly to wrest Canada from the British and make it the fourteenth colony.

It was an inglorious exit for a man lauded in Europe and America for his experiments with electricity and the invention of the lightning rod. Some admirers, like William Goforth, a young captain in the occupying army, seemed to think he had superpowers. "I understand you are a great man that you Can Turn the Common Course of nature, that you have power with the Gods and Can Rob the Clouds of their Tremendious Thunder," Goforth had written Franklin in February 1776. He urged the "old Trojan" to come to Canada and show the American army "how to Extract the Electric fire from the Center — then perhaps we may be able to draw a Vein athwart their Magazene and Send them upwards Cloathd as Elijah was with a Suit of fire."[1] Unfortunately for Franklin and his fellow commissioners, the easy conquest that congressional delegates envisaged had degenerated into a debacle before they arrived. The congress had bungled its first military invasion by not sending enough men, money, and provisions north, gullibly believing that tens of thousands of French Canadians in the British colony would welcome the invaders with open arms.

Franklin had suspiciously little to say about his dismal Canadian adventure, then or later. There is a gap in the flow of his personal correspondence that covers his entire stay in Montreal. Perhaps he was too busy or too ill to put pen to paper. What is more likely is that he wanted the whole miserable affair forgotten because it reflected badly on him as an individual and on the prospects for the American Revolution. Once back in Philadelphia, he moved on to other tasks, such as editing the Declaration of Independence, made after the failed invasion. Toward the end of the year, he sailed for France to plead for money, ships, and men for the revolt against Britain. And yet this silence on his part, which likely contributed to a subsequent lack of interest by historians and biographers, underplays the position Canada had long held in his imagination. Canada was where French and Indigenous raiding parties came from during his Boston childhood, a vast territory ripe for American expansion in his middle years, and a pawn to be played at the negotiating table in Paris toward the end of his life.

Over the course of his long career, Franklin made multiple attempts to make Canada American, sometimes by force and sometimes by guile. At times he was part of a chorus calling for it to be joined to the thirteen colonies. At other times, such as when he made a play for Canada while conducting preliminary negotiations in Paris to end the American Revolution, he worked alone. His desire to acquire the vast territory to the north and west of the thirteen colonies rose and fell on his list of priorities throughout his life, but it never disappeared. Even when he was pursuing more urgent goals — security for the American colonists, a union of the thirteen colonies, independence from Britain — he regularly worked possession of some or all Canadian territory into his proposed solutions.

His interest in Canada is notable because he was the most famous American colonist of his age and continues to be a revered founding father. Although some of his contemporaries sporadically shared his desire to possess Canada, he alone had a series of public platforms and positions he could use to vigorously promote and then actively pursue this goal. This was not an idea he fancied for a while and then discarded, unlike, for example, his belief that Britain and the rebellious American colonists would be able to resolve their differences and keep the empire intact. He came to it early on, most likely because French Canada posed a security threat to the thirteen colonies. But in the following decades, he went on to find other reasons for its annexation. His musings about population growth in the 1750s led him to believe that the swiftly growing American colonies needed space to expand, preferably the entire continent. He shared his thinking with the British public in his 1760 *Canada Pamphlet*, written while he was in London. He lent his formidable weight to the invasion of Canada by American colonists in 1775–1776, in the hope that American possession would deprive the British of a base from which to attack the thirteen colonies. Toward the end of the revolution, he asked Britain to hand over Canada as compensation for the damage caused by British troops during the revolution. "Annexation" is not too strong a word for what Franklin had in mind. He wanted the land, not the people. The French Canadians would be encouraged to leave or be assimilated, their lands sold to the highest bidder, and the territory populated by American colonists. Yet each of his efforts was stymied, often because those with the power to support him had other priorities. Illness, incompetence, and bad timing also played a part.

Franklin's long-standing interest in Canada does not feature highly in the many books, movies, television series, comic books, and plays about him written by Americans. During most of the period between the 1750s, when Franklin first pondered how to take over bits of Canada, and the 1780s, when he went for the lot, American colonists had bigger fish to fry. They were preoccupied with pushing France out of North America, fighting a revolution against imperial Britain, and finally, securing recognition of their independence from France and Britain. The bright glow from these successes all but obscured Franklin's failure to win Canada. His achievements in science and diplomacy and his position as a founding father shielded his lack of success from too much scrutiny. As with all icons, elements that showed Franklin in a less favourable light or did not contribute to the American founding myth were glossed over or left out by future historians.

But that does not explain why his efforts to join Canada to the thirteen colonies received the same offhand treatment from Canadians, for whom he posed an existential threat. Had the British given in to Franklin's entreaties in Paris, the colonies that make up modern Canada would have been absorbed into the newly created United States.

It would be wrong to say that Canadian historians have been completely silent on Franklin. There are Canadian works that provide snapshots of him at work on his Canada project. William Renwick Riddell, a prolific amateur historian and judge, focused on events in 1776 in his 1923 address to the Empire Club, titled "Benjamin Franklin's Mission to Canada and the Causes of Its Failure." Quebec historians Gustave Lanctôt and Marcel Trudel cover the Montreal mission and Franklin's activities in Paris in their separate books, *Canada and the American Revolution, 1774–1783* by Lanctôt and *La Révolution américaine: Pourquoi la France refuse le Canada, 1775–1783* by Trudel, but not the development of his thinking about Canada and his earlier attempts at annexation. More recently, Jeffers Lennox, a Canadian who teaches in the United States, picked up the story of 1776 in his book

North of America: Loyalists, Indigenous Nations, and the Borders of the Long American Revolution. None draws together the separate episodes, examines why Franklin tried, how he failed, and why his quest for Canada, despite its import, is not part of the story Canadians tell themselves about who they are and how they came to be.

This book is not a biography of Franklin. His major accomplishments in scientific, journalistic, diplomatic, and political realms are well covered in hundreds of other histories and biographies. It is an account of the times when his thoughts turned to Canada, an analysis of what drove his actions, and the results. Readers in both Canada and the United States will see a side of Franklin — and of themselves — not normally covered in books and films about this period.

Americans will likely celebrate the 250th anniversary of their Declaration of Independence in 2026 with all the hoopla that surrounds the centrepiece of their origin story (unless the current political and social turbulence sets that country on a far different course). What is lost amidst all the usual fireworks and flag-waving of Independence Day is that the revolution that Franklin helped bring to a successful close was also a foundational moment for Canada.

The 1783 Treaty of Paris, which officially ended the revolution, created not one but two political entities out of Britain's possessions in eastern North America. To the south of the border drawn by Franklin and his fellow negotiators in Paris lay the freshly minted United States of America: thirteen former British colonies whose new western boundary was the Mississippi River. These colonists were proudly republican and mostly Protestant. To the north lay the remnants of British North America: the colonies of Nova Scotia, Newfoundland, Quebec, and St. John's Island (now Prince Edward Island), and Prince Rupert's Land, the territory controlled by the Hudson's Bay Company. These colonists had largely remained loyal to the British Crown. The majority were French-speaking Catholics. They had little in common with the tens of thousands of royalist refugees from the United States and the Indigenous Peoples in Canada except that all three groups had made a conscious choice not to join the Americans. The Paris treaty set out the terms of bilateral relations between the United States and its northern neighbours, who later joined together to form the Dominion of Canada. Franklin's idea that Americans were destined to control the continent continued to resonate long after he died in 1790. Americans invaded Canada again during the War of 1812. They wanted to punish the British for not honouring the terms of the 1783 Paris treaty, but some of the invading generals declared they intended to stay. The term "manifest destiny" was coined in the 1840s, when the dream of continental control re-emerged in the United States. The creation of Canada as a country in 1867 was spurred on by the fear that armed Americans would turn their sights north after their civil war. The United States and Britain had plans for a possible conflict between Canada and the United States right up to the eve of the Second World War.[2] Donald Trump's ridicule of Canada as the fifty-first state and Justin Trudeau as its governor does not seem like gentle ribbing when seen in this context. The insecurity of the northern border, another of Franklin's concerns, has also resurfaced from time to time, although it is overshadowed by bigger problems on the border with Mexico. There are echoes of this concern in the frequent admonitions by American officials that Canada should contribute more to continental security by spending more on defence.

What Franklin thought of the failure of his Canada project remains a mystery. His later correspondence offers only glimpses of his thinking. After his return from Montreal, he complained to his sister Jane Mecom about the ignorance of Canadians and their unwillingness to become involved in the revolution. He appeared to be describing his experience in Canada in a 1779 letter to John Jay when he said that entering a country with no money and seizing provisions, horses, and carriages by force was a sure way to "disgust, offend, and by Degrees make Enemies of the whole People."[3] Money was again on his mind when he wrote his sister years later, agreeing with her that wars in general were costly and wrong. Referring to the Seven Years' War, in which Britain drove France out of North America with the aid of the American colonists, he remarked, "I am confident, that Canada might have been purchased from France for a tenth part of the money England spent in the conquest of it."[4]

Had Franklin finished his memoirs, he might have given a more detailed account of his overall quest. His autobiography ends shortly after he arrived in Britain in July 1757. The outline he sketched indicated he had more to say, including a proposed section labelled "Canada delenda est," which translates as "Canada must be destroyed." (Educated writers in that age were fond of sprinkling Latin phrases throughout their letters.) That was to be followed by sections on his *Canada Pamphlet* and its impact, projects he described as "drawn from me concerning the Conquest," and his 1776 trip to Canada.[5]

He never got around to writing any of it, so we are left to parse his letters and official reports he contributed to, such as the ones the commissioners wrote from Montreal. There is a certain wistful quality to the comment he made about Canada to a British friend in 1777. By that date, Franklin was in Paris and had time to catch up with his correspondence while he waited for ministers in the French court to officially recognize his existence as an American envoy. In Canada, he wrote his British friend, he had been "a Piece of a Governor, and I think a very good one, for a Fortnight; and might have been so till this time if your wicked Army, Enemies to all good Government, had not come and driven me out."[6]

How did it happen that the most famous American of his time, a man thought to have superpowers and who at one point held the fate of Canada in his hand, was unable to satisfy his desire? This book tells that story.

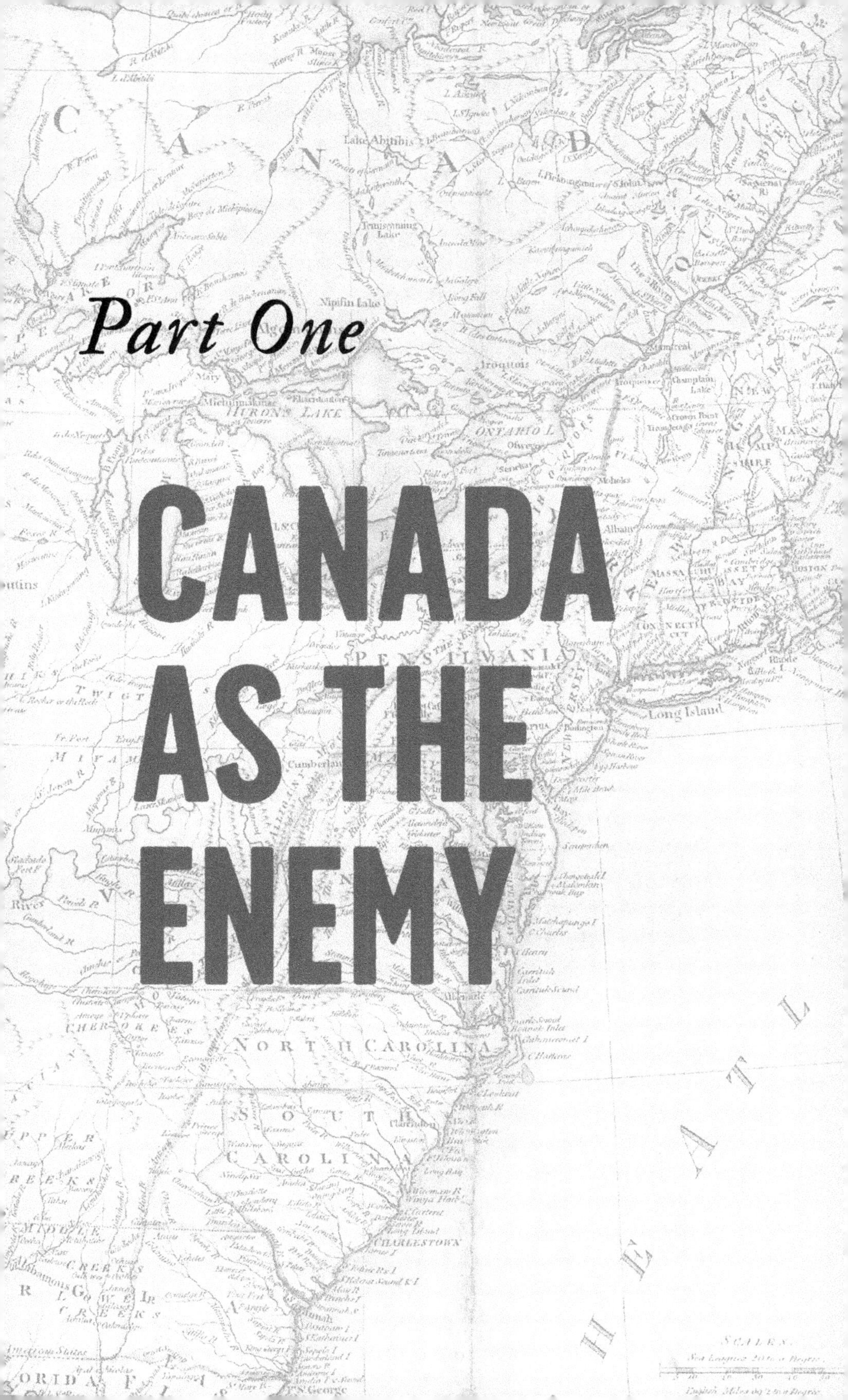

Part One

CANADA AS THE ENEMY

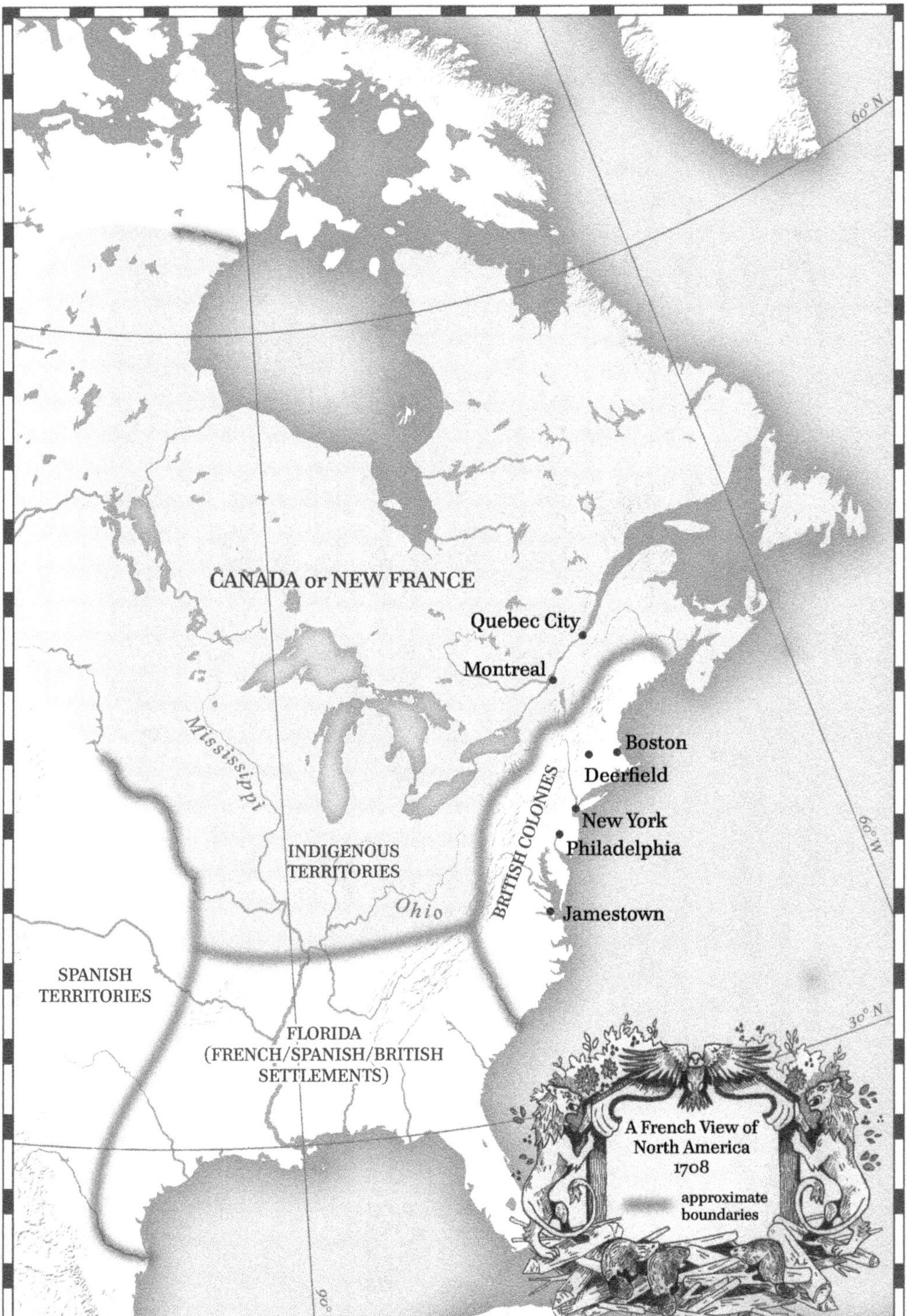

60° N
CANADA or NEW FRANCE
Quebec City
Montreal
Mississippi
Boston
Deerfield
New York
Philadelphia
BRITISH COLONIES
INDIGENOUS TERRITORIES
Ohio
Jamestown
60° W
SPANISH TERRITORIES
FLORIDA (FRENCH/SPANISH/BRITISH SETTLEMENTS)
30° N
90° W
A French View of North America 1708
approximate boundaries

CHAPTER 1

The Threat from the North: Boston 1706–1723

While the French retain their influence over the Indians, they can easily keep our long extended frontier in continual alarm, by a very few of those people; and with a small number of regulars and militia, in such a country, we find they can keep an army of ours in full employ for several years.[1]

— *Benjamin Franklin*

IN 1706, THE YEAR FRANKLIN WAS BORN, A BRIGANTINE CALLED *HOPE* sailed into Boston harbour, carrying fifty-seven hostages from Canada. They were part of a prisoner exchange arranged by the French governor of New France and the English governor of Massachusetts Bay. On board was John Williams, a Puritan minister. He, along with six of his children, had been captured two years earlier by French soldiers and their Indigenous allies in a bloody attack on the village of Deerfield, Massachusetts. Williams was a prize hostage. The governor of New France, Philippe de Rigaud, Marquis de Vaudreuil, bought him and two of his children from their Indigenous captors and then grimly hung on to them as bargaining chips until Joseph Dudley, governor of Massachusetts Bay, reluctantly agreed to exchange Captain Pierre Baptiste, a man the Boston merchants wanted hanged as a pirate.[2]

The arrival of the hostages attracted attention in Boston, then a seaport of less than ten thousand people. There was the controversial exchange of a minister for a pirate, which caused muttering in the fiercely Puritan colony. There was the forceful sermon about God and war Williams preached a few months after his return[3] to an assembly that included the governor. It was published and distributed in town. And there was his horrific, first-hand account of the attack on Deerfield and its sad aftermath, which he wrote about in his book, *The Redeemed Captive Returns to Zion*.

Williams said that about fifty French soldiers and two hundred Abenaki and Caughnawaga (Mohawk) had ransacked the frontier hamlet; murdered an untold number of people, including two of his children; and burned most of the dwellings. The captives were then forced to march almost five hundred kilometres (three hundred miles) north to Canada through snow that came up to their knees in places. Those who were too weak or ill to go on were killed and left by the trail. The slain included Williams's wife, who he said died when "the cruel and bloodthirsty savage who took her, slew her with his hatchlet at one stroke." About nineteen of the original one hundred people taken were dispatched along the way, he said, and another two starved to death. His tale was the stuff of frontier nightmares.

Franklin was far too young to hear first-hand of the brigantine's arrival. But such hostage exchanges and the bloody attacks that preceded them were commonplace during his childhood. Much later in life, he marvelled at how far he had come from the days when he cut wicks for his father, a tallow chandler and soap maker in Boston. "I did not think that I should ever literally *stand before kings*, which, however, has since happened," he wrote in his unfinished autobiography, "for I have stood before *five*, and even had the honor of sitting down with one, the King of Denmark, to dinner." Yet despite the outward change in his material circumstances and standing, events that took place in his youth made a deep impression and continued to influence him later in life. Understanding the environment in which he grew up, especially the religious and geopolitical context, offers clues to his later thinking about Canada.

The Backdrop of Franklin's Youth: French and English Relations in North America

Historians pinpoint different times in Franklin's adult life when he first focused on Canada, including when he was in his forties and his son marched off to battle, and even in his seventies, when he made a difficult, overland journey to Montreal. Yet Franklin would have been aware of Canada much earlier because of the dark shadow it cast over New England in his youth. It posed a physical threat because of frequent raids like the one in which Williams was captured. And it was seen as a threat to the Puritan religious movement and the colonial way of life. The colonists thought their French counterparts lived under the double tyranny of an absolutist monarch, who claimed power by divine right, and the Catholic pope in Rome. The English felt they possessed civil liberties denied to the French colonists and that their settlements were a refuge against absolutism. While they, too, swore allegiance to a monarch, royal powers in England were checked by Parliament. For much of their existence, the colonies had largely been left to their own devices by England. This enhanced their feeling of liberty.

Franklin was born at a time when England and France were actively trying to push each other out of North America. This was the local face of a global battle for supremacy between the Protestant English and Catholic French empires and their allies, a violent struggle for territory suffused with religious overtones. France was the pre-eminent power in Europe. The Dutch, British, and Austrians attempted to constrain it during the first half of the eighteenth century. Throughout Franklin's youth, the frontier conflict waxed and waned, depending on whether war had been declared in Europe between England and France. But it never went away.

The English colonies were strung out along the Atlantic coast, encircled by territory claimed by France and its allies, some of which was also claimed by Britain. Spain claimed Florida and parts of the southwest, north of Mexico. Sandwiched between the European powers were the original inhabitants, the Indigenous Peoples. They struck alliances, sometimes only temporary, with one side or the other or struggled to remain neutral. They in turn had their own internal rivalries and alliances that determined what role in the conflict they chose to take.

New France, according to the French, extended in an arc from Labrador in the northeast to the Gulf of Mexico in the southwest, encompassing Acadia (now parts of present-day Nova Scotia, New Brunswick, and Prince Edward Island), the St. Lawrence River Valley, and the Mississippi River Valley from its source to its mouth. The vast majority of French Canadians lived in or near the three major settlements of Montreal, Quebec City, and Trois-Rivières. There were scattered fur-trading posts in the area surrounding the Great Lakes, which the French called the *pays-d'en-haut* (the upper country). Often these posts were on Indigenous lands also claimed by England or Spain. For example, the 1609 charter for Virginia, given by King James I to the Virginia Company of London, stipulated its borders to the west and northwest stretched from "sea to sea." This jostling for land among representatives of the imperial powers made the situation ripe for conflict, especially in Franklin's time, when settlers from the English colonies began to move westward across the Appalachian Mountains toward the Mississippi River.

England and France took different approaches to colonizing North America. Almost all the English colonies were set up by corporations or by private individuals in search of profit. In exchange for a charter given by the reigning monarch, the individual or group of investors promised to settle the new colony and share its wealth with the monarch. This was empire-building on the cheap, with the financial risk largely assumed by private interests. The Virginia charter of 1609 lists gold, silver, pearls, and precious stones among the wealth the king expected the corporation to find. He was to receive one-fifth of the gold and silver ore. It also included the proviso that no person affecting "the Superstitions of the Church of Rome" be allowed into the colony.

France experimented with chartered corporations in the early 1600s, but they struggled financially and did not meet their obligations to attract sufficient colonists to Canada. After initially allowing French Protestants to immigrate to the new world, France became increasingly intolerant of non-Catholics. The articles for the Compagnie de la Nouvelle-France, issued by King Louis XIII in 1627, called for the corporation to people the colony with French Catholics and to provide and support priests who would serve the inhabitants and convert "les Sauvages" (the savages). Instead of pearls and precious stones, the articles mentioned beaver pelts, whales, and fish as the riches the company would now control. They do not specifically mention any payment to the king from what turned out to be a money-losing colonial gamble. The company had a rough start when a private English expedition funded by London merchants captured New France in 1629. It never fully recovered, even after England gave the colony back to France as part of a peace deal signed in 1632. New France reverted to the French crown in 1663 and remained a royal domain until the British conquest almost a century later.

How and where colonists settled affected relations with the original inhabitants. The importance of the fur trade to New France meant it needed to maintain civil and mutually beneficial relations with the Indigenous groups who sold the pelts of beavers and other animals in exchange for European goods. These sales took place in Montreal or at thinly manned fur-trading posts in the interior, which meant the French colonists could remain grouped along the St. Lawrence instead of further encroaching on Indigenous territory. The French also encouraged the Indigenous Peoples to settle at locations where they could help defend the colony from attack by the English and their allies. The fur trade was much less important in most of the English colonies. Colonists wanted land to farm or mine. When they arrived in Indigenous territory, they came to stay. This led to a more adversarial relationship with some Indigenous Peoples and made them uncertain allies in times of war. But while France had a lighter footprint in North America than England, it shared the same goal of imposing European values and religion on the Indigenous Peoples.

The Central Role of Indigenous Peoples

Indigenous Peoples were important players in Franklin's youth. They held the balance of power because their support could make or break either

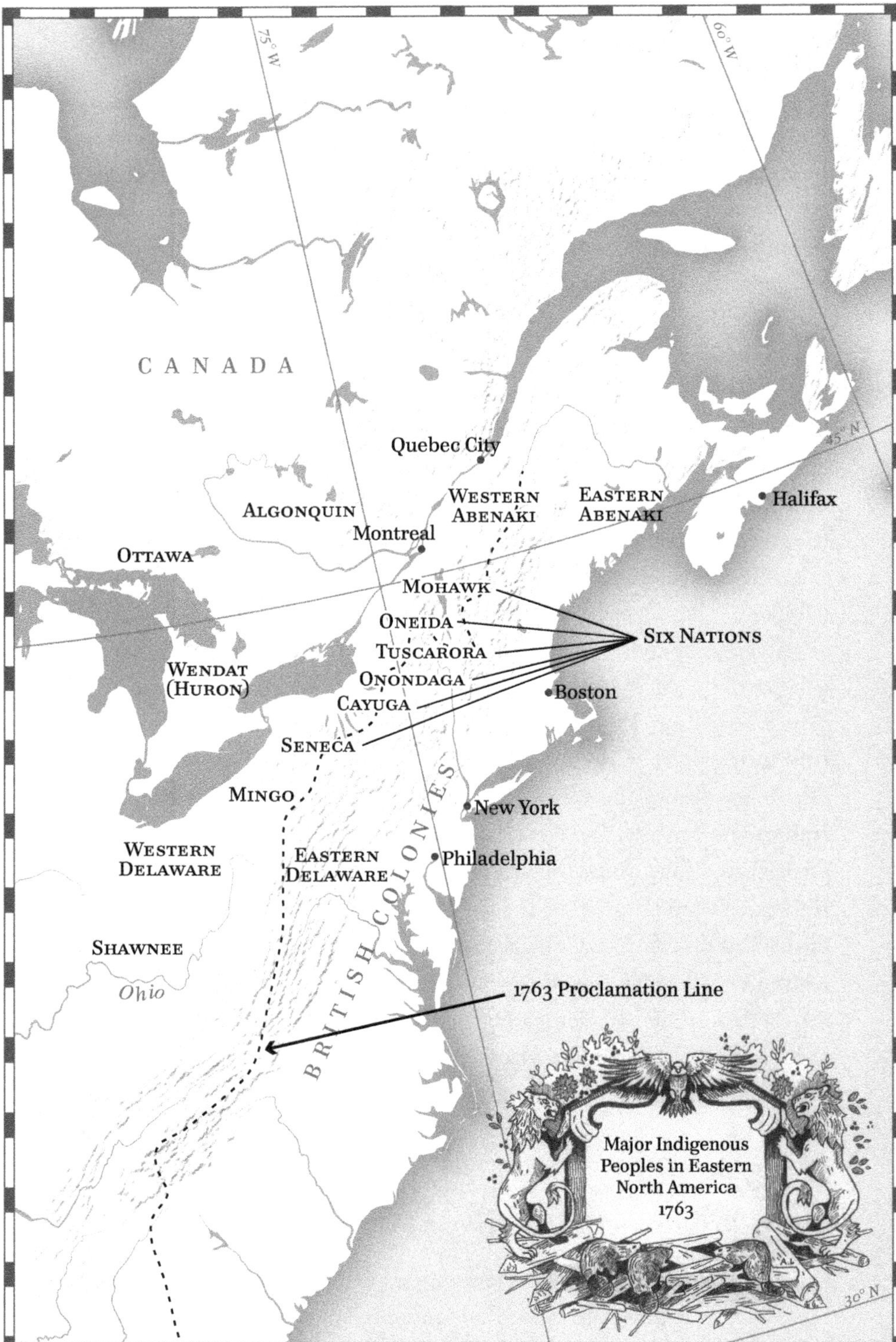

75° W
60° W
45° N
30° N
CANADA
Quebec City
Western Abenaki
Eastern Abenaki
Halifax
Algonquin
Montreal
Ottawa
Mohawk
Oneida
Tuscarora
Onondaga
Cayuga
Seneca
Six Nations
Wendat (Huron)
Boston
Mingo
New York
Western Delaware
Eastern Delaware
Philadelphia
Shawnee
Ohio
British Colonies
1763 Proclamation Line
Major Indigenous Peoples in Eastern North America 1763

side. Three groups were particularly prominent in the conflict between the French and English. The first was the Five Nations, composed of the Mohawk, Oneida, Onondaga, Cayuga, and Seneca. They became the Six Nations when the Tuscarora joined in 1722. They called themselves the Haudenosaunee. The Europeans called them the Iroquois Confederacy. Their territory, centred in what is now upper New York State, was a buffer zone between the French and English. The second was the Algonquian, who lived north and west of the thirteen colonies and was allied with the French. The Wendat also formed part of this alliance. The third was the Abenaki, who lived north and east of the Six Nations. They were allies of the French, although less reliable from the French point of view than the Algonquian and Wendat peoples to the north and west.

The Five Nations pledged in the early 1700s to be neutral in the imperial rivalry. The French wanted to keep it that way. In a letter Governor Vaudreuil wrote in 1704 to a French minister in Paris, he remarked that he had not sent war parties in the direction of Albany, New York, because he did not want to cause a rupture with the Haudenosaunee, or Iroquois. At the same time, he wrote, "We must keep things astir in the direction of Boston, or else the Abenaki will declare for the English."[4]

In battles with the French involving more than one colony, the English had an advantage in terms of numbers but a disadvantage in terms of organization. Each colony considered itself a separate entity and was sometimes loath to contribute men or money to a neighbouring colony if its own interests were not directly at stake. New France, in comparison, had a unified government, with troops and militia under a single command. The citizens of Montreal did not have to go, hat in hand, to the citizens of Quebec City if they were threatened. Uniting the disparate colonies so they could mount a common defence would become a preoccupation for Franklin.

The lack of a unified force probably mattered more in the larger fights between the French and English colonists and their allies than in the frontier attacks on villages and settlements. Yet small fights could lead to bigger ones. Governor Dudley of Massachusetts was so incensed by the attack ordered by the French on Deerfield that he contemplated a much larger attack on New France. In a 1704 letter written after the attack, he said: "In the last two years the Assembly of Massachusetts has spent about £50,000 in defending the Province, whereas three or four of the Queen's ships and fifteen hundred New England men would rid us of the French and make further outlay needless."[5]

A Long History of Hostility

Relying on support from the home country, however, had its downsides. The tale of a proposed attack on Canada, organized by Samuel Vetch, is instructive. Vetch, a former Scottish soldier who married well and settled in Boston, was convicted in 1706 of illegally trading with the enemy French. Such trade went on despite ongoing hostilities. His offence took place during Queen Anne's War in North America (1702–1713), which was part of the larger War of the Spanish Succession in Europe (1701–1714). Vetch sailed to England and successfully appealed his conviction. While there, he decided to put his knowledge of New France to use and wrote a six-thousand-word tract, *Canada Survey'd*, in which he described how Britain could successfully attack Montreal and Quebec City and drive the French from the continent. Vetch's plan became official British policy in 1708.[6]

Vetch arrived back in Boston in April 1709, clutching instructions from Queen Anne to the governors of Connecticut, New England, New Jersey, New York, Pennsylvania, and Rhode Island to raise, arm, and provision about three thousand men and invite what were then the Five Nations to take part. The troops were to be ready by mid-May, when the colonial forces would be joined by a fleet from England, carrying three thousand regular troops. Queen Anne asked Vetch to assure the governors that any government that contributed to "the Reduction of Canada," as conquests were then called, would have a preference on "the Soil and Trade of the Country."[7] The colonials were assembled by June, but the British fleet failed to arrive. In October news came it had been diverted to Portugal. The colonial troops went home bitterly disappointed.

Vetch did succeed in getting some British aid the following year for a successful attack on the smaller target of Port-Royal in Acadia. It looked like Vetch's plan of conquest would finally take shape in 1711, when a British fleet arrived in Boston primed to lead an assault on Canada. Vetch was to command colonial troops from Massachusetts, New Hampshire, and Rhode Island. But disaster struck near Anticosti Island when the fleet was en route to Quebec. Eight transport ships were wrecked, with the loss of about nine hundred men. The British decided to abandon the expedition, over the protests of Vetch and other colonial officers.

The French pursued their own continental dreams. In the 1690s, they captured key English fur-trading posts on Hudson Bay; seized and burned thirty-six English settlements on the island of Newfoundland, including St. John's; and built forts near the mouth of the Mississippi River to consolidate their grip on the river and contain the English colonists to the Atlantic seaboard. Pierre Le Moyne d'Iberville, a French Canadian adventurer, led or took part in all these actions. In 1700 he sent the French king a new and audacious proposal to attack and burn Boston in the winter, when the English colonists would least expect an attack. A force of about eighteen hundred young and vigorous men made up of Canadians, French soldiers, and Indigenous allies could take the city, he wrote. Wearing snowshoes, they could go through the woods and walk over frozen rivers to reach Boston undetected. Taking Boston and burning the grain stored there would weaken New York, drive the Bostonians away, and force the English to focus on rebuilding their establishments rather than attacking Canada, he said. Unfortunately, d'Iberville died while leading another expedition against the English in the Caribbean. Boston was spared from attack.[8]

An Official End to the War: The Treaty of Utrecht

The Treaty of Utrecht signed by Britain and France in 1713 marked the official end to this particular war in North America. In it, France made significant concessions to Britain. It ceded much of Acadia to its opponent but kept Cape Breton Island, which it called l'Île Royale, where it proceeded to build the fortress of Louisbourg. It agreed to restore the area draining into Hudson Bay to the Hudson's Bay Company and compensate it for losses during the war. It ceded all claims to Newfoundland but retained some fishing rights. And it acknowledged that the Haudenosaunee, or Five Nations, were British subjects.

Yet the treaty did not resolve the border between New France and the now British Acadia. Nor did it decide which imperial power should hold the territory surrounding the Mississippi River and the Great Lakes or whether the Abenaki in northern New England were British or French subjects or allies. Enough was left undone to keep colonial conflicts simmering even when Britain and France were officially at peace. Decisions avoided in 1713 would spark a broader conflict in 1754.

A Boy in Boston: Growing Up Among Puritans

How much of this long-standing conflict percolated into young Franklin's consciousness is a matter of speculation. He was five years old when the British fleet arrived in Boston to take part in the 1711 attack on Canada and seven years old when the Treaty of Utrecht was signed. Both events would have caused a stir in his hometown. Up until he left the city at age seventeen, he would have read and heard about the European strife and the much more immediate local attacks by either side on farms and villages. The Deerfield attack, later called a massacre, remained a topic of conversation for years. And in a city controlled by Puritans, he would have been constantly exposed to talk of the religious element of the conflict between England and France.

The Puritans were Protestants who believed the Church of England had not gone far enough in removing the vestiges of Catholicism, or what they called popery, from its practices. Their influence in England peaked after the English Civil War and the rule of Oliver Cromwell. But they remained a dominant force in New England throughout Franklin's childhood. Puritans were not tolerant. Members believed the world was divided between the people whom God would save and those who were damned no matter what they did on Earth. In the first group were the Puritans. In the second was everyone else. In the mid-1600s, Quakers and Baptists could be banished from the colony. Returnees were punished by cutting off one ear for the first offence, then the other, then piercing the tongue with a hot iron, and finally, being hanged if they were foolish enough to return for a fourth time. King Charles II ordered that such punishments cease. The Puritans obeyed grudgingly. They continued to dislike and distrust non-Puritans, including fellow Protestant dissenters from the Church of England, but reserved a special loathing for Roman Catholics.

They wanted the word of God to be presented simply through scripture and sermons, and they abhorred the hierarchical structure of Catholicism that had the pope in Rome at its head, a wealthy and entitled clergy in the middle, and the common folk far below. The Puritans had formed part of the opposition to King Charles I that led to his beheading amidst a civil war and a short-lived republic based on their beloved scripture. Those in England had their hopes dashed by the return of monarchy in 1660. Those in North America had more freedom to pursue their ideals, which included vanquishing religious enemies and eventually forming the republic they were denied in England. They kept a wary eye on the machinations of France, which officially supported the return of a Catholic king to Britain's throne until the 1713 Treaty of Utrecht and unofficially for many years afterward.

Catholicism in their eyes was a danger to their bodies and souls. Having Canada, a French Catholic colony, on their doorstep was akin to sharing the continent with the anti-Christ.

This came through in Williams's account of his captivity in Canada following his capture at Deerfield. His French and Indigenous captors made multiple attempts to convert him and other captives to the Catholic faith, he wrote, attempts that they resisted even when threatened with death. When Williams heard that his son Samuel had "turned to popery," he wrote him to say that he was almost overcome with grief and sorrow to hear that "cunning, crafty enemies" had persuaded him to embrace a damnable doctrine. "Oh! I pity you, I mourn over you day and night!" he wrote. "Oh! I pity your weakness, that through the craftiness of man, you are turned from the simplicity of the gospel. I persuade myself you have done it through ignorance."[9]

Franklin was exposed to similar views from his fellow Bostonians at an early age. There was a constant flow of people at the house where he grew up, at the corner of Hanover and Union Streets. His father, Josiah, ran his business of making candles and soap and selling bulk tallow from his home. Franklin started working for his father full-time at the age of ten, after two years of schooling. Married twice, Josiah had seventeen children, of which thirteen survived. Through his membership in the South Church, Josiah rubbed elbows with men from all stations in life, including Simon Bradstreet, a former governor of the colony, and Samuel Sewall, who owned a printing press and was a Superior Court judge. (Sewall had been a judge at the Salem witch trials of the late 1690s, although he later recanted.) According to Franklin, his father was often visited by "leading People" asking for his opinion on public and private affairs. Josiah sometimes played host to the congregation's prayer meetings, and he frequently invited friends and neighbours to dine and discuss topics he thought would improve the minds of his children.

With all this contact, it would have been strange if the struggle for the continent between the English and the French and the related attacks by Indigenous Peoples were not frequent topics of conversation. Franklin touches on them in the section of his autobiography that focused on his Boston childhood. He refers to "the Indian wars, and other calamities that had befallen our country," in the 1600s. And in writing about Pennsylvania in 1743, he bemoaned the lack of a colonial militia to defend the colony from attacks. By the time he reached the year 1744 in his autobiography, he described his pamphlet *Plain Truth*, which urged the colonies to unite for common defence, and his project to form a voluntary militia.

The diary kept by Sewall, his father's acquaintance, made frequent mention of French and Indigenous adversaries to the north. In an entry from before Franklin's birth, Sewall said his young son Joseph told him he had "news from Heaven, the French were come, and mention'd Canada." In another entry, Sewall noted an express letter arrived, saying that "2000 French and 1000 Indians" were planning to attack Albany or New England. And in another he wrote about the "dismal News of the slaughter made at Deerfield," saying it meant "our congregation was made a Bochim."[10] This referred to a verse from the Bible in which the angel of the Lord told the Israelites that the inhabitants of the land he had given them would become "thorns in their side" because the Israelites had not followed God's orders.

Speaking of Franklin's Autobiography ...

It is worth saying a word or two about Franklin's autobiography, because it is one of the few sources on his early years. It is, however, unreliable, incomplete, and heavily focused on current concerns rather than the problems of the past. He began writing it in 1771, when he was sixty-five years old, looking back at his youth from the vantage point of late middle age. The autobiography started as a letter to his illegitimate son, William, then governor of New Jersey. Franklin had had almost fifty years to curate his memories of his time in Boston, presenting those that supported the story he wanted to tell of a self-made man born in "poverty and obscurity" who through his own efforts at self-improvement rose to become an international diplomat in London, where he represented several of the colonies. Memories that did not directly contribute to fleshing out that image received scant attention. For example, when Franklin worked as a printer's apprentice for his brother, helping to publish the *New-England Courant*, Boston was in the midst of a smallpox epidemic. The newspaper was heavily involved in the noisy debate about inoculation. The *Courant* was against it, printing items decrying it as a "dubious, dangerous Practice."[11] Franklin, who later became an advocate of inoculation after his young son died of the disease, makes no mention in his autobiography of the smallpox controversy.

By 1771 he was adept at crafting stories to suit the argument he was making. Walter Isaacson, one of his many biographers, called Franklin "the country's first unabashed public relations expert."[12] Failures and subjects he found painful got short shrift. His writing reflected the prevailing circumstances in 1771. England and France were at peace. Britain had conquered Canada and driven France out of mainland North America in 1760, gains made official in the 1763 Treaty of Paris. The threat from the north had receded, temporarily as it turned out. The conflict that preoccupied Franklin in his paternal missives was the one brewing between Britain and the thirteen colonies, not the one between American colonists and New France. He was fast making a name for himself in France with his scientific discoveries, which had been translated into French and published several decades earlier. He had visited Paris in 1767 and 1769 and made contacts in scientific circles. It seems natural, given the context, that he would not want to offend his new friends by delving too deeply into the dire deeds of the French and their Indigenous allies in his youth. Better to draw a veil across the matter.

French Canada was far from the only topic that did not receive in-depth treatment in the section on Franklin's formative years. There is remarkably little on the Puritans and Puritanism. Boston was no longer the complete theocracy it once was, but the Puritans still had influence on Franklin's public and private life when he was young. His father was not just an ordinary member of the South Church. At one point he was appointed a tithingman, which meant enforcing attendance at church, admonishing people for inattention and napping, and policing what they wore. Massachusetts no longer strictly enforced its sumptuary law, passed in 1651, which banned persons of "meane condition" from taking on "the garbe of gentlemen." This included wearing gold, silver, silk, lace, or "great bootes" unless the wearer had an estate worth £200 or belonged to one of the privileged groups named in the regulation. Yet the Puritans continued to favour simple and conservative dress in muted colours long after the sumptuary laws fell into disuse. Franklin would don such a garb in France to promote his image as a rustic philosopher. It was a useful disguise for him, whereas John Adams, a founding father and Massachusetts Puritan, retained the hope as late as 1778 that Congress would pass a sumptuary law governing all the colonies.

Franklin says little about how his father's religion influenced his own views. He later described himself as a deist, or someone who rejects organized religion but believes that a single god created the world. In his autobiography, he dismissed his father's small library of religious books as "polemic divinity" and bemoaned the fact that "more proper books" had not fallen his way during a time when he was a voracious reader. Still, he admitted that he read most of his father's books. They would have given him a firm understanding of Puritan beliefs, as would the sermons and essays he read, including those by Cotton Mather, an influential minister and prolific author of more than 450 books and pamphlets. This was information he would put to use later.

Franklin's father had intended that his son become a minister but dropped the idea when his son was still young. It is unclear why. Franklin pointed to money as a problem. His father took him out of grammar school, where courses in Latin and Greek would have prepared him for college, and sent him to a school for writing and arithmetic. Franklin said his father was burdened with a numerous family and "was unable without inconvenience to support the expense of a college education." One biographer disputes this reasoning, saying Latin school was almost free and Harvard gave scholarships to those with exceptional ability.[13] Another speculated that while Franklin was intellectual, he was not pious.[14] Franklin admitted in his autobiography that he "early absented himself from the public assemblies of the sect, Sunday being my studying day." He was more intent on reading everything he could lay his hands on and practising his writing style by imitating others. His younger sister Jane said Franklin could read the Bible by the time he was five years old. Franklin credits his bookishness as the reason his father eventually decided he would become an indentured apprentice to his older brother James, a printer, when Franklin was twelve years old.

The Launch of a Long Publishing Career

The move to his brother's printing shop gave Franklin access to more books. He could borrow from the shop's library, which included *Shakespeare's Works*, Herman Moll's *A System of Geography*, *The History of France*, and collected volumes of *The Guardian* and *The Spectator* from Britain. He could borrow new works from other printers and read works being printed by James, such as *English Liberties, or The Free-Born Subject's Inheritance*. Henry Care, the author of *English Liberties*, was a noted critic of Roman Catholicism.

It was during the time he worked for his brother that Franklin began to develop and hone writing skills he would later use in politics, diplomacy, and his pursuit of Canada. Four years into Franklin's apprenticeship, James established the *New-England Courant*, the fourth newspaper in the colonies. Like other early newspapers, the *Courant* printed excerpts of news from abroad, essays on religious or moral themes, and unsolicited letters from the public. Some news items were many months old by the time they made the voyage across the Atlantic and appeared in print. Franklin was keen to try his hand. He wrote, without his brother's knowledge, a series of well-received letters to the editor under the pen name Silence Dogood. It was common practice at the time for contributors to use pseudonyms. By disguising his handwriting and slipping the letters under the door of the printing house at night, he tricked his brother into printing them. Some even made the front page of the weekly newspaper, which was usually just two pages.

In these pieces, Franklin contented himself with attacking local institutions, like Harvard College (then a training ground for clergy), or social issues, such as drunkenness, or the plight of widows in Boston. But the newspaper also dealt with the wider world, from events in the neighbouring colonies to European affairs. For example, the issue of February 5–12, 1722, described the "impious and detestable practices" of the Hellfire Club in London, where young men of high birth reputedly indulged in immoral acts. It also included news on an outbreak of plague in Alexandria and Cyprus, the sighting of Algerian Rovers in the Strait of Gibraltar, and an account, datelined Boston, of colonial forces discovering a letter from the governor of Canada "directing the Indians to use their utmost Force, to keep the English from settling at the Eastward, and promising to supply them with Powder and Ball for that End." Readers would understand the implicit message that Canada remained an enemy even though the imperial powers were supposedly at peace. The issue of June 18–25 carried news from London that the grand master of Malta had asked for assistance from the viceroys of Naples and Sicily if the Turks attacked. It also ran an account, datelined Boston, that "Indians" had burned houses, killed cattle, and taken five men prisoner somewhere near Annapolis Royal. The July 16–22 issue had a front-page letter from Silence Dogood on political hypocrites. Inside, an anonymous writer raised the question of whether the colonists should defend settlements outside the boundaries of the province for the honour of the king. Not doing so, the writer asserted, would allow "popish missionaries" to set "the Indians" on the western borders of the province.

Talking Up the Threat Posed by Catholics and Indigenous Peoples

Franklin took charge of the newspaper when his brother was jailed for running an item the local authorities regarded as a criticism. James was briefly banned from publishing a newspaper. Issues released between February 4 and September 30 were labelled "Printed and sold by Benjamin Franklin in Queen Street, where Advertisements are taken in."[15] It is not clear whether he was just a figurehead, with James running things behind the scenes, or whether he was fully in charge. In his autobiography, he took the credit, saying that while he had management of the paper, he "made bold to give our rulers some rubs in it." His brother supported his actions, he wrote, but "others began to consider me in an unfavourable light, as a young genius that had a turn for libelling and satyr."

One of the threads that ran through the issues Franklin published was the threat posed to King George I by James Stuart, the Roman Catholic son of James II, whose supporters thought was the rightful heir to the throne. The *Courant* printed in February 1723 the speech the king had made to Parliament the previous October in which he talked of the "dangerous Conspiracy" against him and the "wicked Design" of the "Popish Pretender." The newspaper faithfully followed the discovery of conspiracies, both real and imagined, and the trial, acquittal, execution, or exile of those involved. The items left no doubt that popery, a condition shared by the French Canadians, was a sin.

A second thread was piracy. Peace meant the navies of Britain and France had shed much of their wartime manpower, leaving sailors to find their own way in the world. Many turned to piracy. The *Courant* carried frequent items about pirates worrying and sometimes seizing vessels along the coast. Most did not identify the homeland of the pirates, although some of them would be French. In an unusual item in the issue of June 17–24, 1723, the newspaper listed thirty men taken from the pirate ship *Ranger*. They were a mixed lot, coming from the colonies of Connecticut, New England, New York, Rhode Island, and Virginia but also from London, Exeter, Londonderry, Wrexham in Wales, and the Isle of Man. The newspaper followed their trial and the subsequent execution of most of the men. Blood and guts sold newspapers, even in those days.

The third thread was the threat from hostile Indigenous Peoples, or "Enemy Indians," which the newspaper contended were supported by the "Governour of Canada." The first issue Franklin edited carried an item about 200 men under the command of Captain Harmon going to Norridgewock "in quest of the Indians," while another 170 under Colonel Westbrook were heading to Penobscot for the same reason. An issue in April carried a letter from an officer at Richmond Fort about an "attack by Indians" in which one of his men was shot through the body and the hand. That same month there was another item about "Indians" near Casco Bay shooting a Sergeant Chub, "lodging 11 bullets in his body." In May the newspaper reported that two men were killed by "Indians, who afterwards barbarously cut and mangled them with their Hatchets." Over the next couple of months, four more attacks were reported. Then in August, there was news the "Eastern Indians" told the Five Nations they did not need them anymore as mediators with the English, "and 'tis said the Reason of this Message is grounded on a late Promise from the Governour of Canada and the Jesuits, that they will supply them with all Necessaries for carrying on the War except Men." The next issue carried news of attacks at Northfield and at Rutland, where Rev. Mr. Willard, the minister of the town, was taken. According to the newspaper, Mr. Willard's body was later found and he "was scalped, his Throat Cut, one side of his Face cut off, stabb'd in the Body with Knives, and had his fingers cut off on one Hand and his Thumb on the other." This same issue also reported that the government had received a letter from the "Governour" of Canada, who "pretends abundance of Friendship to this Province in the Affair of the War; tho' we are inform'd by one Hamilton, lately a Captive among the Indians, that the most of them spent the Winter at Canada, and that the Governour supply'd them with Provision and Ammunition." Scalping was a recurring theme in Franklin's later writing about enemies, both French and English.

Not all the reports about Indigenous Peoples cast them as hostile to the colonists. The *Courant* also told its readers about conferences between Indigenous leaders from the Five Nations and the Massachusetts General Assembly in August and September. The discussion centred on whether they would "take up the Hatchet against the Eastern Indians." It also wrote of entertainments put on by British and colonial leaders for the Indigenous leaders. But these positive events were overshadowed, often in the same issue, by news of yet more bloody attacks by Indigenous Peoples, supported by Canada. The last issue Franklin put together, at the end of September 1723, had an item about two "Eastern Indians" being captured by a fisherman from Marblehead when they boarded his boat.[16]

Leaving Boston Behind

Franklin left Boston shortly after he composed that last issue, slipping away in the night to board a sloop to New York. He said in his autobiography that his brother's "harsh and tyrannical treatment" led to his departure, but he also admitted that he had made himself "a little obnoxious to the governing party" and that it might have been difficult for him to stay and work in Boston. He also wrote that a friend persuaded the sloop's captain to take Franklin on board by telling him that Franklin, then seventeen years old, had made "a naughty girl" pregnant and her friends wanted him to marry her. This apparently was untrue. It would not be the last time he lied to achieve a particular end.

Canada was an ever-present threat during Franklin's early years in Boston. When he took the helm of his brother's newspaper and felt the power of being a publisher for the first time, he printed articles that left his Boston readers in no doubt that the French in Canada were dangerous and duplicitous. His thoughts on how to deal with the northern menace would come much later, after he had gained more experience of the wider world. After a brief stay in Philadelphia, the teenaged Franklin set out for London. There he would see how the conflict between French Catholics and English Protestants fit in the imperial context. This was knowledge he would use to his own ends many decades later.

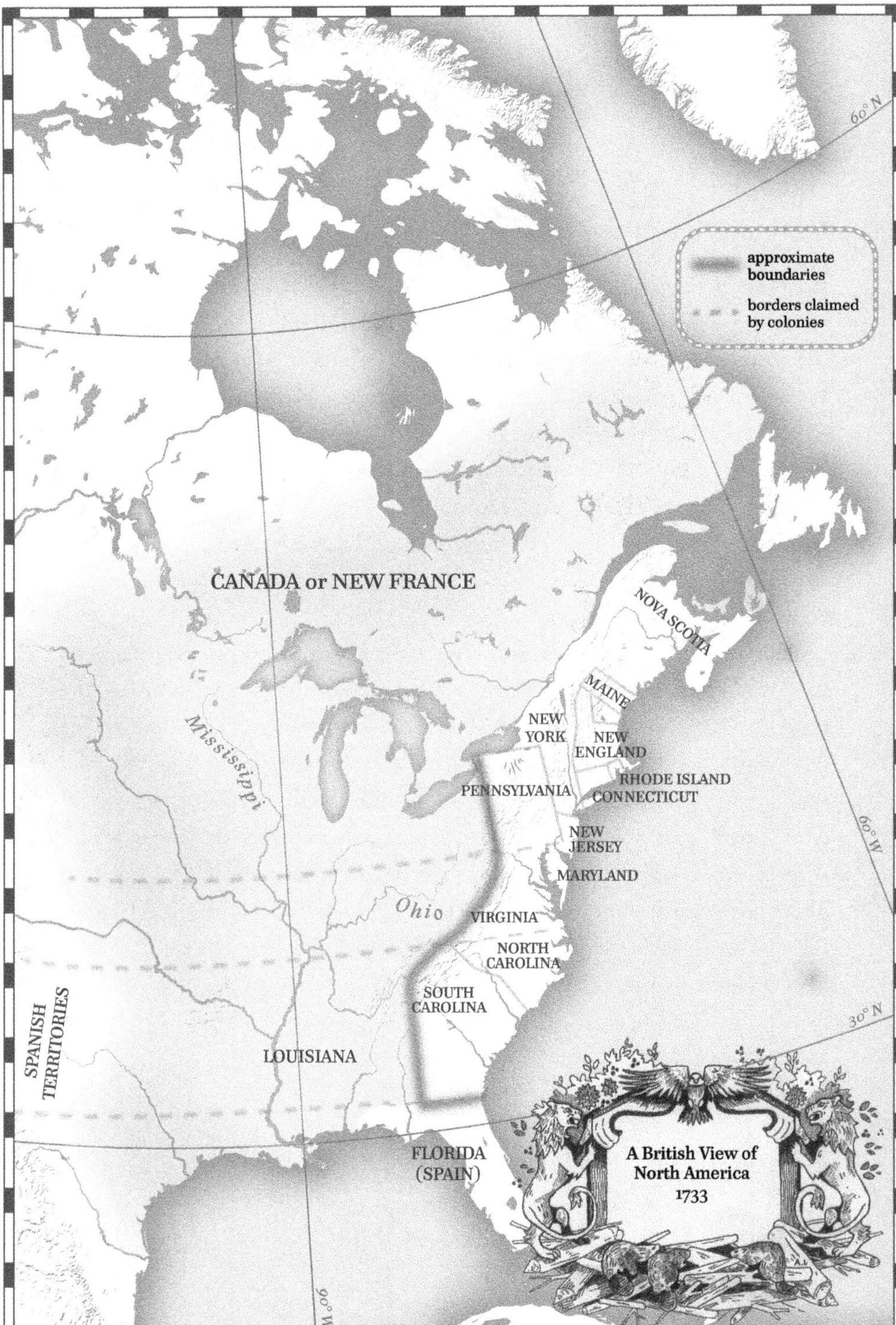
A British View of
North America
1733
approximate boundaries
borders claimed by colonies
CANADA or NEW FRANCE
NOVA SCOTIA
MAINE
NEW YORK
NEW ENGLAND
RHODE ISLAND
CONNECTICUT
PENNSYLVANIA
NEW JERSEY
MARYLAND
VIRGINIA
NORTH CAROLINA
SOUTH CAROLINA
LOUISIANA
SPANISH TERRITORIES
FLORIDA (SPAIN)
Mississippi
Ohio
60° N
30° N
60° W
90° W

CHAPTER 2

Papist Conspiracies: London 1724–1726

> But shall we imitate idolatrous Papists, we that are enlightened Protestants?[1]
>
> — *Benjamin Franklin*

WHEN THE EIGHTEEN-YEAR-OLD FRANKLIN WENT LOOKING FOR LODGings in London in 1725, he did something extraordinary for someone raised a Puritan — he rented a room from a Roman Catholic. Not only was his elderly landlady Catholic, so, too, was an old woman who lived in the attic. A Catholic priest came daily to hear her confession. The building on Duke Street (now Sardinia Street) was opposite "a Romish chapel." Franklin said in his autobiography that he moved there because it was closer to his work at the printing house of John Watts. He had previously shared rooms in Little Britain with his friend James Ralph, who had accompanied him to London, leaving behind a wife and young child. After Ralph left, first to move in with a woman and then for a teaching post in a village, Franklin looked for a cheaper room. Franklin described pleasant evenings with his landlady, who had lived among "people of distinction" and knew a thousand anecdotes.

"Our supper was only half an anchovy each, on a very little strip of bread and butter, and half a pint of ale between us; but the entertainment was in her conversation," he wrote.

Franklin may not have been a staunch Puritan, but he considered himself a Protestant, and there was immense hostility toward Catholics in England at the time. The same could be said of the Boston of his childhood, where colonists who regarded themselves as British readily adopted the prejudices of the mother country, and the Puritans damned anyone not of their faith. (Franklin regarded himself as British until it became clear independence was inevitable.) But there was a different flavour to the enmity felt in the colonies, where French Catholics and their Indigenous allies were a physical, as well as a spiritual, threat. They could emerge from the woods at any moment to burn and slaughter Protestant settlers or waylay unwary fishermen off the coast. In Britain, the external threat existed in the shape of Catholic France, but there were also internal challenges from the Jacobites. They questioned the legitimacy of George I, the Protestant from Hanover who became the British king in 1714, and supported the claim of James Stuart, a Catholic in exile in France. The British authorities also kept a wary eye on the Catholics in Ireland.

In Franklin's time, what church you attended and what god you prayed to mattered, both in Europe and the colonies. Religion determined political alliances and individual fates. In our more secular age, its full import is hard to grasp. In London, Franklin was constantly exposed to British anti-Catholicism, or anti-popery, but he also mingled with more liberal thinkers. It is fair to say his religious views evolved but not to the point that he regarded Catholics as equals. His London sojourn was also useful in that it gave him first-hand knowledge of how the British thought, how their stratified society worked, and how the popular press could make an impact. This was knowledge he would put to use throughout his life and especially in his campaign to procure Canada.

And yet he chose to defy the conventional thinking of his Protestant peers in his choice of dwelling. Financial necessity might have played a larger role than he wanted to admit. Catholic landladies in Protestant London would not attract many Protestant tenants. Franklin initially paid three shillings and sixpence a week for his room, but he talked his elderly landlady down to one shilling and sixpence a week by threatening to move elsewhere. He said she complied because she liked having a man about the house. She was a widow and crippled with gout. The tale does not reflect well on him. After a brief mention in his autobiography of his landlady's faith, he moves on to his love of swimming. This was before pollution and raw sewage were thought to make the Thames hazardous to bathers.

How Franklin Got to London

After leaving Boston in late 1723, Franklin passed briefly through New York, spent some months working as a printer in Philadelphia, and then boarded a ship for London. Sir William Keith, governor of Pennsylvania, had taken a shine to him, promising him money and letters of introduction in London so that he could procure what was needed to set up a printing house when he returned to Philadelphia. Printers in the colonies needed to import much of what they needed to set up shop, including typefaces, paper, and ink. It was not until he reached London that Franklin discovered neither the money nor the letters existed. Yet with his printer's skills, he readily found work, first with the master printer Samuel Palmer in Bartholomew Close and later with Watts at his premises in Wild Court.

Franklin's autobiography is woefully short of details on daily life in London during this formative stage in his life. We learn something in passing when he mentions food but nothing about how he experienced the great, sprawling metropolis that had become the largest city in Europe. London, with an estimated population of more than six hundred thousand, was at least sixty times larger than the Philadelphia he had left behind. It was a city divided geographically into Westminster, the preserve of royalty, politicians, and the aristocracy; the City of London, where trade, manufacturing, and finance took place; and the Borough of Southwark, a centre of industry south of the river. It was a place of massive inequality, with the rich living in opulence and the poor in squalor. Some streets were open sewers and pedestrians had to dodge the contents of chamber pots emptied out of windows. Even in the monied parts of town, street sweepers earned a pittance by clearing a path through the refuse from one side to the other. The air was foul with coal smoke, and great piles of rubbish and street filth could be found along the banks of the Thames. Franklin lived within the City of London and close to Lincoln's Inn Fields, an open square surrounded by the homes of the wealthy and a gathering place for thieves and beggars at night. He was within walking distance of the theatres on Drury Lane, where he and his friend Ralph entertained themselves for the price of one shilling if they sat in the uppermost galleries.[2] His memories of this time focus on his work in the printing shops, the people he met, and his swimming.

An Uneasy Peace Between Britain and France

Franklin had arrived in London when Britain was technically at peace with Catholic France but at war with Catholics, especially those within its borders. Official war with France had stopped with the 1713 Treaty of Utrecht, one of a series of treaties that ended the War of Spanish Succession. This is the same treaty that restored Hudson Bay and its surrounds to Britain, as well as territories held by France in Newfoundland and in Acadia. It called for "universal perpetual peace" between Great Britain and France — a somewhat hopeful ambition, given it followed almost two centuries of conflict. France, in the form of "the most serene and potent prince Lewis XIV" (Louis XIV), acknowledged that Anne, a Protestant and a "most serene and potent princess," was the rightful queen of Great Britain. France would no longer meddle in Britain's internal affairs by supporting the Catholic claimants to her throne.

France and England had once been closely entwined. French was the language of the court, the aristocracy, and those aspiring to join it. The divide between the French and English courts began to widen when Henry VIII broke with the Church of Rome in 1534 and made himself head of the rival Church of England with the Act of Supremacy. Not coincidentally, this gave him access to the wealth of the church, which he used to wage war on France. The gulf widened further in 1688, when the Catholic King James II was replaced by his Protestant daughter Mary and her husband, William of Orange, in what was called the Glorious Revolution. By Franklin's time, Protestant Britain and Catholic France were characterized as inveterate enemies despite periods of shared history.

Religious differences were only a part of the struggle between the two. As their overseas empires grew, they competed for territory in Africa, India, North America, and the Caribbean and for the wealth that came from exploiting the people and resources of the colonies and exporting manufactured goods. The sugar trade with island colonies in the Caribbean was especially lucrative for both imperial powers. The sugar-producing island of Guadeloupe would later figure in the horse-trading over Canada's future. Focusing on the religion of the enemy often masked other, more mercenary incentives to go to war.

Anti-Catholicism: The Glue That Held Britain Together

There were domestic reasons within Britain to play up the Catholicism of the French. Beginning in 1707, when the Act of Union united the kingdoms of Scotland and England, creating Great Britain, the monarch and their ministers struggled to find the glue that would hold together the disparate parts of the British realm (Wales had been annexed by England in 1284 and incorporated into the realm in 1536). Protestantism fit the bill. It helped the British define themselves in opposition to the Catholic French. They were a Protestant, island-dwelling people, who, with their Parliament, enjoyed freedoms that the Catholic, continental French, ruled by an autocratic king and an equally autocratic pope, could only dream of. Or so the British, both at home and abroad, were encouraged to think. Painting these features onto the face of an external enemy drew the realm together and helped paper over internal differences.

Catholics were persecuted when a Protestant was on the throne. The reverse was also true. Catholics were blamed, often rightly, for welcoming the arrival of the Spanish Armada; for the execution of Protestants under Mary Tudor, the Catholic daughter of Henry VIII; and for the Gunpowder Plot of 1605. There were rumours Catholics had infiltrated high office and masterminded the Civil War and the execution of Charles I in 1649.

Laws passed in the late 1600s meant Catholics could not vote, could not hold a seat in either of the Houses of Parliament, and were excluded from state offices. (There were milder but still real restrictions on Protestants who dissented from the Church of England.) An Act Against Popery in 1700 promised a reward of £100 for information that led to the capture and conviction of Catholic priests. Catholics paid higher taxes, could not possess arms, had fewer rights to education, and could not legally purchase property. The Act of Settlement of 1701 prohibited a Catholic or anyone married to a Catholic from ascending to the throne. Behind all these penalties was the Protestant fear that the foremost allegiance of English Catholics was to the pope in Rome and not to the king in England.

It did not help the standing of Catholics in Britain that Jacobites wanted to put a Catholic on the throne and had been threatening an armed insurrection against the English Crown since William of Orange deposed James II in 1688. The Jacobites, so named because "James" in Latin is "Jacobus," mounted an unsuccessful rebellion in 1715, the year after George I began his rule. As his legitimacy rested on the fact that he was a Protestant, this gave him and his ministers ample reason to fuel anti-Catholicism and to talk up the Protestantism of the British. They had the support of London merchants who fretted that Jacobite success would end up helping France, Britain's foremost imperial and commercial rival. France had supported the exiled James III and given him refuge for long periods of time. Despite a pledge made in the 1713 Treaty of Utrecht to end that support, it continued, albeit less openly. During the reign of George I, authorities uncovered countless papist conspiracies, some more real than others. Franklin was aware of them because he set many of these stories in print when he managed the *New-England Courant* in Boston for his brother.

The Free Press Routinely Targets Catholics

During Franklin's first stay in London, from late December 1724 to July 1726, the existence of a peace treaty between Britain and France muted overt attacks on the French in printed publications. But Catholicism (or popery, as it was commonly called) was fair game for writers of pamphlets, newspapers, and especially almanacs, which regularly outsold the Bible. The majority of books printed in London in the early 1700s were religious works. In contrast to France, which heavily regulated publishing, Britain enjoyed a relatively free press. There had been an attempt to regulate newspapers through the Printing Act of 1662, but the act was not renewed when it lapsed in 1695. It is difficult to ascertain what Franklin did or did not read during his time in London, except for the few works he mentioned in his autobiography and letters. But there was enough anti-popery about that Franklin would have been exposed to it constantly in the printed material available at the coffee houses and bookshops he frequented and in some of the works he set in type at his printing jobs.

Almanacs catered to popular opinion and presented a mix of useful information, sensational stories, and predictions for the year to come. Often these optimistic forecasts included the end of the pope or of the French. One such almanac by John Partridge for 1724 promised readers the moon's sign for every day of the year, the daily motions of the planets, high water at London Bridge, astrological observations, "and other Things fit for such a Work." It also contained "The Protestant Remembrancer continued," which it identified as a dissertation on the increase in papists and the decrease in Protestants. The author of the dissertation, according to the almanac, talks of "the implacable Enmity which the Church of Rome has entertained against Protestants" and the nations "more or less drench'd with the blood of Protestants at the instigation of the Pope and the Papist clergy." The title page of the almanac noted that it had been thirty-six years since "Protestants Deliverance by King William from Popery, and Arbitrary Government."[3]

Cato's Letters, a collection of essays by the influential writers John Trenchard and Thomas Gordon, was first published in the *London Journal*, a weekly, and then in book form in 1724. The essays were widely republished in the American colonial newspapers. Trenchard and Gordon thought liberty was constantly threatened by conspiracies fomented by those seeking power, including the Catholics. In one essay, they attacked the papacy, calling it "a Fairy Dominion, founded upon Non Entities, Inventions, and Abominations; supported by Lies and Terrors; exercised with Cruelty, Craft, and Rapine; and producing Meanness, Delusion and Poverty, where-ever it prevails." They reminded their readers of the "mighty difference" between them and other nations: "We are not the Prey of Monks, or Janizaries, or Dragoons, nor the blind Slaves of unaccountable Will and Pleasure. Our Lives and Properties are secur'd by the best Bulwark in the World, that of Laws, made by our selves, and executed by our Magistrates, who are likewise made by us; and when they are dishonesty executed, or wilfully neglected, our Constitution affords a Remedy, a tried and practicable Remedy."[4]

Newspaper items cast Catholicism and, by implication, Catholic France in a bad light. For example, the *London Journal* of Saturday, June 13, 1724, carried an item about Jesuits in France, saying they were gaining power at the French court:

> A most severe Edict has ben published there against the Profession of any Religion in that Kingdom but that of the Roman Catholick. By which Protestant Preachers, that exercise their Function, are to be punished with Death; and their Auditors, if Men, are to be sent to the Gallies for Life; if Women, to be shaved, and confined for ever in such Place as the Judges shall think fit. The Children of Protestant Parents are to be christen'd in 24 hours after their Birth, in their own Parish Church; and as they grow up are to be educated in the Roman Catholick Religion, under severe Penalties of Failure, &c.

It would be an exaggeration to say these items dominated the newspapers. They were dotted amongst other news meant to catch the eye. The same copy of the *London Journal* that carried the warning about growing Jesuit power in France had items on the crowning of the czarina in Moscow, accompanied by the dispersal "of no less than 15,000 Gold and Silver medals among the populace," and news of the "Persian Rebel Meriweys making an alliance with the Great Mogol against Prince Tochmas, son of the late King of Persia." There was English news: a riot in Devonshire by a great rabble of weavers and woolcombers, four hundred workers taking the Duchess Dowager of Marlborough to court for not paying for building work on

Blenheim House. And there was human interest: a brewer in Southwark dying after he fell "into the boiling Copper" and a rash of suicides in Worcester, including the wife of a clergyman who hanged herself while her husband was at his parish church. Yet there were enough anti-Catholic items to give readers the clear impression that the Catholics were their enemies.

Those who could not read were exposed to anti-Catholic messaging at church services, where sermons referred to the mistreatment of Protestants abroad, especially in France and Spain. There was some truth in these depictions. Through an edict in 1685, Louis XIV made Protestantism illegal, forcing its adherents to convert or flee the country. Many of the Huguenots forced to flee France became bitter exiles in England and North America. In Spain the inquisition against heresy, created by a papal bull in 1478, did not end officially until 1834. Tomás de Torquemada, the fanatical grand inquisitor who authorized torture, property confiscation, and grisly executions, provided plenty of fodder for English sermons. Tirades from the pulpit about Catholic excesses and Protestant martyrs usually failed to mention that other countries, including England, had also tortured and killed those they considered heretics.

Works That Influenced Franklin in London

In his autobiography, Franklin named two works he read during his first visit to London. One was a recently published satire written by Edward Young, whose writing style and views had an impact on the young printer. Young was a poet, a playwright, an unsuccessful politician, and eventually a Church of England clergyman and chaplain to King George II. He published seven satirical poems, starting in 1725, which were gathered together and republished in 1728 with the title *Love of Fame, The Universal Passion*. Franklin did not identify which of the satires he copied and sent to his friend Ralph, only that it "set in a strong light the folly of pursuing the Muses with any hope of advancement by them." That is, Franklin felt Ralph's own poetry was not nearly as good as Young's and that Ralph therefore lacked the talent to make it as a poet. (Franklin's efforts to push him into a more lucrative career might have been influenced by the fact that Ralph owed him money.)

Young cultivated a particular style in his popular satires, not unlike the one Franklin later adopted as his own. He was good-natured in his criticism, and used humorous allusions, thinking this would have more effect and gain him a broader audience. Franklin later reprinted some of Young's work in *Poor Richard's Almanack*, which he edited and published after his return to Philadelphia, telling readers that rather than giving them his bad lines, he would reproduce the best he could find. In his works, Young upheld the official line about the superiority of Protestant Britain over Catholic France. For example, in "Reflections on the Public Situation of the Kingdom," written in 1745, he talked about "the weight of British wrath" cleaving "the papal mitre, or the Gallic chain" and of a "pope-bred princeling" who had suckled "malice with his milk, Malice, to Britain, liberty, and truth" and was trying to "cut his passage to the British throne." In a sermon he preached to members of the House of Commons in 1728, he said it had long been reputed to be "the most powerful Assembly in the World: And why? Because the most free; for Power and Freedom are one." To enjoy Young's writing, as Franklin did, was also to absorb his world view.

The second printed work that Franklin referred to had a direct impact on his London life. It was *The Religion of Nature Delineated* by William Wollaston, a philosopher. Franklin took issue with Wollaston's arguments about the nature of right and wrong and whether morality exists independently of religion. He decided to write, print, and distribute a pamphlet of his own, *A Dissertation on Liberty and Necessity, Pleasure and Pain*. What was important about the pamphlet was not Franklin's argument. He later considered it juvenile and its publication a mistake. But the pamphlet did open doors for him in London, at least those of some radical thinkers who thought Franklin shared their beliefs. These men included Dr. William Lyons, who wrote *The Infallibility of Humane Judgment, Its Dignity and Excellency*, and Bernard Mandeville, who wrote *Fable of the Bees*. Lyons "took great notice of me, called on me often to converse on those subjects," wrote Franklin in his autobiography. He took Franklin to a "pale ale house" called the Horns in Cheapside to meet Mandeville, "a most facetious, entertaining companion." Lyons and Mandeville were deists and freethinkers who challenged religious and political orthodoxy. Deists believed God existed, but they followed no particular religion and thought nature and reason influenced human events. Mandeville further believed that no government or church was entitled to automatic obedience or loyalty.

This was radical stuff in the Western world, where the established Christian religions feared they were being undermined by philosophers who questioned the essentials of Christianity, including whether God had ordained the existing system of monarchy and ecclesiastical authority.

Franklin's Religious Beliefs Start to Take Shape

Did Franklin share these beliefs? There were signs even before he reached London that he no longer adhered to the Puritan faith. In relating his departure from Boston, he said his "indiscrete disputations about religion began to make me pointed at with horror by good people as an infidel or atheist." When he arrived in Philadelphia for the first time, he sought shelter not in a Puritan church but in a meeting house for Quakers, a group the Puritans scorned. In London, as mentioned, he took lodgings with a Catholic landlady in a house frequented daily by a Catholic priest. And the pamphlet he published in London verged on atheism and drew him to the notice of the deists.

Franklin wrote in his autobiography that he was never without religious principles but that some Puritan dogmas seemed unintelligible or doubtful to him. He believed, he wrote, that there was a deity, that he made the world, governed it by his providence, and that the most acceptable service to God was doing good to man. He also believed that souls were immortal and that crime would be punished and virtue rewarded. He thought all the religions in the colonies had these essentials but then mixed them with other articles that served to divide the people. He had found that members of most sects felt they were the only ones who possessed the truth and that all others were wrong. This, he wrote, was like a man travelling in a fog who could see his immediate surroundings clearly but only blurry outlines of people ahead of him and behind him, "tho' in truth he is as much in the Fog as any of them." This awareness of the potential divisiveness of religion led him "to avoid all Discourse that might tend to lessen the good Opinion another might have of his own Religion."

His reticence to engage in religious debate seemed suspicious to fervent believers, including John Adams, a New England Puritan. Adams wrote a letter to the *Boston Patriot* newspaper in 1810 in which he portrayed Franklin as a religious shape-shifter. "The catholics thought him almost a catholic. The church of england claimed him as one of them; the presbyterians thought him half a presbyterian and the friends believed him a wet quaker. The dissenting clergymen in England and America were among the most distinguished asserters and propagators of his renown. Indeed all sects considered him, and I believe justly, a friend to unlimited toleration in matters of religion." Franklin's apparent flexibility did not go down well with someone who believed the only true religion was theirs.

Max Weber, the nineteenth-century German sociologist and theorist, and a critic of Franklin's, described Franklin as a "colourless deist" who more than anything exemplified the spirit of capitalism. In his book *The Protestant Ethic and the Spirit of Capitalism*, Weber wrote that Franklin embraced virtues, or at least left the impression he had embraced them, when they would be useful to him in the pursuit of money and success. His decision to drink water rather than beer in the daytime when he worked at Watts's might fit with this criticism, although Weber did not mention it. Franklin said in his autobiography that he persuaded some of his fellow workers to follow his lead and replace their regular breakfast of beer, bread, and cheese with "a large porringer of hot water-gruel sprinkled with pepper, crumb'd with bread, and a bit of butter in it," because it was cheaper and better for them. But it also left him with more money to buy books, and he made money from the interest he charged on loans to fellow workers who continued to drink beer and ran out of money before payday.

The Limits to Franklin's Tolerance

Franklin's religious beliefs had a bearing on how he viewed Canada because its population was close to 100 percent Catholic. If we take him at his word, he emerged from his Puritan childhood and his stay in London without strong prejudices against any Christian religion. It is hard to square that with his subsequent use of anti-Catholic language. *Poor Richard's*

Almanack, his popular creation, was sprinkled with allusions to the greatness of Protestantism and the baseness of Catholicism. It may be that he still considered Catholics inferior and his tolerance only extended to other Protestants. An entry under the month of November in the 1749 issue is a good example. It noted that November 5 was a lucky day for the English church and British liberty, "for on that day in 1604, the popish gunpowder treason was detected; and on the same day in 1688, our glorious deliverer from popery and slavery, King William, landed at Torbay." The quote that begins this chapter comes from a 1764 pamphlet attributed to Franklin titled *A Narrative of the Late Massacres*. It was written following the slaughter by settlers in Pennsylvania of peaceful members of the Six Nations, some of whom were being sheltered by colonists. Franklin was trying to bring calm to Philadelphia, which was divided on how to respond. In the pamphlet, he used his knowledge of the religious leanings of his fellow colonists to make his case. "These were not Enemies," he wrote of the victims, "they were born among us, and yet we have killed them all. But shall we imitate idolatrous Papists, we that are enlightened Protestants?"

A reasonable explanation is that while Franklin embraced religious tolerance to a certain extent, he recognized that intolerance or the appearance of it could be used to influence public opinion or sell almanacs to a largely Protestant public in the colonies. He could don a religious guise like a cloak and then discard it when he was dealing with those of a different persuasion. That would explain Adams's description of him as a religious chameleon and Weber's view that he did and said whatever he thought would help him achieve his goals. It also fits with Franklin's later dealings with Catholic France. But his life in Paris was still far in the future when he left London for Philadelphia in 1726, returning to a world where the French Catholics in Canada and their Indigenous allies remained a constant threat.

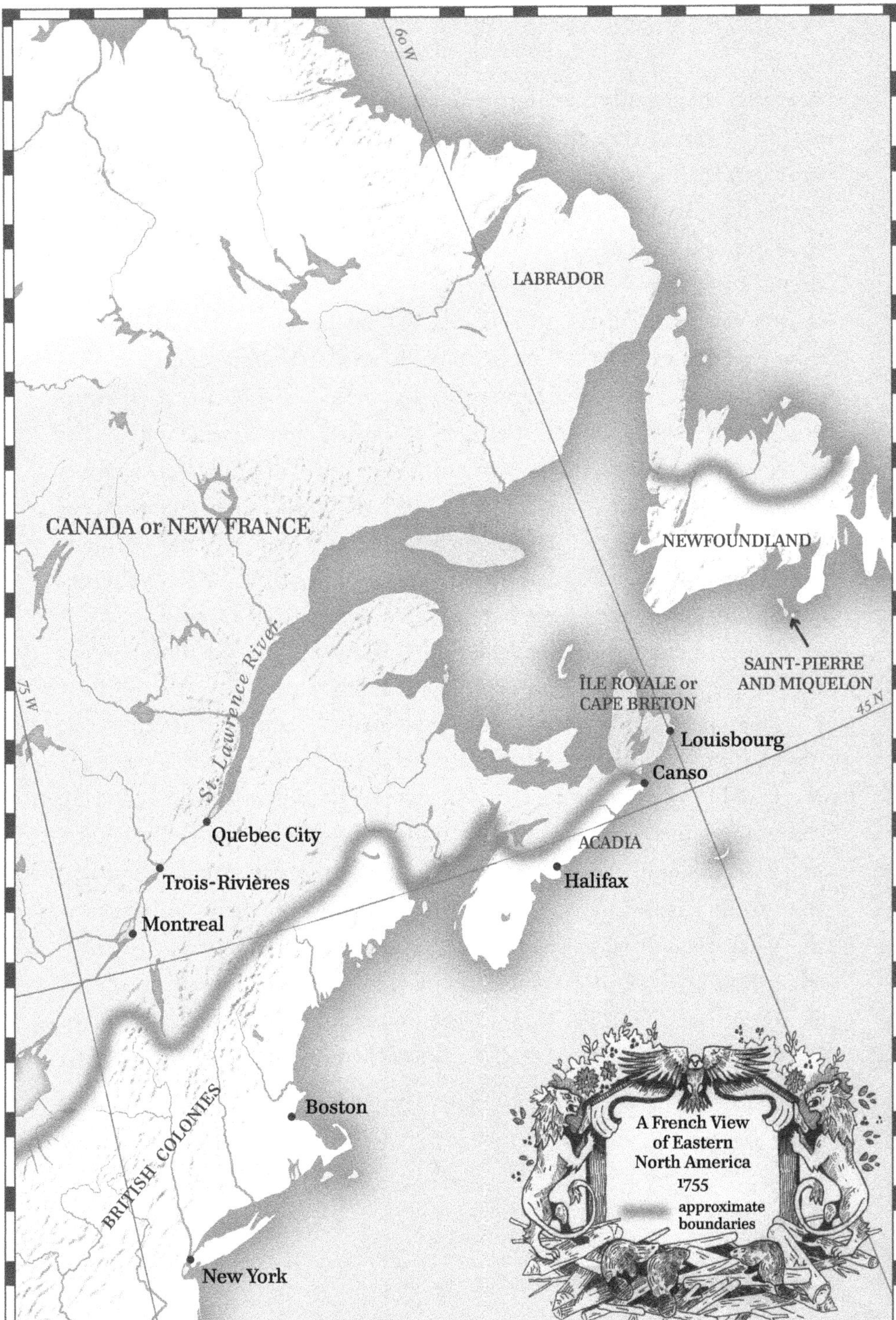

LABRADOR
NEWFOUNDLAND
CANADA or NEW FRANCE
St. Lawrence River
SAINT-PIERRE
AND MIQUELON
ÎLE ROYALE or
CAPE BRETON
Louisbourg
Canso
Quebec City
ACADIA
Trois-Rivières
Halifax
Montreal
Boston
BRITISH COLONIES
New York
60 W
75 W
45 N
A French View
of Eastern
North America
1755
approximate
boundaries

CHAPTER 3

A Dangerous Man: Philadelphia 1726–1748

> I had on the whole abundant reason to be satisfied with my being established in Pennsylvania. There were, however, two things that I regretted, there being no provision for defense, nor for a complete education of youth; no militia, nor any college.
>
> — *Benjamin Franklin*

IN MARCH 1748, MORE THAN TWO DECADES AFTER LEAVING LONDON, Franklin set off with a group of emissaries from Pennsylvania to beg the British colonial governor in New York to lend them cannons. Britain was at war again with France. Enemy privateers were prowling the waters of Delaware Bay, close enough to alarm even the pacifist burghers of Pennsylvania. Franklin spearheaded an effort to persuade reluctant Pennsylvanians to organize and pay for some sort of defence or face what he told them would be a horrible fate at the hands of the French from Canada and their Indigenous allies. Acquiring cannons from New York was part of this campaign.

How had it happened that the young printer who left London for Philadelphia in 1726 was securing arms and helping organize the defence of

Pennsylvania in 1748? It was not a straightforward progression. For many of those years, Britain and France were technically at peace. During that time, Franklin built his business empire.

Success as a Printer

Franklin had worked briefly for a merchant when he returned to Philadelphia before turning back to printing, first in the printing house of Samuel Keimer, where he had passed some months before leaving for London, and then in a shop he set up with Hugh Meredith, a coworker he persuaded to leave Keimer's employ. Their new business prospered. In 1729 Franklin and Meredith took over the newspaper started by Keimer, simplifying its title, *The Universal Instructor in all Arts and Sciences: and Pennsylvania Gazette*, to the *Pennsylvania Gazette*. When the partnership ended, Franklin continued on his own. In 1732 he started *Poor Richard's Almanack*, which would help make his fortune. He used the format he had seen in London, using a mix of factual information interspersed with homespun philosophy. Entries under specific dates reinforced the idea that the French and the Catholics were the enemies. For example, he would mark the date of the French king's birth, writing, "He bids fair to be as great a mischief-maker as his grandfather." The Duke of Cumberland's 1746 victory over Scottish rebels at Culloden would be commemorated with the remark that the rebels had been assisted by "the kings of France and Spain, the Pope and the Devil," who planned to put "a pretended prince" on the throne and make everyone Catholic. "I endeavour'd to make it both entertaining and useful," Franklin wrote of the almanac, "and it accordingly came to be in such demand, that I reap'd considerable profit from it, vending annually near ten thousand."

These were busy years for Franklin, in both his public and private life. He set up house in 1730 with Deborah Read, a woman he had courted then abandoned when he left for London. Their union was common law because Deborah had married a man who turned out to be an unsuitable husband and whose whereabouts were unknown. Around the same time that the couple began living as man and wife, Franklin fathered an illegitimate son,

William. The mother's identity was never revealed. Franklin and Deborah raised William as their own. The couple also had a son, Frankie, who died of smallpox when he was four, and a daughter, Sarah (a.k.a. Sally), who survived. Even as an old man, Franklin castigated himself for not having Frankie inoculated with the live virus from an infected person, a popular but not foolproof treatment.

Using Public Office for Private Gain

Alongside his printing business, Franklin took on the role of clerk of the Pennsylvania assembly in 1736 and became deputy postmaster of Philadelphia in 1737. He set up a discussion club, the Junto, and persuaded its members to establish a subscription library. They pooled funds to buy books, which subscribers could take home to read. Much like his father, who sold candles to the watchmen he supervised in Boston, Franklin was adept at combining public works with private gain. The clerkship led to contracts to print the votes, laws, and other business of the assembly. Being deputy postmaster helped him boost the circulation of his newspaper, which led to more advertisements. The subscription library gave him access to more books, a boon for such a voracious reader. He wrote an anonymous pamphlet, *A Modest Enquiry into the Nature and Necessity of a Paper-Currency*, in support of those assembly members arguing for its creation and was rewarded with a contract to print the new currency. As one biographer concluded, "In business Franklin was extremely alert to the main chance." Another biographer wrote that he was a "consummate networker," always mixing civil and social life and leveraging both to further his business interests.[1]

Franklin was supremely conscious of his image as a businessman, making sure not only to be diligent and hard-working but also to appear to be so. He recounted in his autobiography that he personally carried paper for his print shop in a wheelbarrow down the street, where others could see him. This was work more naturally done by a shop apprentice. "Thus being esteem'd an industrious, thriving young man, and paying duly for what I bought, the merchants who imported stationery solicited my custom; others proposed supplying me with books, and I went on swimmingly," he wrote.

His calculated use of appearance would resurface again in his life as a diplomat in London and Paris.

Turning to Public Affairs

Once he felt financially comfortable, Franklin turned his active mind to public affairs, starting with small projects, like regulating the city watchmen and organizing fire companies, or brigades. A visitor to Philadelphia in 1744 said that while the State House, the Assembly House, and a church on Second Street were good buildings, the majority of houses were "mean and low, and much decayed," and the streets were "generally not paved, very dirty and obstructed with rubbish and lumber."[2] Franklin's initiative was welcomed because fire was much on the minds of Philadelphians. He attempted in 1743 to set up an academy to educate the youth of Pennsylvania. By 1747 he decided to step back from running what had become a publishing conglomerate, with printing shops in other cities. Franklin had helped promising apprentices set up shop in return for a share of the profits. He officially handed over day-to-day operations to his foreman, David Hall, at the start of 1748 and later told a friend that he hoped to have time to read, continue his scientific experiments with electricity, and converse with interesting people. This proved a faint hope, if indeed it was genuine. He was already deeply embroiled in his multipronged effort to push a reluctant Pennsylvania into fortifying itself against anticipated attacks by the French and their allies.

War Returns to North America

Full-fledged war had returned in stages. Britain declared war on Spain in 1739 after a British naval captain told the House of Commons that the Spanish had boarded his ship off the coast of Cuba and sliced off part of his ear. Although there was more at stake than this personal assault, it became known as the War of Jenkins' Ear. That war was subsumed into the War of Austrian Succession in Europe, where France, Spain, Prussia, and Bavaria fought Britain, the German state of Hanover, and the Dutch Republic over who should succeed Charles VI, the Holy Roman emperor and ruler of the Austrian Habsburg monarchy. He had died in 1740 without a male heir. The European conflict spilled over into North America in 1744, when France declared war on Britain after their troops had clashed in Europe. In what was to be called King George's War, the two imperial powers officially resumed their armed struggle for control of North America.

In those days, news travelled at the rate of a sailing ship crossing the Atlantic. The fort at Louisbourg on Cape Breton was closer to Europe than Boston and got wind of the outbreak of war first. The French governor of the fort decided to strike the first blow, sending troops to capture an English fishing village at Canso, about 110 kilometres (70 miles) south on the coast of what was then British Nova Scotia. This incensed the British authorities in Massachusetts Bay. William Shirley, the governor, wrote his superior in London, the Duke of Newcastle, asking for permission to launch an immediate attack on Louisbourg. The French used the harbour there as a base for their fishermen, which depleted British fishing stocks, Shirley wrote, and for their warships and privateers, which disrupted British trade all along the coast, from Newfoundland to the sugar colonies in the Caribbean. Louisbourg also guarded the mouth of the St. Lawrence River, the gateway to Canada and the interior of the continent. Taking it "would probably in a little time be attended with an easy Reduction of that Country," leaving the British in control of the continent. Shirley reckoned that the acquired territory, with its fish, furs, lumber, and promise of security for the British colonies, would be "a more valuable Territory to Great Britain than what any Kingdom or State in Europe has belonging to it."[3]

His was not the only voice in New England calling for a new war of conquest. Robert Livingston, the son of a prominent New York merchant, said assaulting French Canada would be a "noble" undertaking. "The French aim at nothing less than to have the whole Continent," he wrote to a friend in 1746. "I think we ought to have the Same Views and prosecute them, and everyman in his Station should act with Emulation & the utmost vigour and diligence." One Boston newspaper compared the North American war between France and Britain to the epic struggle between Rome and Carthage. Like Carthage, Canada must be conquered.[4]

A combined force of about four thousand men from Connecticut, Massachusetts, and New Hampshire duly set out in the spring of 1745, intent on capturing Louisbourg. Rhode Island offered to supply a vessel. Pennsylvania declined to supply men.

Franklin followed the expedition avidly from Philadelphia. He wrote his brother John in Boston in May 1745. "Our people are extremely impatient to hear of your success at Cape Breton," he wrote. "My shop is filled with thirty inquiries at the coming of every post. Some wonder the place is not yet taken." Franklin mused in the letter about how fortified towns like Louisbourg were "hard nuts to crack" and warned that some of the men in the French garrison were likely to be "devils." There was a certain religious element overlaid on the attack. New England was in the midst of a religious revival called the Great Awakening, which promoted the Puritan spirit against the increasing secularization of society. George Whitefield, one of the leading proponents of this awakening and a friend of Franklin's, provided a motto and a flag for the New Hampshire troops: *Nil desperandum, Christo Duce* (No need to despair, Christ is our leader). Samuel Moody, the chaplain for the expedition, was said to have taken an axe with him, intent on attacking the altars of the Catholic "Antichrist" in Louisbourg.[5]

The *Pennsylvania Gazette*, which Franklin printed and sometimes wrote, carried what news it could glean of the expedition. On May 23, 1745, it ran an essay outlining the economic benefits to be gained if Louisbourg were captured. A couple of weeks later, it printed an illustration of Louisbourg so its readers would have an idea of the situation of the town under siege "by our Forces." That item also talked of how the French king had begun "the present unjust War against the English." It went on to say that the French were preparing a great number of privateers to attack British shipping and they had boasted they would not need to cut firewood on shore because "the Jackstaves of English Vessels would be a Supply sufficient."

The siege did not last long. The French garrison at Louisbourg was weak and in desperate need of provisions. Its commander capitulated June 17, 1745. When the news reached Philadelphia almost a month later, it prompted "upwards of 20 Bonfires" in the streets and much feasting, according to the *Gazette*. Throughout the colonies, it was seen as a great victory for the colonists, because Britain had provided little help. The loss inflamed the French, who increased their attacks on the British colonies. In a two-month period in the spring of 1746, at least thirty-five war parties involving French soldiers and Indigenous allies were sent from Montreal to strike at British colonial settlements near the border.

John Norton, yet another Puritan minister taken captive, wrote a hair-raising account of a 1746 attack and his captivity. He was in Fort Massachusetts with about thirty men, women, and children when it was captured by French and Indigenous fighters, commanded by Pierre de Rigaud de Vaudreuil. The French commander stood by while a group of Indigenous fighters seized the corpse of one of the British defenders, which they subsequently scalped before cutting off the head and arms, wrote Norton. One of the French then took an arm, flayed and roasted it, and offered it to one of the captives to eat. He refused. "The Frenchman dressed the skin of the arm (as we afterwards heard) and made a tobacco pouch of it."[6]

The Franklin household was personally affected by the onset of this new war when William, the illegitimate son, enrolled as an ensign in the army in 1746 and marched off for a projected assault on Canada, involving colonial and British troops. The plan was to have one body of troops sail up the St. Lawrence to Quebec City while the other travelled up Lake Champlain to attack Montreal. It was cancelled at the last minute and the assembled colonial troops were sent home when the promised eight battalions from Britain failed to arrive. The British ministry had decided to redirect them to what it considered more pressing problems in Scotland, the Low Countries, and the Caribbean. This was not the first time the British ministry had left the colonists high and dry. It left them bitter at the seeming neglect of their concerns by the mother country. Some elements of the plan would be used almost thirty years later, when Americans once again set their sights on Canada.

Philadelphia Threatened

French privateers did not seem deterred by the loss of their base in Louisbourg. They resupplied and refitted their vessels in the Caribbean for cruises up the Atlantic coast. In the spring of 1747, they were sighted near the mouth of Delaware Bay. In July a French privateer entered the bay and plundered plantations near Bombay Hook, about 120 kilometres (75 miles) downstream from Philadelphia. The privateers seized four enslaved people, bedding, clothes, and furniture and roughed up several colonists. This set off alarms in Philadelphia. By the time news of the raid reached the city, popular rumour had increased the number of armed attackers to one hundred from about twenty. There was talk that Spanish prisoners, enslaved people, and other desperate men were plotting to seize a ship in the harbour to join the enemy. There was a clamour for increased protection, which ignited a debate in the colony over who should pay for its defence.

Pennsylvania was one of the few remaining colonies whose charter was held by an individual or proprietor rather than a company. William Penn had received the original charter in 1681 to set up a colony, partly as a religious refuge for fellow Quakers. His son Thomas was now the proprietor. Thomas lived in Britain and consistently resisted paying taxes on the family estates in Pennsylvania, money that was needed if the colony was going to mount a credible defence. Pennsylvania had an assembly, selected by the colonists and dominated by Quakers, and it held the purse strings. It also had a governor, appointed by the king or queen and sworn to uphold the Penn family interests, and a council, whose members were selected by the governor. The debate over what to do next pitted the Penns and much of the assembly against the council. The council urged the Quakers to set aside their pacifist principles for the sake of the safety of their fellow colonists. The governor was missing in action because he had returned to Britain for his health.

Anthony Palmer, the president of the council, tried to prod the assembly into action on August 17, 1747, saying the successful attack near Bombay Hook would embolden the enemy, who could descend on the city next spring. The people of Pennsylvania could no longer rely on the length and depth of the Delaware River for protection because the enemy had learned to navigate its twists and turns with the aid of river pilots. "The Terror and Confusion, the Ruin of vast numbers of Families, the Destruction of the Trade, the Bloodshed, Cruelty, & other fatal Consequences which must unavoidably attend the plundering or burning of this City, are too obvious to need a Discription," Palmer told the assembly members. He added that all parts of the government must do something to protect the people of Pennsylvania. The assembly was not to be moved. It responded with a letter on August 25, dismissing the supposed threats as "so many Bravados," which the enemy had no power to undertake. It took issue with Palmer's mention that the colony was defenceless, because using such words would alarm the colonists and Palmer's speech could fall into enemy hands. Erecting fortifications or building ships would cost a lot, yield little benefit, and was against their principles, the letter continued. And even if all these obstacles were removed, the request "is not best timed when our Treasury is low."[7]

The First Successful Public Relations Campaign?

Franklin decided to take things into his own hands. What followed was a carefully constructed and executed campaign, in which he drew on his power as a newspaper publisher, his penchant for planning, his knowledge of human nature, his growing expertise in military matters, and his extensive network of friends. In early November, he published a piece in the *Gazette* aimed at moderate Quakers, who realized something must be done despite their pacifist principles. It argued that Quaker doctrine was opposed to an aggressive war but not to a defensive one. This was a distinction the American colonists would use again in the future. He then wrote and published a pamphlet, *Plain Truth: or, Serious Considerations On the Present State of the City of Philadelphia, and Province of Pennsylvania*, in which he laid out the reasons to invest in defence and countered as best he could the arguments being made against doing so.

Franklin, like Palmer, noted that some Pennsylvanians felt that the war that "rages over a great Part of the known World" would not touch them because of "the Length and Difficulty of our Bay and River" and because they were protected by the northern colonies from French attacks and by colonies to the south from Spanish aggression. He argued this was no longer true. Philadelphia's growing wealth made it a tempting target for the enemy, who had learned the secrets of the river and were informed of the city's defenceless state by spies and traitors. Franklin went on at some length about spies, including their use in Biblical times, citing numerous passages from the Bible. After one such passage that mentioned a priest, he suggested Catholic priests in Pennsylvania were encouraging the enemy. "'Tis well known, that we have Numbers of the same Religion with those who of late encouraged the French to invade our Mother-Country," he wrote. This was a reference to a planned invasion of Britain.

He went on to talk about the Six Nations, the Indigenous confederacy with which the British colonists were at peace. This might not last, he wrote. "The French know the Power and Importance of the Six Nations, and spare no Artifice, Pains or Expence, to gain them to their Interest." He worried the Six Nations might join the enemy forces "when they see that the French, and their Indians, boldly, and with Impunity, ravage the Frontiers of New-York, and scalp the Inhabitants." (British colonists often referred to scalping, although they and their Indigenous allies also indulged in the practice and paid a bounty for scalps.) If the Six Nations changed sides, he wrote, the consequences would be "deserting of Plantations, Ruin, Bloodshed and Confusion!" The colony's trade was also at risk, he wrote. If enemy ships continued to seize ships going out and ships coming in, no one could afford to trade. Businesses would collapse, tradesmen would lose their jobs, and people would move to safer colonies.

Franklin then imagined what would happen to Philadelphia if the enemy, tempted by its riches, sacked and burned the place. The rich would be able to flee, but the "middling People, the Tradesmen, Shopkeepers, and Farmers," could not leave with their families. Those left behind would be lucky to be captured by officers of the French navy; otherwise, they could be left in the hands of "licentious Privateers" and subject "to the wanton and unbridled Rage, Rapine and Lust, of Negroes, Molattoes, and others, the vilest and most abandoned of Mankind."

Having painted this exceedingly dark picture of the future, Franklin turned to the reasons the colony was defenceless and what could be done. He blamed the "wealthy and powerful people" who sat in the assembly. If they could not overcome their religious scruples, he said, referring to the Quakers, they should retire and let others take charge of government. Wealthy members of the opposition were no better in his view. They did not want to spend money on defences that would protect Quaker trade. It seemed that both parties in the assembly "had sworn the Ruin of the Country, and invited the French, our most inveterate Enemy, to destroy it."

If their leaders would not do their duty and protect Pennsylvania, it fell to the people to make their own arrangements, he concluded. "All we want is Order, Discipline, and a few good Cannon." After all, great numbers of them came from the "British Race," whose ancestors "made so glorious a Stand for our Religion and Liberties, when invaded by a powerful French Army, join'd by Irish Catholicks, under a bigoted Popish King!" As for the large number of Germans in Pennsylvania, they were brave and steady and would likely want to defend their newly acquired liberty and prosperity. "The Way to secure Peace is to be prepared for War," he said. He had some ideas on how to do this and would make them known in a few days. Franklin signed the pamphlet "A Tradesman of Philadelphia," neatly positioning himself with the "middling people" who were most at risk, as opposed to the wealthy and the Quakers.

Rousing the public was only the first step. Franklin followed through with detailed plans on how to establish an association, separate from the colonial assembly, under which volunteer militia companies could form and a lottery that would raise funds for the necessary equipment, especially cannons. He was careful to consult widely before presenting his schemes, ensuring that none of this came as a surprise to the men in positions of power. Franklin later estimated that about ten thousand men signed up for the militia. They armed themselves, elected their officers, and met for militia training every week. The Philadelphia regiment wanted him to be their colonel, but he declined, saying he was not the best choice. At the end of November 1747, Franklin wrote Cadwallader Colden, a New York friend with whom he mainly discussed scientific experiments, to say that *Plain Truth* "has wonderfully spirited us to up and defend our selves and Country" and to tell him a lottery was being set up to raise £3,000 "for erecting a Battery of Cannon below the City."

He kept the need for defence and the consequences of not having it in the public eye by running items in the *Gazette*. In December, the *Gazette* ran a letter from Conrad Weiser, the colony's authority on Indigenous groups, saying the French had induced two groups living near the Mississippi to make war on Pennsylvania. There was an advertisement in that same issue for *The New Manual Exercise*, a military handbook useful for militia training, that Franklin published and sold. The following month, the *Gazette* ran a story about how eight hundred of the voluntary militia, with "Drums beating and Colours flying," assembled before the State House in Philadelphia on January 1 to elect their officers and present their choices to the president and members of the council. Franklin had left nothing to chance. He designed the devices and mottos on the standards and ran descriptions of them in the January 12 issue of his newspaper. Many of these symbols and sayings are still used today. One had an eagle descending from the skies with the motto *A Deo Victoria* (Victory from God). Another had a coronet and plume of feathers, with the words "In God We Trust."

Presenting the officers to the president and council gave the volunteer militia a semi-official gloss, even though it was not backed by the Quaker-dominated assembly. Franklin observed in his autobiography that he believed the defence of the colony "was not disagreeable to any of them, provided they were not required to assist in it." Some seemed to have bought his argument that a defensive war was different than an offensive one. He kept his job as clerk of the assembly. In private letters to friends, he passed on rumours of invasion. In January 1748, he wrote his friend James Logan about two prisoners who had escaped from Canada, bringing news that the French were readying three thousand men and "a great body of Indians" to attack Albany. Unnamed people in New York believed these rumours to be true, he wrote.

The Search for Cannons

Forming the militia was only one part of the solution. The colony still needed cannons. Petitions had been sent to Pennsylvania's proprietor, Thomas Penn, in London. The merchants of Philadelphia petitioned the Lords of the Admiralty in London to send a warship armed with cannons to patrol Delaware Bay. Anticipating there would be no help coming from the proprietor, the lottery organizers sought to purchase cannons in Britain with the £3,000 that had been raised. But getting them across the ocean would take time. The council wrote the governors of other colonies, including Massachusetts Bay and New York, asking for the loan of cannons. They even wrote the temporary commander-in-chief at Louisbourg to see if he could spare a few. Franklin contacted his friend Colden to find out whether New York would be willing to grant their request. George Clinton, the New York governor, had responded to the initial request by saying he would get back to them. New York was anticipating a visit by an engineer from Britain, who was to advise on the colony's defences. When the council in Pennsylvania learned the engineer had arrived, it decided to immediately send a delegation to meet with Clinton.

Franklin described in his autobiography how the New York governor was initially noncommittal. Pennsylvania did not get much sympathy from the other colonies because its Quaker-dominated assembly resisted spending money on anything that smacked of war and did little to help other colonies defend the frontier. The governor of Massachusetts Bay, whose colony was a frequent target of the raids, had refused outright to lend the Pennsylvanians cannons. The emissaries turned to New York, making an arduous two-day journey to dine with the governor and his council, a group of senior advisors. Copious amounts of Madeira wine, drunk from generous glasses called bumpers, led the governor to change his mind. The governor said he would lend them six cannons, Franklin recounted. But as the meal continued and the Madeira flowed, he raised it to ten, and then finally to eighteen. "They were fine Cannon, 18 pounders, with their Carriages," Franklin wrote, referring to the approximate weight of the cannon balls. They were "soon transported and mounted on our Battery, where the Associators kept a nightly Guard while the War lasted: And among the rest I regularly took my Turn of Duty there as a common Soldier."

The loan did not go quite as smoothly as Franklin implied. The New Yorkers insisted the Pennsylvanians put up a £1,000 bond to back their promise to return the cannons within three months of any request from New York. The transport to Philadelphia by ship was delayed and then rerouted overland when the *Don Pedro*, a Spanish warship, was sighted off the coast. But it went well enough that the cannons eventually arrived and were installed on one of the fortified emplacements, or batteries, on the waterfront. By May the governor's council in Pennsylvania announced with some satisfaction that the colony was no longer defenceless and could protect itself "against the Designs of our Enemies."[8] Franklin was careful to ensure credit for this accomplishment was shared. But it was widely known he was the driving force. He was now seen as a military expert. According to Sally F. Griffith, an academic who studied American boosterism, Franklin set the template for such public campaigns. The first step was to persuade people there was an emergency and that they must unite to face a common threat. The second was to call a public meeting, present a plan, and keep the issue in the public eye. The third was to ensure a broad number of citizens were on board and to raise money through individual donations. There must be a leader, which in this case was Franklin, but by keeping in the background, he ensured that the creation of the militia was seen as a community initiative and credit was widely shared.[9]

Not everyone was pleased with Franklin's efforts. Penn, the proprietor, fretted that the volunteer militia was founded on a contempt for government. In a March 1748 letter to Richard Peters, the secretary and a member of the council who was loyal to the proprietor's interests, he predicted it would all end in anarchy and confusion. "The People are so fond of what they call Liberty as to fall into Licenciousness," Penn observed. Once they saw they could act in a military manner independent of government, he asked, why would they not act against it? In a subsequent letter to Peters in June, Penn took direct aim at Franklin. "He is a dangerous Man and I should be very Glad he inhabited any other Country, as I believe him of a very uneasy Spirit. However as he is a Sort of Tribune of the People, he must be treated with regard."

With the militia formed and at least some cannons in place, Pennsylvania waited for the anticipated attack by the French. Instead, news came in August 1748 that Britain and France had negotiated a peace treaty at the end of April. The *Gazette* ran a brief announcement on August 18 about "His Majesty's Proclamation for a Cessation of Arms." The Treaty of Aix-la-Chapelle, involving Britain, France, and Austria-Hungary, was officially signed in October 1748. It brought peace, which was welcome in the colonies, but included an exchange of conquered territories, which was not. The fort at Louisbourg, whose capture was a source of pride for the colonial forces, was given back to France. Britain regained Madras in India. The question of which empire controlled the lands west of the Appalachian Mountains was left undecided, making a future rematch between Britain and France in North America likely, if not inevitable.

Although his militia never tasted battle, the experience of organizing a fighting force and securing weapons was not a wasted one for Franklin. It gave him a deeper understanding of military matters, which he would lean on in subsequent years. It gave him practice in using his pen to rally the public to his cause, which in this case was the proper defence of Pennsylvania. As part of this process, he learned it was effective to tap into local prejudices, such as anti-Catholicism. And it established, or perhaps re-established, the idea in his mind that the French in Canada were a threat to the security of the colonies, which set him to thinking about how that threat could be removed.

CHAPTER 4

Casting a Covetous Eye: Philadelphia 1749–1756

No rest and no hope of rest for our thirteen colonies as long as the French remain the masters of Canada.[1]

— *Benjamin Franklin*

FRANKLIN SPENT HIS FIFTIETH BIRTHDAY LEADING 130 POORLY clothed and badly armed men over rough terrain in the Blue Mountains of Pennsylvania. They had slept in a barn the previous night and set out that morning hoping to reach Gnadenhutten, the site of a recent massacre, before nightfall. Franklin stayed dry on that rainy, cold day in January 1756 because he had a good coat, unlike most of his men. Their clothes were soaked and their gunpowder wet, leaving them vulnerable to attack. Three kilometres (two miles) into the miserable march, they turned back to spend another night in the barn. When they reached Gnadenhutten the following day, they were greeted with "one continued Scene of Horror and Desolation," wrote Thomas Lloyd, a doctor who accompanied the expedition. Since the raid in November, the mangled corpses of the villagers had been rotting in the open, amongst the charred remains of their houses and

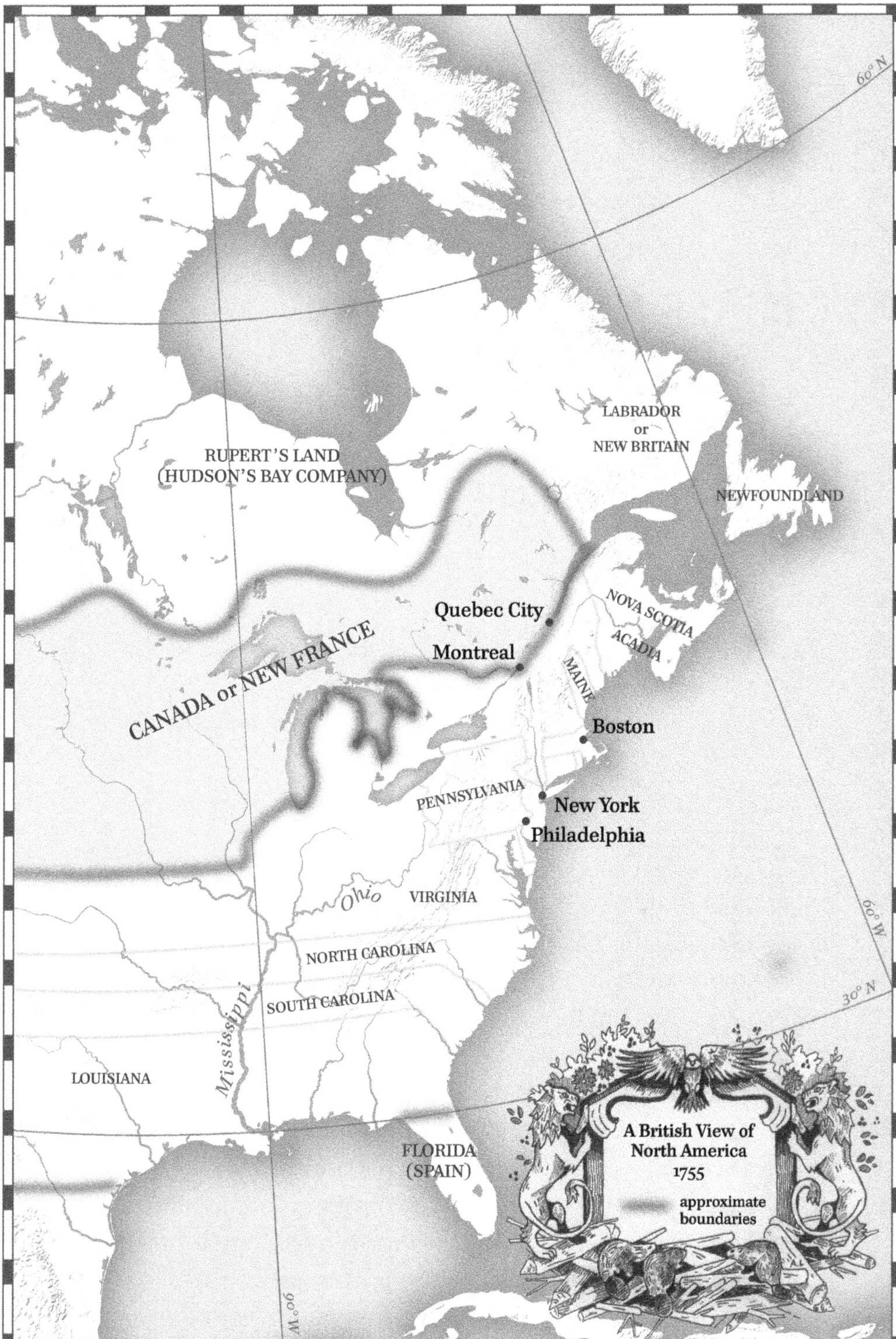

60° N
LABRADOR
or
NEW BRITAIN
RUPERT'S LAND
(HUDSON'S BAY COMPANY)
NEWFOUNDLAND
Quebec City
NOVA SCOTIA
ACADIA
CANADA or NEW FRANCE
Montreal
MAINE
Boston
PENNSYLVANIA
New York
Philadelphia
Ohio
VIRGINIA
60° W
NORTH CAROLINA
30° N
SOUTH CAROLINA
Mississippi
LOUISIANA
FLORIDA
(SPAIN)
90° W
A British View of
North America
1755
approximate
boundaries

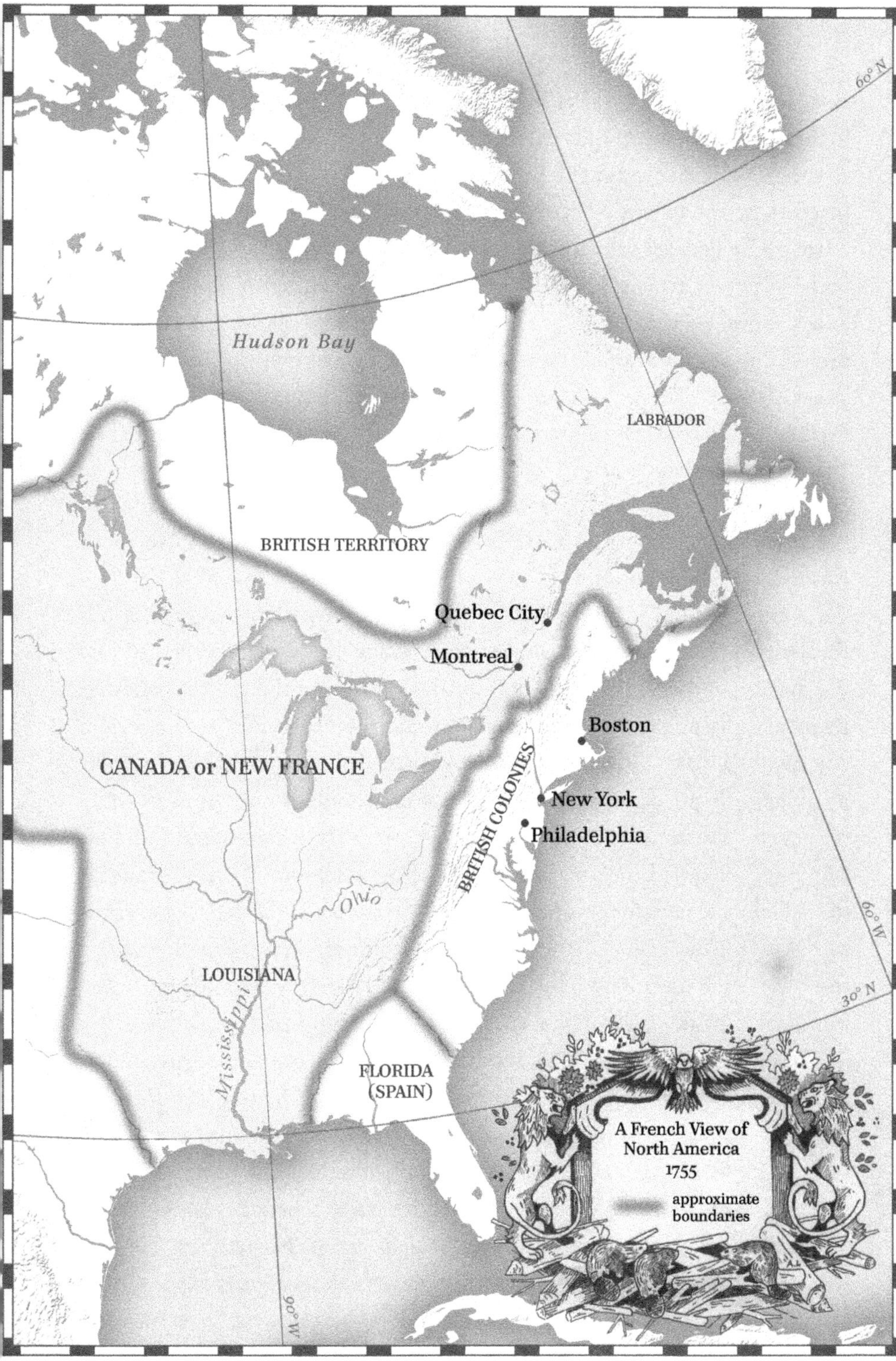
60° N
Hudson Bay
LABRADOR
BRITISH TERRITORY
Quebec City
Montreal
Boston
CANADA or NEW FRANCE
BRITISH COLONIES
New York
Philadelphia
Ohio
60° W
LOUISIANA
30° N
Mississippi
FLORIDA
(SPAIN)
A French View of
North America
1755
approximate
boundaries
90° W

church. The "wanton Cruelty" of the slaughter left Lloyd so angry he wanted to "scalp all I lay my Hands on with unrelenting Rage."[2]

The grisly assault on the mission settlement was one of many taking place along the colony's northwestern frontier as grievances that had been festering for decades were avenged. Indigenous warriors, including Shawnee and Delaware, attacked American settlers encroaching on their territory and the new British outposts built to protect them. The war parties were armed, incited, and sometimes accompanied by the French. These bloody skirmishes on the Pennsylvania frontier and in Nova Scotia, the former French Acadia that was now a British colony, eventually merged into the French and Indian War in North America. It in turn became part of the Seven Years' War, when Britain and France expanded their land and sea battles to coastal Africa, the Caribbean, India, the Mediterranean, Northern Europe, and the Philippines.

When war looked like a certainty, Franklin helped push a militia bill through the Pennsylvania assembly, where he had been a member since 1751. He overcame Quaker qualms by inserting a clause in the bill that allowed members of the pacifist sect to opt out, and he proceeded to organize a colonial militia for a second time. It was still voluntary. This was a point of pride with the colonists, who thought paid soldiers could not possibly be as good as men who were fighting to protect their homes and families. But this time it had the official approval of the assembly. Then, as Franklin described in his autobiography, Robert Hunter Morris, the deputy governor of Pennsylvania, "prevail'd with me to take charge of our North-western frontier, which was infested by the enemy, and provide for the defense of the inhabitants by raising troops and building a series of forts."

Franklin believed in public service, but as with so many of his public-spirited activities, he had additional motives for leaving comfortable Philadelphia for a few rough weeks on the frontier. He had his eye on the rich, arable land beyond the Appalachian Mountains, known as the Ohio country, thinking it the perfect place to create two new British colonies. Shoring up the frontier defences would help make that happen. He had thought long and hard over the preceding five years about the expansion of the colonies and was convinced their future lay to the west. This was first and foremost Indigenous territory, but it was also claimed by New France and sparsely inhabited by French fur traders and military outposts. The British had rival claims but less of a physical presence. The imperial powers had not resolved the question of who owned the Ohio country in previous treaties. An answer was urgently needed now that settlers and speculators were crossing the mountains, hungry for land. Franklin had cut his military teeth organizing a militia and procuring arms. Now he was taking an active part in driving the French out of a part of North America they considered to be part of New France. He would eventually throw his considerable weight behind ensuring that Britain had it all.

Franklin's Practical Approach on the Frontier

In writing about his time on the frontier, Franklin showed none of the emotion displayed by Dr. Lloyd about Gnadenhutten. Perhaps it had diminished in the interval between the event in 1756 and when he started writing his autobiography in 1771. But even in his letters to Governor Morris at the time, he mostly stuck to the facts. In his autobiography, he called the settlement "desolated" and then moved on to more practical matters, such as finding wood to build huts. He wrote about indulging his scientific curiosity by timing how long it took two men to fell a pine tree (six minutes) and investigating how the unseen Indigenous watchers in the area dug holes for fires and hung their feet over the edge to keep them warm. The horror of the slaughter did not deter him from his work. "The Indians had burned Gnadenhut, a village settled by the Moravians, and massacred the inhabitants," he wrote in his autobiography, "but the place was thought a good situation for one of the forts."

Franklin approached his other tasks with the same practical bent. He sent a remarkably detailed set of instructions to Captain John Van Etten, who was leading one of the colonial militia companies posted in the area. Franklin told Van Etten how many men should be posted and exactly where they should stand; how much bread, pork, beef, and rum they should be allotted and when the rum should be doled out; and how much the men should be paid, including extra amounts for those who supplied their own blankets and guns. He pointed out that the colonial government offered forty dollars "for each scalp of an Indian Enemy."[3] Also on offer, but not mentioned, was an extraordinary bounty of $700 for the heads of two Delaware Chiefs. He clearly condoned scalping at this juncture but would later try to make enemies appear barbarous when they used the same tactic.

Dealing with the frightened settlers was another part of Franklin's job. He tried to stop people fleeing the area by threatening to disband or remove militia companies sent there to protect them. Settlers should "behave like Men, do something for themselves, and assist the Province's soldiers," he grumbled in a January letter to Morris. And it was his clever suggestion to the militia chaplain, who bemoaned low attendance at prayers, that part of the daily rum ration should be doled out at the end of divine services. "And never were prayers more generally and more punctually attended," he observed with satisfaction in his autobiography. Throughout this period, he kept the public in Philadelphia, 120 kilometres (75 miles) to the southeast, fully abreast of developments through frequent reports in the *Pennsylvania Gazette*.

He wrote the governor again on January 25, telling him the men had completed a wooden "Stockado" about 38 metres long by 15 metres wide (125 feet by 50 feet). From his description, the fort sounds similar to those depicted in movies about the American west — a solid row of thick logs, pointed at the top, set in a ditch about one metre (three feet) deep. He was responsible for three such forts, spaced across close to fifty kilometres (thirty miles) of frontier. "This Day we hoisted your Flag, made a general Discharge of our Pieces, which had been long loaded, and of our two Swivels," Franklin told Morris. In a letter sent the same day to his common-law wife, Deborah, he thanked her for sending him roast beef, roast veal, and minced pies and said he expected to complete his work within the next ten days, after which he planned to return home.

Sleeping in a barn, or in a hastily constructed hut, was a far cry from Franklin's regular life in Philadelphia, where he was a member of the colonial assembly and deputy postmaster general of British North America. He obtained that royal appointment in 1753, after paying a friend in London to lobby for him. These duties were not onerous and left him plenty of time to conduct his electricity experiments, already gaining him renown in scientific circles in Britain and France, and to develop his thinking on the future expansion of the colonies.

Building a Rationale for the Possession of Canada

Three papers Franklin wrote in the early 1750s reveal why he thought that some of, if not all, the territory claimed by France in North America was needed for the British colonies to fulfill their promise and what had to be done to achieve this goal. The first was *Observations Concerning the Increase of Mankind, Peopling of Countries, &c*, a paper ostensibly about population growth that was written in 1751 and circulated among friends before being published in 1755. It was followed by *Short Hints towards a Scheme for Uniting the Northern Colonies*, his plan for the colonies to unite so they could defend themselves against French Canada, written for the Albany Congress of June–July 1754. The third was *A Plan for Settling Two Western Colonies in North America*, written after the congress in 1754, which built on the previous two papers and spelled out his intention to take some of the contested territory west of the Appalachian Mountains, claimed and partially occupied by the French.

Observations, the first of the papers, was described by one historian as one of the earliest formulations of manifest destiny, a phrase coined in 1845 to express the idea that Americans were fated to control the continent.[4] In it, Franklin argued that population expansion depended on land being available for men to purchase, so they could farm it and support a family. Because land was more plentiful in America than in Britain, men were encouraged to marry. There were more marriages per hundred people in the colonies each year than in Europe; couples married at a younger age; and they had more children. He reckoned the colonial population would at least double every twenty years and would eventually exceed that of Britain. (He turned out to be correct.) The key was continued access to more and more land to accommodate this growth. At one point in the pamphlet, he switched from talking about America to talking about North America, saying: "But not withstanding this increase, so vast is the Territory of North America, that it will require many ages to settle it fully." It is unclear whether this was just a slip of the pen — even then Americans frequently conflated America with North America — or whether he was already seriously contemplating British control of the top two-thirds of the continent. Toward the end of the pamphlet, Franklin referred to negotiations between Britain and France over the boundaries between the British and French colonies in North America that had begun after the last war. The pamphlet was written before the French and Indian War started and before the boundary talks had broken down. "How important an affair then to Britain, is the present treaty for settling the bounds between her Colonies and the French, and how careful should she be to secure room enough, since on the room depends so much the increase of her people?"

In the last two paragraphs of his original *Observations*, which he dropped in later versions on the advice of friends, he argued for America to be "purely white." That meant excluding people from Africa, whom he described as "black or tawny," and people from Asia, who were "chiefly tawny." He did not stop there. The Spaniards, Italians, French, Russians, and Swedes had "a swarthy Complexion." He showed special contempt for Germans, already present in Pennsylvania in great numbers. Not only were these "Palatine Boors" swarthy by his reckoning, but they also "swarm into our Settlements, and by herding together establish their Language and Manners to the Exclusion of ours." That he could now attack the Germans after calling them brave and steady in his 1747 pamphlet *Plain Truth* is an example of how he would shift his opinion to suit the goal at hand. His attack on the German colonists would later come back to haunt him.

Some historians have suggested that Franklin was motivated to write his *Observations* because he was irritated by British legislation restricting iron manufacturing in Pennsylvania and by Britain's refusal to consider a Pennsylvania law that limited how many convicts could be sent to the colony. He ensured his views were known in London by arranging to have many of his papers reprinted there. *Observations* appeared in two popular British publications, *The Gentleman's Magazine* and *Scots Magazine*.

He certainly bristled at Britain's attempts to stymie manufacturing in the colonies so that British merchants could buy colonial raw materials, transform them into goods, and sell them back to the colonists at a profit. Imperial policy was all about what worked best for Britain, an attitude that would eventually spark the revolution.

Franklin suggested Britain's worries about competing with colonial manufacturers were unfounded because the colonists were more interested in farming than manufacturing, if they had access to land. The empire would benefit from the growing number of colonists, he continued, because they represented a growing market for British goods. The separate decision to ignore Pennsylvania's limits on convicts irritated him because he blamed them for crimes, such as arson, murder, and theft, and thought Britain's decision was high-handed. Even then, England had a long history of making its undesirables someone else's problem by shipping them abroad. Franklin made these points in a satirical piece that appeared in the *Gazette* in 1751, in which he proposed sending a shipload of rattlesnakes to Britain as a token of colonial gratitude for British felons.

Franklin's Plan for Union Looks a Lot Like the One Later Used for Canada

Franklin's *Short Hints towards a Scheme for Uniting the Northern Colonies* and the accompanying *Reasons and Motives for the Albany Plan of Union* argued that the colonies had to set aside their petty grievances and jealousies and unite to defend themselves against attacks by the French in Canada and their allies. In *Reasons*, an explanatory piece he wrote around the same time, Franklin noted that in times of danger, the various legislative assemblies often waited to see what the others would do, fretted about doing more than their share, or refused to do anything if they were not immediately at risk. When Virginia asked seven other colonies for assistance in countering French attacks in the Ohio country, six of the seven did nothing, he wrote. He concluded that "one principal encouragement to the French, in invading and insulting British American dominions, was their knowledge of our disunited state." Overarching control of Indigenous policy was needed, he said, to avoid the disputes that had arisen under the current disjointed system, which hindered settlement, and to keep the Indigenous Peoples from being cheated, which had led to attacks. The plan envisioned an expansion of the colonies by establishing new settlements on land purchased from Indigenous Peoples in the interior of the continent.

Franklin pushed hard for union at the congress of seven colonies held in Albany, New York, in June and July 1754. The British ministry had originally approved the congress, thinking it would allow the delegates to meet with leaders of the Haudenosaunee Confederacy, or Six Nations. Indigenous support, or at least neutrality, was crucial if the British colonies were to win a war with New France. The Six Nations still held the balance of power in the region. Franklin, one of four commissioners from Pennsylvania, thought it a good opportunity to present the plan of union he had been thinking about for a number of years. Westward expansion was impossible unless the French and their allies were defeated by the united colonies.

An item that appeared in the *Gazette* in May 1754 and was attributed to him helped prepare the ground. It said the French were confident of gaining control of the Ohio country, because unlike the disunited British colonies, they had "the very great Advantage of being under one Direction, with one Council, and one Purse." The item was accompanied by the now-famous illustration of a snake cut in pieces along with the warning "Join or Die."

His proposed remedy makes interesting reading for Canadians because the structure he suggested is similar to the one used when the Dominion of Canada was created more than a century later. In Franklin's plan, the colonies would have jurisdiction over most matters but would form a Grand Council to oversee areas where unity would better serve the common interest, such as defence and Indigenous policy. Above the Grand Council would be a senior official appointed and paid by the British Crown. Franklin originally called this official the governor general but later changed the title to president general at the request of the delegates. Union would be achieved through an act of the British Parliament. The British North America Act of 1867, which established the Dominion of Canada, had many of these same elements: a governor general appointed by the Crown, a legislative body called the House of Commons instead of Grand Council, and a division of powers between that body and the provinces.

The delegates to the Albany Congress broadly supported Franklin's idea. Several had sketched out similar thoughts prior to the meeting. But the legislative assemblies in the colonies, whose agreement was necessary, still jealously guarded their own prerogatives and would not lend their support. The British ministry was opposed. It was wary of the colonies gaining too much military might. Writing in 1789, Franklin observed that had his plan or something like it been adopted in 1754, "the subsequent Separation of the Colonies from the Mother country might not so soon have happened." The united colonies could have organized their own defence without the need of British troops, he wrote.

Although Franklin does not say so, inspiration for his governance idea might also have come from the Haudenosaunee, whose confederacy consisted of six nations: Cayuga, Mohawk, Onondaga, Oneida, Seneca, and Tuscarora. At the 1744 treaty negotiations in Lancaster, Pennsylvania, Canasatego, an Onondaga Chief, said that the unity and understanding between the confederacy members gave them "great Weight and Authority" with neighbouring nations. "We are a powerful Confederacy," Canasatego told the representatives of Pennsylvania, Maryland, and Virginia, "and, by your observing the same Methods our wise Forefathers have taken, you will acquire such Strength and Power; therefore whatever befalls you, never fall out with one another."[5] Franklin would have been aware of Canasatego's speech because he had edited and printed the proceedings of treaty conferences since 1736. It would take several more decades before the American colonists would follow the Haudenosaunee lead.

Linking Land Speculation to Security

In his *Plan for Settling Two Western Colonies in North America*, Franklin went from justifying the need for more land to laying out a concrete proposal for taking some of the contested territory from the French. "The great country back of the Appalachian mountains, on both sides of the Ohio, and between that river and the lakes; is now well known both to the English and the French, to be one of the finest in North America," he wrote. The French were "making open encroachments on these territories, in defiance of our known rights." If these encroachments were not stopped, the French population would increase because they had access to more land, he reasoned. This would confine British colonists to the strip of land between the mountains and the sea. Worse still, the French would undoubtedly persuade Indigenous Peoples to "kill and scalp our people" and push the settlers on the frontier back to safer ground in established colonies. "If two strong colonies of English were settled between the Ohio and lake Erie," it would protect the existing colonies and would prevent "the dreaded junction of the French settlements in Canada, with those of Louisiana." The new colonies would also be good places from which the British could "annoy" both Louisiana, by going down the Ohio and Mississippi Rivers, and the southern part of Canada, by sailing over the lakes. "Such settlements may better be made now, than fifty years hence," he counselled, "because it is easier to settle ourselves, and thereby prevent the French settling there, as they seem now to intend, than to remove them when strongly settled." In this paper, he linked colonial expansion to the union outlined in his Albany Plan.

Franklin had done all this thinking and theorizing about future colonial expansion before he found himself marching through the frontier wilderness. He would repeat elements from all three papers in the years ahead, as his vision expanded to include all of Canada. For the time being, he was focused on the Ohio country or territory, a loosely defined region west of the Appalachians and south of Lake Erie, which the French considered to be part of Canada.

In July 1756, after he had returned from the frontier, Franklin wrote the British preacher George Whitefield, a business client and friend, saying how wonderful it would be if the two of them jointly settled a colony on the Ohio. "What a glorious Thing it would be, to settle in that fine Country a large Strong Body of Religious and Industrious People! What a security to the other Colonies; and Advantage to Britain, by Increasing her People, Territory, Strength and Commerce." Franklin had it on good authority that it was a "fine" country because he had sent his son, William, on an expedition to the interior in 1748 with a fur trader. William returned with glowing reports of a rich country ripe for settlement beyond the mountains.[6] This joint project never came to fruition. Franklin may have written Whitefield about westward expansion in the hope that the preacher would win converts to the idea in London. British investors had been important backers of land speculation companies from the beginning. Franklin would later advocate in London on behalf of some of these companies, including a proposal put forward by William for two colonies in the vaguely defined Ohio and Illinois territories. The Illinois territory lay west of the Ohio territory, southwest of Lake Michigan. It was considered by the French Canadians to be part of the *pays-d'en-haut* (upper country). Franklin became personally involved with other land speculation schemes, as did many of the founding fathers. He had significant landholdings in the Ohio country and Nova Scotia when he died.

Why There Were Competing Claims over the Ohio Country

The "known rights" Franklin accused the French of trampling in the Ohio country were mainly in the eye of the beholder. Which European power claimed title to what was Indigenous land was hopelessly muddled because of the penchant of both French and English monarchs to grant charters to individuals and companies without reference to each other, let alone the Indigenous Peoples whose land they were parcelling out. For example, Louis XIII of France issued an edict in July 1626 giving the Compagnie des Cent-Associés the entire continent, without any reference to the 1609 charter given to the Virginia Company by James I of England. It granted the company a massive swath of territory that stretched from the Atlantic to the Pacific and overlapped with the French grant. In the boundary talks that began in Paris in 1750, French commissioners Étienne de Silhouette and Roland-Michel Barrin, Marquis de La Galissonière, spent considerable time refuting claims to territory made with equal ferocity by the British commissioners, William Shirley, governor of Massachusetts, and William Mildmay. One point they squabbled over incessantly was whether John Cabot, or Giovanni Caboto, established an English claim when he sailed to North America in 1497, as the British maintained, or whether he was a Venetian, as the French replied, who undertook the voyage at his own expense and could not be credited with a territorial claim because he was really looking for the northwest passage to China.[7]

The squabbling was not confined to the imperial powers. There were disputes among and within British colonies whose claims overlapped. Six British colonies had charters that suggested their land extended from the Atlantic to the Pacific Ocean, which they called the Southern Sea: Connecticut, Georgia, Massachusetts, North Carolina, South Carolina, and Virginia. Franklin noted to a friend that his plan to establish two western colonies was designed in part to prevent settlers from Connecticut from invading the area. When the Ohio Company of Virginia, backed by members of the elite in that colony, began surveying an eighty-thousand-hectare (two-hundred-thousand-acre) tract just west of the Appalachian Mountains in 1750, it alarmed not just the French and the Indigenous Peoples but also some colonists in Pennsylvania, Connecticut, and New York. Those in Pennsylvania and Connecticut felt the Virginians were trespassing on their land. The fur traders in New York, rivals to the French Canadian traders, feared settlement would hurt their business by driving fur-bearing animals away. William Douglass, a Boston physician, argued in a widely read pamphlet that the Appalachian Mountains should form the western border of the colonies with French territories and that the St. Lawrence River and the Great Lakes should form the northern border. George III was said to have bought a copy of the pamphlet for his library.

European Squabbles Undermine the Unity of the Six Nations

There were also disputes among the Indigenous Peoples. The Six Nations had defeated Indigenous groups, including the Shawnee and Delaware, as far west as the Mississippi River and claimed that by right of conquest, they alone had the power to dispose of lands in the Ohio country in treaties with the British. This right was disputed by the French but readily accepted by the British as a basis for land deals. The treaties the British negotiated were often exercises in sleight of hand, with names rearranged on maps and vague wording used to disguise the extent of territory being transferred.

The sale of these lands caused friction in the Indigenous world at a time when tensions were rising among the Six Nations. Wooed by French and

British officials with presents and promises, it was becoming harder for the group to maintain its unity and neutrality. The Mohawk in the east were inclined to support the British in a war with the French. The Seneca in the west leaned toward the French. The Onondaga, Cayuga, Tuscarora, and Oneida in the centre largely wanted to remain neutral. Both imperial powers fretted that some or all the Six Nations might support the enemy if it came to war. The pressure they exerted was tearing the Six Nations apart.

Misleading Maps

Britain and France supported their territorial claims with misleading maps. An important one published in 1755 by John Mitchell, who was born in Virginia, showed no western limit to the borders of Georgia, North and South Carolina, and Virginia (see page 62). Virginia, according to Mitchell, also stretched north to Lakes Huron and Michigan. New York and New England extended to the St. Lawrence. A large chunk of unnamed territory north of the Great Lakes, encompassing most of what is now southern Ontario, was marked British. New France (or Canada, as it was labelled on the map) only began north of the Ottawa River as far as Mitchell was concerned. The map had been commissioned by Lord Halifax, head of the Board of Trade, one of the governmental bodies responsible for the affairs of the colonies. At the time, Halifax was agitating for war with the French in North America. The map would later be used in the Paris peace negotiations, which resulted in Britain recognizing American independence, and again during the negotiations at Ghent, which ended the War of 1812 in North America. This was not a neutral interpretation of existing borders.

The French were no better. A map done that same year by Jacques-Nicolas Bellin, chief engineer of the cartographic section of France's Ministère de la Marine, drew a hard line down the spine of the Appalachian Mountains for the western border of the British colonies (see page 63). Louisiana, a French possession, began just west of those mountains and merged seamlessly in the north with Canada, which on this map went well below the Great Lakes. According to Bellin's map, the Ohio country was French. Bellin does not appear to have ever visited New France, but he had access to maps, both official and those submitted by explorers, that the French ministry had carefully compiled over the centuries. This dispute might have continued indefinitely, with each side issuing increasingly fanciful maps, but the inability of the boundary commissioners to reach agreement, the increase in fort-building and colonial settlement in the disputed area, and changes in imperial thinking about the importance of North America nudged the two sides closer to outright war.

Britain and France See Their Colonies in a New Light

The colonies had long been pawns in an imperial chess match, often valued more for how they could be used against the other player in the struggle for European or global supremacy than for any intrinsic worth. There was a dawning recognition in Britain that the colonies were important to British manufacturers, both as a market for their goods and as a source of raw materials, but Britain's position in Europe remained the paramount concern. By one estimate, British exports to North America rose from about 6 percent of exports in 1700 to about 26 percent by the early 1770s. Access to the rich fishing grounds off Newfoundland was prized by both imperial powers, not just for the fish and seals but also as a training ground for sailors who could be employed by their navies in times of war. Having trained sailors at the ready became more important to both powers after the French navy went on a shipbuilding spree, producing thirty-seven warships between 1749 and 1755. France and Britain each saw a presence on the mainland of the continent as extra protection for their respective sugar islands in the Caribbean, which some in Europe considered more of a prize than anything the continental colonies had to offer.

French attitudes toward their North American colonies mirrored those of the British. If the British thought the colonies were important, then so did the French. French ministers were informed by reports written by the two boundary commissioners: de Silhouette, an agent of the foreign ministry who became familiar with British views during his time in Britain as a tobacco merchant, and La Galissonière, a former naval officer and one-time commandant-general of New France. "It cannot be denied that this Colony has been always a burden to France, and it is probable that such will be the case for a long while," La Galissonière wrote in a December 1750 report to his superiors in Paris, "but it constitutes, at the same time, the strongest barrier that can be opposed to the ambition of the English." That ambition, he said, was "superiority in Europe." Maintaining a strong French presence would leave the British colonists fearful of attack; prevent the British from moving against Saint-Domingue and Martinico (Martinique), France's valuable Caribbean colonies; and help protect the possessions of France's ally, Spain, in America, he wrote.[8] La Galissonière was commandant-general of New France when Captain Pierre-Joseph Céloron de Blainville set out on a nearly five-thousand-kilometre (three-thousand-mile) journey through the Ohio country in 1749, planting lead plates along the way that proclaimed it a French territory. De Silhouette thought North American trade was important and worried that if the British gained a monopoly, it would open an economic gap France could not close. For all these reasons, both men supported the idea of holding on to the Ohio country by building more forts, a policy that backfired when it helped provoke the French and Indian War.

In the lead-up to that war, Britain and France both built forts in strategic locations, attacked those of the rival power, and sometimes retook those that were captured. This was when the French established Fort Toronto, which has since grown into the city of that name, on Lake Ontario. The fort was designed to waylay Indigenous fur traders coming from the north on their way to the British trading post at Chouegen (Oswego) on the other side of the lake. La Galissonière was particularly scornful of the traders at Chouegen giving the Indigenous Peoples rum, which the French king had forbidden. Franklin saw the strategic significance of the Oswego post and recommended in his 1754 plan for colonies that it be strengthened and provided with some "armed half-gallies" that could cruise Lake Ontario. France also built a fort at Crown Point on Lake Champlain, well within what the British colonies considered their territory. Britain built Fort Halifax in Nova Scotia.

Washington Defends the Land Speculators and Provokes a War

One incident from this period stands out because it involved George Washington, then a young lieutenant colonel in the Virginia militia leading troops for the first time. The Ohio land speculation company had decided to build a fort at the forks of the Ohio River, near where Pittsburgh is today. Washington, with about 160 men, was ordered by the governor of Virginia in late 1753 to go and defend it. Before he could arrive, the French and their Indigenous allies took the company outpost without firing a shot. More than a month later, the French commander heard that Washington was approaching and sent an emissary to talk to him. But when Washington and his men encountered the French force, they killed the emissary, Joseph Coulon de Villiers de Jumonville, and nine of his men. How this happened was disputed. The British said the French fired first. There were reports that Tanaghrisson, a Seneca Chief who supported the British, split Jumonville's head with his hatchet and washed his hands in his brains. The French claimed that Washington had assassinated their emissary. "This murder is unique and can be avenged only by shedding blood," the governor of New France told one of his military commanders.[9] A French expedition was mounted in July 1754 to go after Washington, who was at nearby Fort Necessity. With half his men drunk, Washington was forced to capitulate to the superior French force. He signed an instrument of surrender in which he acknowledged that he was responsible for the assassination of Jumonville.[10]

Britain and France were still technically at peace, but news of British losses in the Ohio country turned the thoughts of the British ministry, led by Thomas Pelham-Holles, the Duke of Newcastle, to war. Negotiations over the ownership of the Ohio country and the boundary between Nova Scotia and New France had failed. Now was the time to use force. Newcastle decided in late 1754 to send Major General Edward Braddock to the colonies, along with two regiments. Braddock's orders were to remove the French from the Ohio country, destroy the French forts on Lake Champlain, and take the French forts on the Nova Scotia peninsula. This was a tall order, given the difficulty in travelling through wilderness, where there were few good roads. Hearing of the British plans, the French arranged for massive reinforcements to be sent to North America in the spring of 1755. Braddock would get there earlier because he could land in Virginia. The French had to wait until the St. Lawrence River was free of ice.

Franklin said the Pennsylvania assembly sent him in his role as deputy postmaster general to meet Braddock and offer to ensure the general's dispatches reached the colonial governors quickly. But when he caught up with Braddock in Maryland, he found the British troops lacked horses and wagons to carry their supplies and provisions. When the general suggested he would confiscate what he needed along the way, Franklin took charge, advertising for horses, wagons, and drivers and advancing some of his own money to acquire them. He said he warned the general about the danger of "ambuscades [ambushes] of Indians," but his warning was brushed aside. "These savages may, indeed, be a formidable enemy to your raw American militia," Franklin quoted the general, "but upon the king's regular and disciplin'd troops, sir, it is impossible they should make any impression." The army was indeed ambushed on its way to the Ohio country. Two-thirds of the men on the march were killed. Braddock later died of his wounds. His papers, with his orders, instructions, and correspondence, fell into French hands, revealing Britain's hostile intentions. "This whole transaction gave us Americans the first suspicion that our exalted ideas of the prowess of British regulars had not been well founded," Franklin wrote in his autobiography. He further noted that Braddock and his troops would not have been needed in the first place if the British government had allowed the colonies to unite for their defence.

Losing Faith in the British, the Colonies Make Their Own Plans for War

Braddock's defeat worsened the mood in the colonies and strengthened support for dealing with the French in Canada once and for all. There were those in New England who still bemoaned the handing of Louisbourg back to New France and wanted to continue their religious crusade. Governor Shirley of Massachusetts, who had organized the expedition that captured Louisbourg, wanted to attack French forts on Lake Champlain, which he said would allow an army to march north "into the very heart of their country."[11] The *Boston Evening-Post* published a letter on September 8, 1755, supposedly sent to a French officer, that said the French were planning to send fifty thousand troops to retake Nova Scotia and subdue the western territory. The plan, according to the letter, was to capture all the English settlements in North America and "fill that Part of the Country with Catholicks, so as to drive Hereticks into the Sea." In Philadelphia, Reverend Reading asked his parishioners what course they should follow "when these dogs of Hell, Popish superstition and French tyranny dare to erect their heads and triumph within our borders?" He said that if they did nothing, the streets of the town would be "trod by the lordly feet of French Conquerors" and they would be asking themselves, "Who is yonder Virgin shrieking in the arms of a lustful Ravisher?"[12]

The conflict between the French, the British, and Indigenous groups for control of the Ohio country was one of two main flashpoints in the French and Indian War. The other was Nova Scotia, the former French Acadia, ceded to Britain in the 1713 Treaty of Utrecht. Despite the passage of time, its border with New France remained in dispute and Britain's grip on the colony was feeble. The British worried, with some justification, that the mainly French population was untrustworthy and liable to side with the French if there was a war, even though Britain had allowed them to retain their lands and practise their Catholic faith. After four decades of instability, Britain decided to tighten control of the region by capturing some of the larger French forts in the vicinity, excluding Louisbourg for the time being, and deporting as many Acadians as they could round up, seizing their lands in the process. About ten thousand Acadians were expelled during the ethnic cleansing between 1755 and 1763. Some escaped to nearby French territories or into the woods, joining with the Abenaki and Mi'kmaq to mount reprisals on their colonial overlord. Some went to Louisiana and stayed to lay the foundations of Cajun culture.

Franklin would later misleadingly portray the French and Indian War as one fought over British rather than colonial interests. He made these remarks in 1766, when Britain was sparring with the colonies over imposing taxes to pay down some of the enormous debt from the war. The colonists had "no particular concern or interest" in the disputed boundary between Canada and Nova Scotia, Franklin told a hearing of the British House of Commons on February 13, 1766. As for the Ohio country, he said, "The contest there began about *your* right of trading in the Indian country, a right you had by the treaty of Utrecht, which the French infringed." The French had seized traders and their goods, "which were *your* manufactures," he noted, and they took a fort that "*your* merchants" had erected. Franklin was wrong about the Treaty of Utrecht conferring rights and he was economical with the truth when it came to the causes of the war. The New England colonies wanted as much of the fishing grounds as they could take. Where the boundary was drawn between Nova Scotia and French Canada mattered to them. Trade with the Indigenous Peoples in the Ohio country was important, but Franklin knew the real point of contention was land, both for settlers pouring out of the established American colonies, where good farmland was scarce, and for land speculators looking to make handsome profits from colonial expansion.

After he returned to Philadelphia from the frontier in 1756, Franklin was elected colonel by the Philadelphia militia. He accepted the post, and this encouraged the officers in his regiment to give him a military escort out of town when he was leaving for a short trip. They rode with their swords drawn and made quite a show of it, he wrote in his autobiography. Franklin said that when Thomas Penn, the proprietor of Pennsylvania, heard of it, he was offended because no such honour had been paid to him when he had visited from London. Penn already had good reason to dislike him, because Franklin was behind many of the bills that the assembly passed, and that the governor then vetoed, seeking to impose taxes on the proprietor's lands.

The Pennsylvania Assembly Sends Franklin to London

Yet in January 1757, the assembly decided to send Franklin to London to deal directly with Penn, or with the British ministry if Penn would not change his position. Franklin had a growing reputation among amateur scientists, known as natural philosophers, in England and France because of his electrical experiments. He had received a prestigious medal from the Royal Society of London and honorary degrees from the colleges of Harvard, Yale, and William & Mary. Franklin's renown may have led the assembly to overlook, or at least downplay, the effect that tensions between the two men would have on his mission to London. Richard Peters, a member of the Pennsylvania council who supported the proprietor's interests, wrote Penn to warn him of the appointment. Peters thought Franklin would push for a change of government in the colony, giving the king, rather than the proprietor, control. He also warned that "considering the popularity of his character and the reputation gained by his Electrical Discoveries which will introduce him into all sorts of Company he may prove a Dangerous Enemy." Penn dismissed the concern, saying Franklin was not well known in London and "will be looked very coldly upon by Great People, there are very few of any consequence that have heard of his Electrical experiments." Both Peters and Penn turned out to be right. Franklin did struggle to meet "Great People" in London, as Penn predicted. If anything, this led him to support the independence of the colonies. He did prove to be a dangerous enemy, as Peters had foreseen.

The final battle between Britain and France for control of northern North America was just gathering steam when Franklin left for London in April 1757. He was going on colonial business, although one of his critics suggested Franklin had caught wind of attempts to fire him as deputy postmaster general and wanted to make his case to the authorities in person. "They talk of sending the Electrician," John Kearsley wrote disparagingly to the former governor, Morris, now back in England. "He jumps at the chance." Kearsley said Franklin was going to advance his own interests but was "artfully insinuating that he goes on his countrys Service."[13] With Franklin, it was probably a bit of both. One of the interests he would advance while in London was Britain's right to Canada.

Part Two

CANADA CAPTURED

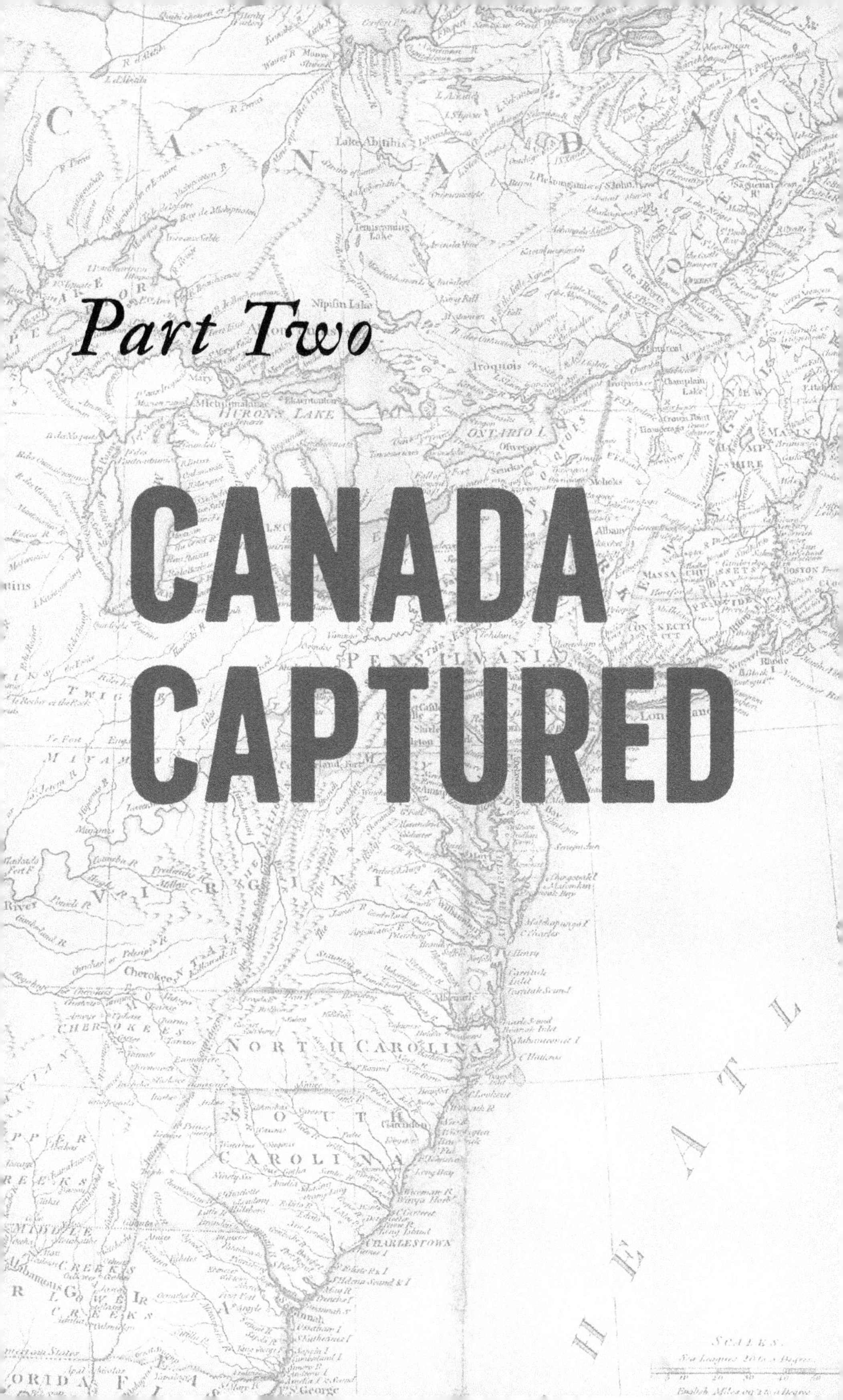

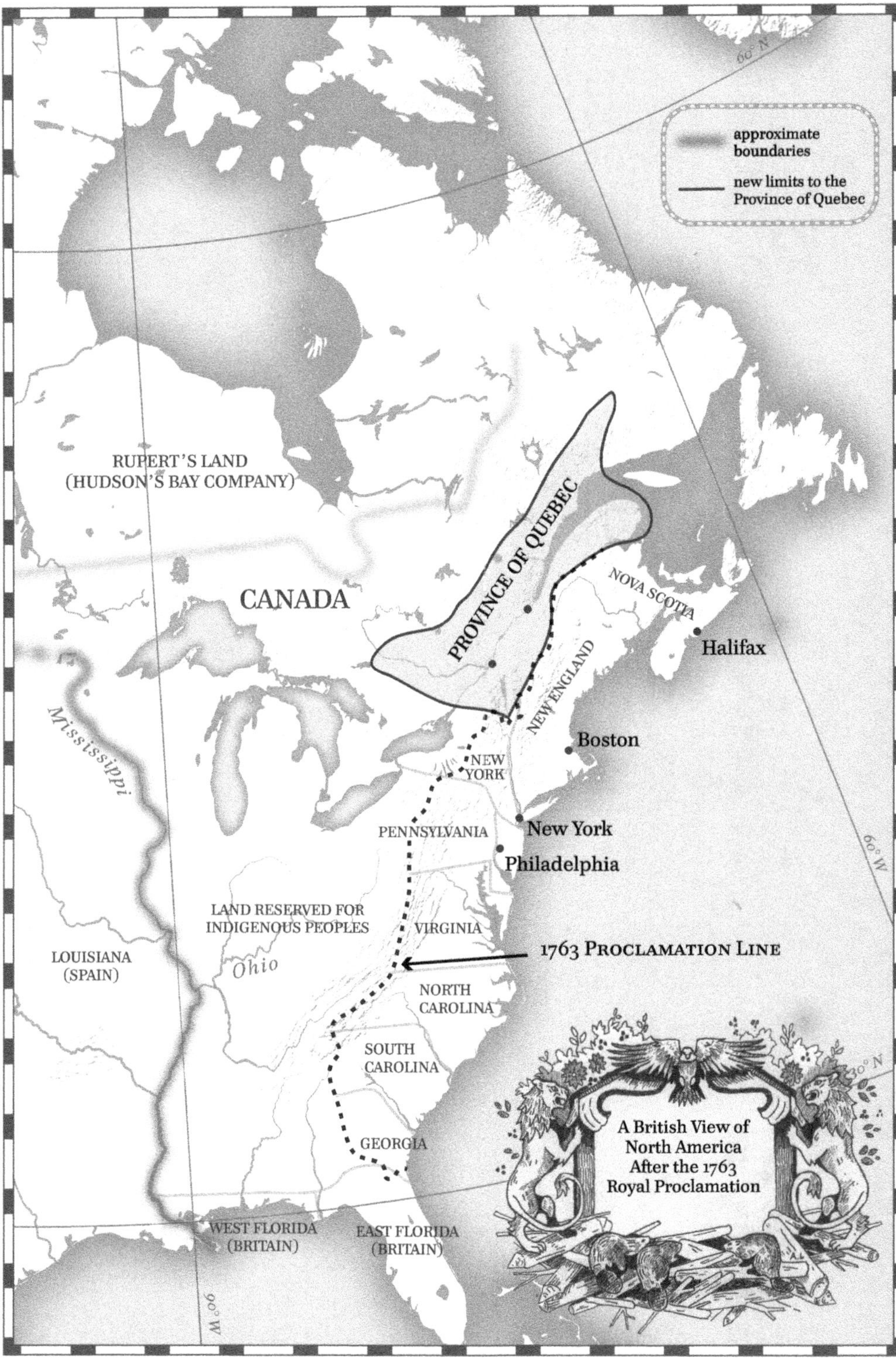

approximate boundaries
new limits to the Province of Quebec
60° N
60° W
30° N
90° W
RUPERT'S LAND (HUDSON'S BAY COMPANY)
CANADA
PROVINCE OF QUEBEC
NOVA SCOTIA
Halifax
NEW ENGLAND
Boston
NEW YORK
New York
PENNSYLVANIA
Philadelphia
Mississippi
LAND RESERVED FOR INDIGENOUS PEOPLES
VIRGINIA
LOUISIANA (SPAIN)
Ohio
1763 Proclamation Line
NORTH CAROLINA
SOUTH CAROLINA
GEORGIA
WEST FLORIDA (BRITAIN)
EAST FLORIDA (BRITAIN)
A British View of North America After the 1763 Royal Proclamation

CHAPTER 5

Ravings of a Mad Prophet: London 1757–1773

> No one can more sincerely rejoice than I do on the reduction of Canada; and this not only because I am a Colonist, but as I am a Briton.[1]
>
> — *Benjamin Franklin*

BENJAMIN FRANKLIN'S DREAM OF ACQUIRING "ROOM ENOUGH" FOR AMERICAN colonists was tantalizingly close as the Seven Years' War neared its end. The British had captured the French fort at Louisbourg in July 1758. After Quebec City fell in September 1759, they were confident all of Canada would be theirs within a year. In January 1760, a delighted Franklin wrote a slightly premature letter to his friend Lord Kames, a Scottish Enlightenment thinker, enthusing over the anticipated conquest of Canada. "If we keep it, all the country from the St. Laurence to the Missisipi will in another Century be fill'd with British people; Britain itself will become vastly more populous by the immense Increase of its Commerce; the Atlantic Sea will be cover'd with your Trading Ships; and your naval power thence continuously increasing, will extend your influence round the whole globe and awe the world."[2]

The 1763 Treaty of Paris that marked the official end of the Seven Years' War still lay in the future when Franklin wrote Lord Kames. In London, where Franklin was now living, politicians and pamphleteers were already conducting a lively debate about how to divide the spoils of a war that had not yet ended. One key question was whether Britain should give Canada back to France and retain the sugar-producing island of Guadeloupe. Franklin, knowing this would deny the colonists the security they yearned for, began a propaganda campaign in favour of adding Canada to the British Empire. The letter to Lord Kames, which Franklin acknowledged might appear to his friend to be the "ravings of a mad prophet," was part of that campaign. Britain would keep Canada in the end, but it would be a short-lived victory for Franklin and his continental dreams.

As previously mentioned, Franklin had been sent to London in 1757 as an agent for the legislative assembly of Pennsylvania because it had reached an impasse with William Denny, the British governor, over taxation. Denny was refusing to approve every money bill the assembly sent him because they included taxing the estates of the proprietor, Thomas Penn. Franklin's task was to meet with Penn in London and persuade him to change his mind. He was not the obvious choice for an agent. He was already on bad terms with the proprietor because he backed previous attempts to tax the estates. Yet he did have a name in scientific circles in Britain and France because of his experiments with electricity and his invention of the lightning rod. He quickly learned that scientific fame did not provide an entree to Britain's elite, just as Penn had predicted.

The London Elite Give Franklin the Cold Shoulder

That was brought home to Franklin in his first meeting on assembly business with John Carteret, Earl of Granville and president of the Privy Council, a group of nobles appointed by the king to be his advisors. Penn, who was distantly related to Granville, had asked the earl to deal with Franklin in his stead. The meeting did not go well. According to Franklin, Granville lectured him on the laws governing the colonies, saying they were drawn up by judges, debated in the Privy Council, and then signed by the king. Franklin should consider them "the law of the land." Americans, continued the earl, did not understand their constitutions and thought themselves "at Liberty to regard or disregard them at [their] own discretion." This treatment clearly rankled Franklin, who by his own admission struggled with humility. With Penn refusing to meet him, Franklin was forced to submit the assembly's complaint in writing to the proprietor's solicitor, who he described as a "a proud, angry man" who had a "mortal enmity to me." The solicitor told him to send the complaint to the offices of the attorney general and the solicitor general of Britain. He did so, and they let it gather dust for almost a year. During that time, Franklin made several attempts to be introduced to William Pitt, secretary of state in the coalition ministry he formed with Thomas Pelham-Holles, the Duke of Newcastle. "He was then too great a Man, or too much occupy'd in Affairs of greater Moment," Franklin observed many years later.[3] The elites made it clear to the colonial emissary that he was beneath their notice.

One upside of this rejection was that it left him time to pursue other company and other endeavours. He attended regular meetings of scientists, historians, philosophers, and explorers in coffee houses, like St. Paul's, the George and Vulture, or the Grecian on the Strand, and met scholars and thinkers through the Royal Society, which had made him a fellow in 1756. Craven Street, where Franklin rented rooms, was in a respectable area but not far removed from the threadbare lodgings of his youth in Wild Court and a world away from the mansions and palaces of the nobility in the west end of the city. Intellectuals met in coffee houses. The ruling elite met in clubs with names like White's, Brooks's, or Boodle's. Their doors were largely barred to Franklin, who carried the double stigma of being a colonial and a former tradesman.

Franklin Furthers the Colonial Cause by Making Friends with Printers

Yet those tradesman credentials helped Franklin in another way. He was still a member of the Worshipful Company of Stationers, the printer's guild, from his time as a printer in the colonies. This helped him make useful connections with printers in the capital. Chief among these valuable contacts was William Strahan, who printed *The London Chronicle: or, Universal Evening Post* and published some of the leading authors of the day, such as

Dr. Samuel Johnson, David Hume, and Adam Smith. Strahan was one of Franklin's three closest friends. The others were Sir John Pringle, a doctor and moral philosopher, and Dr. John Fothergill, a doctor and a Quaker. Franklin had corresponded with Strahan prior to his arrival. Now Strahan's newspapers and printing presses provided an outlet for much of Franklin's writing in London. His articles also appeared in other newspapers, such as the *Public Advertiser* and *The Gazetteer and New Daily Advertiser*, and in magazines such as *The Gentleman's Magazine*. If he could not get personal interviews with Britain's rulers, he would grab their attention with his pen.

Franklin saw himself as chief publicist for the colonies in London, correcting what he considered were British misperceptions. He did this through letters to the editor, short pieces, and longer pamphlets. All were signed with a pseudonym. This was common practice at the time. But it also provided useful cover for Franklin, who wore two hats: he was colonial agent for Pennsylvania and deputy postmaster general for the Crown.

Now middle-aged, Franklin drew on decades of experience in business and politics to inform readers and persuade them to share his way of thinking. At times he favoured the direct frontal attack. One of his first letters to the editor during this stay in London criticized the Pennsylvania proprietor. In other instances, such as the debate over Canada versus Guadeloupe, he used a fuller range of tactics, including satire and appeals to common sense and imperial glory.

Why France No Longer Wanted Canada

In making the case for Britain to retain Canada once peace was declared, Franklin was pushing on an open door. By 1760 France was no longer able to support its colony across the sea and showed every sign of wanting to be rid of it. The battle on the Plains of Abraham in 1759, which Britain won, is frequently portrayed as the turning point for France in North America. It attracted additional attention because of the dramatic deaths of both French and British commanders — Louis-Joseph, Marquis de Montcalm for France, and James Wolfe for Britain — and through the posthumous praise heaped on Wolfe in the House of Commons by William Pitt. A highly imaginative painting of the dying Wolfe done by Benjamin West in 1770 burnished the legend. Wolfe appears as a Christlike figure, surrounded by mourners.

But two other events around the same time helped dim French prospects of keeping New France: the 1758 Treaty of Easton, signed by the British and the Indigenous Peoples in the Ohio Valley, and a 1759 naval battle between Britain and France off the south coast of Brittany. Under the terms of the Treaty of Easton, the Indigenous Peoples of the Ohio Valley agreed to abandon France and make peace with the British. This allowed British and colonial troops to focus their energies on attacking the French troops and outposts, including Fort Duquesne at the forks of the Ohio River. In return the British promised the Indigenous Peoples that they would not establish settlements in the Ohio Valley after the war. They would not honour this promise.

The 1759 naval battle that eroded France's ability to keep Canada took place in Quiberon Bay. The French navy went into that engagement already weakened, with an estimated 47 large warships in its total fleet, compared to 111 for the British navy. Of the twenty-one warships France committed in Quiberon Bay, it lost seven and the remainder were scattered. The British victory scuppered French plans to invade Britain, which really would have put the British on the back foot in the war, and it left France unable to supply and defend New France. Britain now controlled the North Atlantic. The effects of its naval superiority were felt in 1760, when a sizeable French force, which outnumbered the British defenders, had to call off an attempt to retake Quebec City because a British fleet sailed up the St. Lawrence. The British navy had already blocked the French convoy meant to supply reinforcements. Montreal capitulated in September 1760, leaving Canada in British hands.

While this was a blow to France's prestige, dismay was far from universal. The strain of supporting the money-losing colony was lifted, freeing resources for the fight closer to home. Voltaire, the French philosopher, was among those who questioned the value of New France even before the fall of Quebec City. He had denigrated Canada in 1757, describing it as "quelques arpents de glace" (a few acres of ice). He changed that slightly in his 1759 novel *Candide* in which a character said France and Britain were at war over "quelques arpents de neige" (a few acres of snow). In October 1760, he wrote a French marquis who had the ear of King Louis XV, saying that if France lost Canada, it lost almost nothing.[4] And in September 1762, he wrote Étienne François, duc de Choiseul, then French minister of war, marine, and the colonies, saying that he, like most Frenchmen, liked peace better than Canada and he thought France could be happy without Quebec.[5]

Choiseul had come to the same conclusion. The conflict in North America had competed for his attention during the war, with battles along the coast of Africa and in the Caribbean, Europe, India, and the Mediterranean. His overriding concern was how to strike a blow that would stagger Britain and leave France the pre-eminent power in Europe. The invasion of Britain was supposed to be that blow. But France no longer had the necessary sea power after the Battle of Quiberon Bay. When Britain proposed peace negotiations less than a week after the naval engagement, confident it now had the upper hand, France agreed to preliminary discussions.

It was the practice at that time for the main belligerents in a war to negotiate an end to hostilities. It was during such talks that they would exchange some territories taken in battle and make other concessions. The concept of winner-take-all or total victory did not emerge until much later. At the end of the previous war, Britain had handed the captured fort at Louisbourg back to France. Imperial politics and domestic considerations determined which pieces were swapped and which were kept in what was a global game with multiple pieces and players.

The first set of talks went nowhere. Choiseul later wrote that Britain was not serious and had made the proposal only to appease its allies, Prussia and the German electorate of Hanover.[6] But Choiseul had also created a stumbling block when he said the peace talks should be divided into two stages, with the first involving Britain and France and the second involving all their allies engaged in disputes on the European continent. Britain insisted on one set of negotiations.

Franklin Wages His Campaign for Canada with His Pen

It was about this time that Franklin decided to write a satiric letter to the editor about whether Britain should keep the not-quite-conquered French colony. It was called "Humourous Reasons for Restoring Canada" and had a wide circulation in London, appearing in Strahan's *London Chronicle: or, Universal Evening Post* on December 25–27, 1759, and later reprinted in *The Grand Magazine* and *The Gentleman's Magazine*. Franklin, using the pseudonym A. Z., claimed to have found a list of reasons why Britain should give the colony back to France in the peace negotiations. They ranged from the danger that keeping it would lead to uninterrupted trade with "the Indians," sparking too great a demand for British goods, to the possibility that the English would appear too vengeful if they destroyed Canada, even though the Canadians deserved it. Some of the reasons were purely humorous, such as the fact that having plenty of beaver would make broad-brimmed hats cheaper for "that unmannerly sect, the Quakers." Others had a more serious intent. One jabbed at the British ministry, saying that if the British kept Canada, it would look as though their statesmen had courage, "but what have statesmen to do with courage?" Another talked of a French plan to burn and ruin the thirteen colonies and said if the British didn't give Canada to the French, it would look like they were afraid of them. Franklin cited the French historian Pierre-François-Xavier de Charlevoix, who had written that the last time Canada was taken by the English, the French court questioned whether it was worth recovering. The court had decided its merits lay in the fact that a French presence in North America would make it harder for the British colonies to grow stronger. "Let us then, oblige them," Franklin wrote. The letter ended with his observation that the French were still holding out at Montreal and Trois-Rivières. One way to avoid having to worry about the restoration of Canada was for the British navy to be "a little too late" in sailing up the St. Lawrence, allowing the French to resupply and recover Quebec.

Franklin adopted a more serious tone in his next major endeavour, a fifty-eight-page pamphlet published in April 1760 and titled *The Interest of Great Britain Considered, With Regard to her Colonies, And the Acquisitions of Canada and Guadaloupe*, more commonly called the *Canada Pamphlet*. In today's terms, the choice between Canada and Guadeloupe appears to be between apples and oranges. At the time, it merited serious consideration. Both Britain and France judged the worth of their colonies based on the value of the products they provided to the respective imperial power and whether those products complemented or competed with existing trade or manufacture. Colonies were expected to feed raw materials to the motherland, where manufacturers used them to create goods for domestic consumption and re-export, sometimes to the same colonies that had provided the raw goods. The trading system was purposely designed with domestic rather than colonial interests in mind. The cost of supporting far-flung outposts was part of this equation. In contrast to more modern views of trade, Britain and France also believed that the total amount of global trade was limited. In such a zero-sum game, depriving a rival power of a lucrative colony would be a powerful blow.

Even before Britain captured Guadeloupe in May 1759, the British debated whether their existing colonies in the West Indies were more valuable than those on the North American continent. The island colonies produced high-value goods, like sugar, making them attractive to British merchants. The colonists purchased enslaved people brought on British ships from Africa, making them attractive to British slavers. They used the profits to build estates in Britain, creating jobs in the motherland. British colonists in the West Indies, while fewer than those on the continent, initially bought more British goods. That began to change around the middle of the 1700s, when demand for these goods in the American colonies rose along with the population. Still, Guadeloupe fit the British idea of a valuable colony. After its capitulation on what were considered lenient terms — under British rule the French inhabitants could keep their laws, property, and the Roman Catholic religion — its sugar merchants redirected their exports to Britain, imported British goods like wrought iron, and purchased people enslaved by the British. By one estimate, Guadeloupe exported more sugar to Britain in the first six months of 1761 than it had ever shipped to France in a full year. In 1760, British ships brought 4,980 enslaved people to the island, and 7,835 the next year.[7] It was clear to British merchants and slavers there was money to be made in Guadeloupe.

Canada was a harder sell. Its most valuable export was cod, followed by pelts from the fur trade, which was already in decline. Cod was shipped to Britain, to its European allies, and to colonies in the West

Indies, where it was used to feed enslaved people and exchanged for island goods such as rum, molasses, tobacco, and sugar. There was no question that the fishery off the coast of the British colonies of Newfoundland and Nova Scotia was a valuable asset, as was the fort at Louisbourg, which guarded the mouth of the St. Lawrence. But what of the rest of it? It was well-known that New France had been a financial drag on France. What contribution would it make to Britain and the empire? Pitt, in charge of defence and foreign policy in the coalition ministry, favoured Canada for strategic rather than economic reasons. He thought driving the French out of North America would provide more security to the colonists and weaken his European adversary by depriving it of the Newfoundland fishery. (He also sanctioned the capture of Guadeloupe in the hope it would severely damage the French sugar trade and give Britain a bargaining chip to exchange for the island of Minorca off the coast of Spain, which the French had taken in 1756. But he had not intended to keep the sugar-producing island.)

The pamphlet debate over which colony would be worth more to the British began in December 1759, when an anonymous writer, thought to be John Douglas, a protégé of the Earl of Bath, wrote *A Letter Addressed to Two Great Men on the Prospect of Peace; and on the Terms necessary to be insisted upon in the Negociation.* Douglas argued that as long as the French remained in Canada, the thirteen colonies would have no security. At some point, there would be another war. That fit with Franklin's thinking. But then came the responses, including *Remarks on the Letter Address'd to Two Great Men*, whose author was believed to be William Burke, a distant relation of Edmund Burke, the Anglo-Irish politician and philosopher. William Burke argued that Britain did not have enough sugar islands and that Guadeloupe also supplied indigo, coffee, and cotton. Canada had little economic value, he wrote. Keeping it might allow the American colonists to grow so strong they no longer needed a connection with Britain and would seek independence. "The Possession of Canada, far from being necessary to our Safety, may in its Consequence be even dangerous," he argued presciently. "A Neighbour that keeps us in Awe, is not always the worst of neighbours." His pamphlet had three editions. This worried Franklin.

More Than Security Lay Behind Franklin's Desire for Canada

Franklin had already developed his rationale for why Canada should be American in the pamphlets he wrote in the 1750s. *Observations* dealt with the burgeoning population of the thirteen colonies and the need for more territory for the next generation of farmers. His *Albany Plan* and his *Plan for Settling Two Western Colonies* suggested that some of this expansion could be accomplished by buying land west of the Appalachians from the Indigenous Peoples. This was land the French considered to be part of Canada, or New France, and which the American colonies claimed belonged to them. Franklin's long-standing preoccupation with the security of the thirteen colonies led him inexorably to think that instead of nibbling away at territory north and west of the colonies, Britain should have the lot. With Canada in British hands, the colonists' security problems would disappear, and a huge new area would be open for expansion.

Franklin added to the growing number of pamphlets — there would eventually be around sixty-five written on this topic, not including newspaper articles and comments — with his *Canada Pamphlet*. With the help of a friend, thought to be Richard Jackson, a lawyer, member of Parliament, and the London agent for the colony of Connecticut, he crafted an argument for keeping Canada that would appeal to British sensibilities. He acknowledged to a friend later that he also wanted to advance the interests of the colonies. He noted in the pamphlet that the ongoing war had started in North America before embroiling the nations of Europe and that as long as Britain and France shared a long border in North America, there was a potential for another war between imperial powers. Defending the "frontier of the British empire" by building more forts and maintaining garrisons would mean "immense" expense, he said, appealing to the British taxpayer. The ongoing threat from Indigenous Peoples, who "murder'd and scalp'd," would disappear once the French influence was removed and the only Europeans left to trade with were British. Peace would lead to a population increase of "British subjects on that side of the water." "Canada in the hands of France has always stinted the growth of our colonies," he wrote. "In the course of this war, and indeed before it, [it] has disturb'd and vex'd even the best and strongest of them, and found means to murder thousands of their people and unsettle a great part of their country." A population increase in the colonies would not cause a population decrease in Britain, he said, touching on the current fear among the ruling class that the world's population was a fixed number and that gains in one part of the world would lead to losses elsewhere. He forecast that the colonial population would double in twenty-five years, not including new immigrants. Supplying them would keep British manufacturers busy for centuries. The new territory would keep this process going even longer. These were arguments he had previously made in his *Observations*, a copy of which was attached to the new pamphlet.

Franklin knew Burke was not alone in raising the idea of colonial independence. The subtext to Franklin's comments about population growth was that if Britain paid heed to the security concerns of the colonies now by keeping Canada, the question of possible separation would be put off for some time. He scoffed at the fear raised by Burke that the colonies would grow so powerful they would separate from Britain. They could not agree to unite for their common defence when the French and Indigenous Peoples were "perpetually harassing their settlements, burning their villages, and murdering their people," he wrote, thinking perhaps of his failed Albany Plan. The possibility of union "is not merely improbable, it is impossible," he wrote, carefully adding the caveat "without the most grievous tyranny and oppression."

Guadeloupe was valuable, he agreed, but it was fully inhabited by French people, who spoke a different language, had different manners, and practised a different religion. Holding it was "hardly tenable" and would cost more than the colony was worth. Profits from the sugar exports would go to the French, adding to the wealth of France not Britain, he continued. The prospects for population growth, and thus future British exports to Guadeloupe, were limited.

Franklin's Plan for the French Canadians

At the time Franklin wrote his pamphlet, Canada was also fully occupied by people who had a different language, culture, and religion. Of the estimated sixty-five thousand to one hundred thousand inhabitants, only a handful were British. But he had a plan to deal with French Canadian Catholics. He would encourage them to leave and assimilate those who refused to go. He did not appear to consider that the French Canadians had spent generations on the land — Quebec City was founded in 1608 — and were unlikely to consider France home. French Protestants, who were few in number, would probably choose to remain, he wrote, while many of the others would choose to leave if they were allowed to sell their lands and effects. After that, people from the American colonies could move in. He predicted that in less than half a century, those who chose to remain would be "blended and incorporated with our people both in language and manners." Franklin did not believe in multiculturalism.

While this debate continued in London, the French Canadians and the British military officials charged with governing them after the conquest existed in a state of limbo. No one knew who would rule Canada once the terms of peace were agreed. Many French Canadians lived in fear because their last governor, the Marquis de Vaudreuil, and their religious leaders had told them that if the British won, they would receive the same treatment as the Acadians, who were deported and their goods and property confiscated. The British wanted to wipe out everything that was Canadian, Vaudreuil had maintained.[8] After the fall of Montreal in 1760, Vaudreuil signed articles of capitulation in which Sir Jeffery Amherst, British commander-in-chief of North America, agreed to provide ships to take Vaudreuil, along with his senior officials and military officers, back to France. Amherst also agreed that anyone else, aside from prisoners and enslaved people, could leave if they wanted. Article XLVII stated that "the Negroes and panis [enslaved Indigenous people] of both sexes shall remain, in their quality of slaves, in the possession of the French and Canadians to whom they belong." The French Canadians who remained would be allowed to keep their property, including furs in transit to Montreal, and would be free to practise the Roman Catholic religion. The articles also included a clause that allowed the governor, who had been born in Canada, to come back if the anticipated peace treaty called for Canada to be returned to France.

Historians differ on how many people left for France or French colonies after the British conquest and whether the colony was left bereft of all its leaders, or decapitated, as some called it. James Murray, the British military officer appointed governor of Canada immediately after the conquest, estimated in 1761 that ten thousand people had left. A more recent estimate cut that figure by more than half.[9] There were no reliable population figures at the time. Regardless, that still left somewhere between sixty-five thousand and one hundred thousand French Canadians, depending on which estimate is used.

Contrary to Franklin's wishes, the British authorities were not planning to deport the French Canadians. Quite the opposite. In 1761 Charles Wyndham, the Earl of Egremont, who had replaced Pitt as the British secretary of state in charge of the region, wrote to Amherst, telling him it was essential to retain as many French subjects as possible in Canada to prevent them from moving to French colonies, where they might still pose a threat to Britain.[10] They were to be "humanely and most kindly treated," Egremont stipulated. He added that soldiers, sailors, and other British subjects should refrain from insulting or reviling the French Canadians by reminding them they had been conquered; criticizing their dress, customs, and manners; or by offering "uncharitable Reflections on the Errors of that mistaken Religion, which they unhappily profess." The spectre of a mass exodus of French Canadians became a theme in the letters Murray sent to the ministry in London, in which he defended concessions made to the local people. The British authorities still had eventual assimilation in mind and were keen to populate their new possessions with loyal subjects. But this would be a long-term endeavour.

France Readily Gives Up Canada in the Peace Negotiations

Negotiations to end the war restarted shortly after Louis XV of France declared in March 1761 that it was time to go back to the negotiating table. Fighting in North America had ended but the war continued in Europe. Britain was now ruled by George III, who ascended the throne in October 1760, following the death of his grandfather, George II. The new king told a combined session of Parliament shortly afterward that he intended to "prosecute this War with Vigour" to obtain "a safe and honourable peace."[11] Despite those words, his ministers were aware that he did not want to prolong hostilities, especially in Europe. Unlike George II, the new king did not want to fight to gain more territory in Germany. The British and French monarchs exchanged ambassadors, who relayed official and unofficial proposals by the ministers in charge of the negotiations — Choiseul in Versailles and Pitt in London.

Choiseul's starting point was that Britain could have Canada. It was the first article in a memo he sent to Pitt dated July 15, 1761. France, he wrote, would not return under any pretext. He never wavered from this position throughout the talks. In return France wanted four things from Britain: that French Canadians be free to practise the Roman Catholic religion; those who wanted to go to other French colonies be free to sell their goods or take them without harassment; the borders between Canada and Louisiana and between Louisiana and Virginia be clearly fixed; and the French be free to fish for cod off Newfoundland, dry their catch on its shores, and shelter on Cape Breton, which the British would give back to France. Choiseul proposed other territorial trades in Europe, Africa, and India, including giving Minorca back to the British in exchange for Guadeloupe and the nearby island of Marie-Galante.

Pitt's reply was blunt to the point of rudeness. "Haughty and despotic" was how Choiseul characterized it. Britain would keep all of Canada, wrote Pitt. France would not get Cape Breton, or any other island in the Gulf of St. Lawrence, nor the fishing rights it sought in the gulf. Britain certainly did not agree that Louisiana extended as far north as Canada nor that it shared a border with Virginia. The lands between Canada and Louisiana, which included the Ohio country, were not French possessions that could be ceded, Pitt stated. It was not all bad news for France. Britain would allow it certain fishing rights off Newfoundland, provided France demolished some fortifications Britain had built when it controlled Dunkirk in France. And once France had given back Minorca, the British would give it the "opulent" island of Guadeloupe and the smaller island of Marie-Galante.[12]

The war continued in parallel with stop-and-start negotiations. Pitt resigned in 1761 and was replaced as principal negotiator by John Russell, the Duke of Bedford. But the decision that Britain would keep Canada remained unchanged. The British made more conquests in the Caribbean, including Martinique and

Grenada in 1762. After Spain entered the war early that year to fight alongside France, the British took Havana. The concentration of sugar islands now in Britain's hands briefly revived the Canada-vs-Guadeloupe debate, with some arguing Britain could now control the whole sugar trade if it kept Guadeloupe. But by that time, the outlines of a peace settlement were in sight.

It is unclear whether Franklin's arguments, or indeed any of the arguments made by pamphleteers, had a major impact on Britain's decision to give back Guadeloupe. The elites famously paid little heed to public opinion. There were rumours in Britain that Pitt was beholden to a group of British sugar planters in the Caribbean, who would face more competition if Britain kept Guadeloupe. When the parties agreed to a preliminary peace deal in November 1762, and then followed it with the "Definitive Treaty of Peace and Friendship between his Britannick Majesty, the Most Christian King, and the King of Spain" in February 1763, it appeared that Franklin got everything he had long sought.

Franklin Sees the Peace Treaty as a Triumph

The final peace agreement, signed in Paris, extended far beyond North America to cover territories in Africa, Europe, India, Sumatra, the Mediterranean, and the Caribbean. It included troop withdrawals from certain captured territories in Europe and territory swaps in Africa and India. The most relevant provisions for Franklin involved the fate of Canada and the contested territory west of the Appalachian Mountains. Britain would keep all of Canada, or New France, a huge territory that covered the St. Lawrence Valley and the Great Lakes, extending south to the Gulf of Mexico. The French would leave North America, keeping only Saint-Pierre and Miquelon, two small islands off the south coast of Newfoundland, where their fishing fleet could shelter. (These remain part of France today.) In return for ceding Minorca to Britain, France regained the islands of Guadeloupe and Marie-Galante. The other French territory on the continent, Louisiana, ended up in Spanish hands after a complicated swap engineered by Choiseul, the French minister. France ceded Louisiana to Spain. Spain then surrendered Florida to Britain and received Havana in return. The Mississippi River was chosen as the dividing line between the British on the east and the Spanish on the west. Choiseul was sanguine about the loss of Canada. He already had his eye on a replacement. He wrote Madame de Pompadour, the influential former mistress of Louis XV, in July that a settlement in Guiana in South America (now French Guiana) would compensate France. It was superior to Canada, he wrote, in that it could produce sugar, cocoa, and indigo, as well as excellent grain, rye, and oats. He had already sent botanists, naturalists, doctors, farmers, and colonists to investigate its potential.[13]

Franklin had left London for Philadelphia in August 1762, before the preliminary peace terms were agreed. There had been a temporary lull in the wrestling match between the colonial assembly and the proprietor of Pennsylvania and a partial victory for the assembly when a bill passed that raised a small amount of taxes on the proprietor's lands. When news of the tentative peace deal reached Franklin early in 1763, he wrote a series of ecstatic letters to his London friends. He told Strahan in February 1763 that it was "the most glorious peace you have ever made, the most advantageous for the British Nation, in my Opinion, of any your Annals have recorded." He congratulated Richard Jackson, who had taken over his duties as agent for Pennsylvania in London, saying the preliminaries "are universally approved in these Parts." Then he started making plans for filling the new territories with British people, starting with the territories immediately to the west of the thirteen colonies. He suggested to Jackson it would be a good time to start thinking of creating colonies along the Mississippi River, now that all the land between it and the Atlantic Ocean belonged to Britain. "What think you now of asking for a Slice of Territory, to be settled in some manner like that I once propos'd?" he asked. In a postscript, Franklin talked of a scheme he was involved in to obtain a grant of land, which he thought might not succeed, but also of another that he thought both Jackson and he could get shares in, which could be profitable. "There appears every where an unaccountable Penchant in all our People to migrate westward," he wrote.[14]

The Devil Is in the Details of the Royal Proclamation

The Royal Proclamation of 1763, which followed the peace treaty, presented a setback to Franklin's immediate plans. It was largely the work of the Lords

Commissioners of Trade and Plantations, also known as the Board of Trade, an eight-person body whose remit was to report to cabinet on the colonies. Its members included William Petty, Earl of Shelburne, who would later play an important role in determining the fate of Canada during negotiations to end the American Revolution. While serving as president of the board, Shelburne defended the terms of the peace treaty for the ministry. He dismissed Guadeloupe as a "trifling object."[15]

Egremont, the secretary of state, had asked the board in May 1763 for advice on how to govern the new acquisitions. The first point he asked them to consider was how Britain could derive "the most extensive Commercial Advantages" from its new territories. He also said there were two questions about the security of North America they needed to answer: how to defend it from attack by another European power and how to preserve internal peace and security "against any Indian disturbances." On the second point, Egremont said the king was keen to impress the Indigenous Peoples with the "Mildness of his government." This meant "protecting their Persons & Property & securing to them all the Possessions, Rights and Privileges they have hitherto enjoyed, & are entitled to, most cautiously guarding against any Invasion Occupation of their Hunting Lands, the Possession of which is to be acquired by fair Purchase only."

The board members were aware that American colonists were already spreading westward into the Indigenous lands. They partly bought Franklin's argument that population growth had caused some of the colonies to become "overstock'd," as they put it in a reply to Egremont in June 1763. But they also thought colonists were looking farther afield for land because speculative monopolies held by "Land Jobbers" had forced up the price of land in the original colonies. New settlements were needed, they agreed. But they wanted colonists to go north to Nova Scotia, rich in fish and lumber, or south to Georgia and Florida, where they thought many of the commodities found in the West Indies could be produced. In their eyes, the greatest gain from the peace treaty was "the exclusive Fishery of the River St. Laurence on all the Coasts in the Gulph of St. Laurence and all the Islands in that Gulph." And they were confident there was more than enough land in Nova Scotia and Georgia to accommodate all the colonists who had settled on the western side of the Appalachian Mountains.[16] It is unclear whether they knew how many colonists this entailed. Franklin had written his friend Jackson in March 1763 about Fort Pitt in the Ohio country (where Pittsburgh is today), saying there were at least two hundred log houses around the fort. But there were no firm figures on the total number of settlers west of the mountains.

New Borders Constrain Canada and the Thirteen Colonies

The Board of Trade drafted the final proclamation, which was published on October 7, 1763. It set new borders for Canada, part of which the British renamed the Province of Quebec, and new western limits for the thirteen colonies. Somewhat confusingly, the name Canada continued to be used interchangeably with Province of Quebec by both the British and the colonists. The Province of Quebec, or Canada, was reduced to a narrow, roughly rectangular territory along both banks of the St. Lawrence. It encompassed the major population centres of Montreal, Trois-Rivières, and Quebec City. Its western edge was a line drawn from Lake Nipissing southeast to a point on the St. Lawrence River roughly where Cornwall, Ontario, is today. Its eastern edge went from the Baie des Chaleurs, which today separates northeastern New Brunswick from the Gaspé Peninsula, to the St. John River, on what was the southern Labrador coast and is now part of Quebec. It included the Gaspé Peninsula in the east but did not include most of what is now Southern Ontario in the west. The vast hinterland surrounding the Great Lakes, or *pays-d'en-haut*, was set aside for the Indigenous Peoples now subject to the king. The board called it "Indian Country." One advantage of restricting the colony of Canada in this way was that it would prevent the "Ancient French Inhabitants" from leaving to settle in remote places, "where they neither could be so conveniently made amenable to the Jurisdiction of any Colony nor made subservient to the Interest of the Trade & Commerce of this Kingdom." The board also advised that those ancient inhabitants were likely to exceed any British settlers in number for quite some time, even if the utmost efforts were made to speed new settlements. The king had wanted the governor of Canada to also have jurisdiction over "Indian Country," but the board objected, saying that among other things, it would give the province an advantage in trade with Indigenous Peoples. They asked, and the king agreed, that the commander-in-chief in North America would oversee it.

The royal proclamation attempted to constrain the thirteen colonies to the eastern seaboard. Their western limits were set at "the heads or Sources of any of the Rivers which fall into the Atlantic Ocean from the West and the North West." This effectively drew a boundary line down the spine of the Appalachian Mountains. Once again, the board thought keeping colonists close to the coast was the best way to keep them accessible to and dependent on Britain. The land to the west and northwest of the mountains was Indigenous territory and would not be open to settlement without explicit permission. Any land sales would go through the Crown. Last-minute changes to the draft proclamation by John Pownall, permanent secretary to the Board of Trade, slightly softened this blow by adding phrases that implied the restrictions were temporary. For example, new land grants were forbidden "for the present, and until our further Pleasure be known," and Indigenous territory was set aside "for the present as aforesaid." Still, this was not at all what Franklin wanted. He believed that confining the colonists to a narrow strip of land between the mountains and the sea would permanently check their growth. It would also impede land speculation schemes.

Land Speculators Continue to Hatch New Schemes

Franklin and his fellow expansionists chose to regard the proclamation line as a temporary setback. He did not explicitly mention it in any of the surviving letters he wrote in the following twelve months. Given that he often repeated the same thing in letters to multiple correspondents, the absence of any reference suggests he was not overly concerned. Richard Jackson made a fleeting comment on the limits in a letter to Franklin in April 1764. Jackson wrote about a land scheme proposal the two were involved in and said he thought there was a prospect that "Prepossessions" against settlements on the Mississippi and what he called the "back country" would be removed. Franklin's letters show that he had not given up on colonial expansion. In them he made frequent reference to possible new settlements, mostly in the prohibited area west of the thirteen colonies supposedly reserved for the Indigenous Peoples. Some he hoped to profit from, but others he supported because they would help friends and relatives and fulfill his vision of North America filled with British subjects. Among his surviving papers is a partial document called "A Scheme for a Western Settlement 1763–1764," which outlines a plan to sell land to settlers, with preference given to those from Connecticut. The document identifies Franklin as the author.

His interest extended to potential land grants in Canada and in Nova Scotia. For example, in May 1764 he wrote Jackson, saying he was interested in obtaining a grant for land in Nova Scotia if it looked like a likely place for a settlement. He obtained a share in Nova Scotia land grants given to a group from Philadelphia in 1765 and received a grant in his own name for twenty-thousand acres in 1767. He still owned the latter when he died, leaving it to his son, William. Franklin also advanced requests by his family, friends, and acquaintances. A group of Nantucket whalers, whom he identified as relations, wanted to set up a whaling station on St. John's Island (now Prince Edward Island). John Baynton and Samuel Wharton, with whom he had other business ventures, wanted two tracts of land in Canada: eight thousand hectares (twenty thousand acres) on Lake Champlain, land which Wharton described to Franklin as "rich pine Country, is of good soil," and another eight thousand hectares on the Baie des Chaleurs, which according to Wharton, "is the best Cod Fishery in this Government." Franklin pressed Jackson to act quickly on these requests, before Governor Murray would grant the land to someone else. "Can you obtain such a Grant for us, and will you share my Third with me?"[17]

While his interest in land settlement and land speculation were constants, they took a back seat to other matters after he returned to Philadelphia. He was busy with his duties as deputy postmaster general, appointing local postmasters, and making a tour of the colonies, from the southernmost part of Virginia to the easternmost part of New England. His travels lasted seven months and covered 2,900 kilometres (1,800 miles). During this trip, which must have been arduous given the lack of good roads in many places, he fell and dislocated his shoulder. This put him out of action for some time. The problem that appeared to consume much of his time, judging from his letters, was the dispute between the assembly, where he was once again a member, and Penn over the payment of taxes on the proprietor's extensive land holdings.

Colonial Security Threatened Again

The British victory over the French had solved one of the security problems faced by the thirteen colonies. Canada could no longer be used as a staging point for French attacks on the colonies. But peace with all the Indigenous Peoples on the frontier still eluded the colonists. Some colonists believed that French traders who remained in the area west of the mountains were inciting Indigenous groups to continue fighting, supplying them with clothing and ammunition. Certainly, some of the Indigenous Peoples of the interior believed the French would return and defeat the British. But it was the increasing encroachment on Indigenous lands by American settlers, despite British promises this would not happen, that was at the heart of this conflict. An uprising, known as Pontiac's War, after the English name for the Odawa Chief who led the attacks, began in 1763 with assaults on British forts at Detroit and elsewhere in the area south of the Great Lakes, including the Ohio Valley. The Indigenous forces drew warriors from a wide range of groups, including the Chippewa, Delaware, Miami, Potawatomi, Seneca, Shawnee, and Wendat. War parties raided settlements in Pennsylvania, North Carolina, and Virginia, causing panic among settlers. Some retaliated by murdering peaceful Indigenous Peoples. A slaughter of Conestoga by a group called the Paxton Boys appalled Franklin.

The Pennsylvania assembly agreed to contribute to the defence of the colonies by paying to raise and equip a force of one thousand men, to be led by Colonel Henry Bouquet, a Swiss-born British officer. Franklin and Bouquet had met almost a decade earlier and had written each other frequently ever since. They now corresponded about the military mission and its financial problems. In one of these letters, Bouquet referred to their joint plan to settle a colony on the Scioto River (which runs through present-day Columbus, Ohio).[18] This was separate from the proposal, made in an anonymous pamphlet published in Britain in 1763, to establish a large, new, western colony. It was to be called Charlotina, after Queen Charlotte, and included the area south of the Great Lakes between the Mississippi and Ohio Rivers.[19] The reason for establishing Charlotina, according to the author of the pamphlet, was to prevent the French from returning to the area once Bouquet and his forces had driven them out. It never came to pass.

Franklin Heads Back to London

When the assembly sent a money bill that included the Bouquet expedition's expenses to the governor, he sent it back — not once but several times — because it did not exclude the proprietor from paying taxes. The old problem had flared up again, only this time it burned more fiercely. The immediate problem was eventually solved when the assembly gave in to the demands of the governor, who took Penn's side. But the bitter argument over the proprietor's refusal to help defend the colony in time of need hardened the hearts of a majority of assembly members. They resolved to petition George III to make Pennsylvania a royal colony, removing governing functions from Penn. They turned to Franklin once again, asking him to return to London to present their case to the king. He would represent the colony as assistant agent to Richard Jackson.

Franklin was still not a popular choice with the supporters of the proprietor, who held a minority of seats in the assembly. He admitted privately to a friend that he disliked and despised Penn.[20] The proprietor's supporters had targeted Franklin for months in a series of pamphlets, which among other things accused him of fraud involving the colony's accounts, of spending immense amounts of the public money during his previous stay in London, and of wanting to trample on their rights by doing away with the colony's original charter.[21] They dug up the unwise comment he had made in the first version of his *Observations* twelve years earlier about Palatine boors herding together, referring to German immigrants. His critics said the comment, which had been excised from the final version, showed Franklin thought the German immigrants were swine. Franklin admitted to a friend the comment had cost him the German vote and his seat in the assembly.[22] He had fought back through his writing and by asking Bouquet to write a letter to him praising all the work he had done on behalf of Britain, a letter he could show to anyone who doubted his probity and loyalty to the king. Bouquet duly complied.[23]

The personal attacks continued even after Franklin set off for London in November 1764. William Smith, an old foe, wrote a particularly vituperative pamphlet in which he said Franklin was "the most unpopular and odious name in the province" and was someone who "truckles for preferment for himself and his family."[24] This might have been a reference to the appointment in 1762 of Franklin's illegitimate son, William, as colonial governor of New Jersey.

Franklin's farewell letters to family and friends gave little indication of the heavy burden he was carrying. He was preoccupied with his immediate task of persuading the king to make Pennsylvania a royal colony and of protecting the colony's interests as Britain tried to extract more money from its possessions in the postwar period. But the personal attacks had found their mark. In his final letter to his daughter, Sarah, before boarding the ship in November 1764, he said that his enemies would magnify her slightest indiscretions into crimes to wound him. She must be "extreamly circumspect" in all her behaviour, he wrote, and make sure to go to church no matter who was preaching.[25]

With Canada now safely in British hands, Franklin wanted to ensure that the captured French territories were settled by British subjects. If he could earn a personal profit from some of the new settlements on Canadian soil, all the better. His next stint in London would be dominated by the rising tensions between imperial Britain and the American colonies. Yet he still found time to promote a series of land speculation schemes and search for wealthy British investors to back them. He would also discover, somewhat belatedly, that Britain's rulers and American colonists really did have widely different views on what should be done with the newly conquered territories in North America.

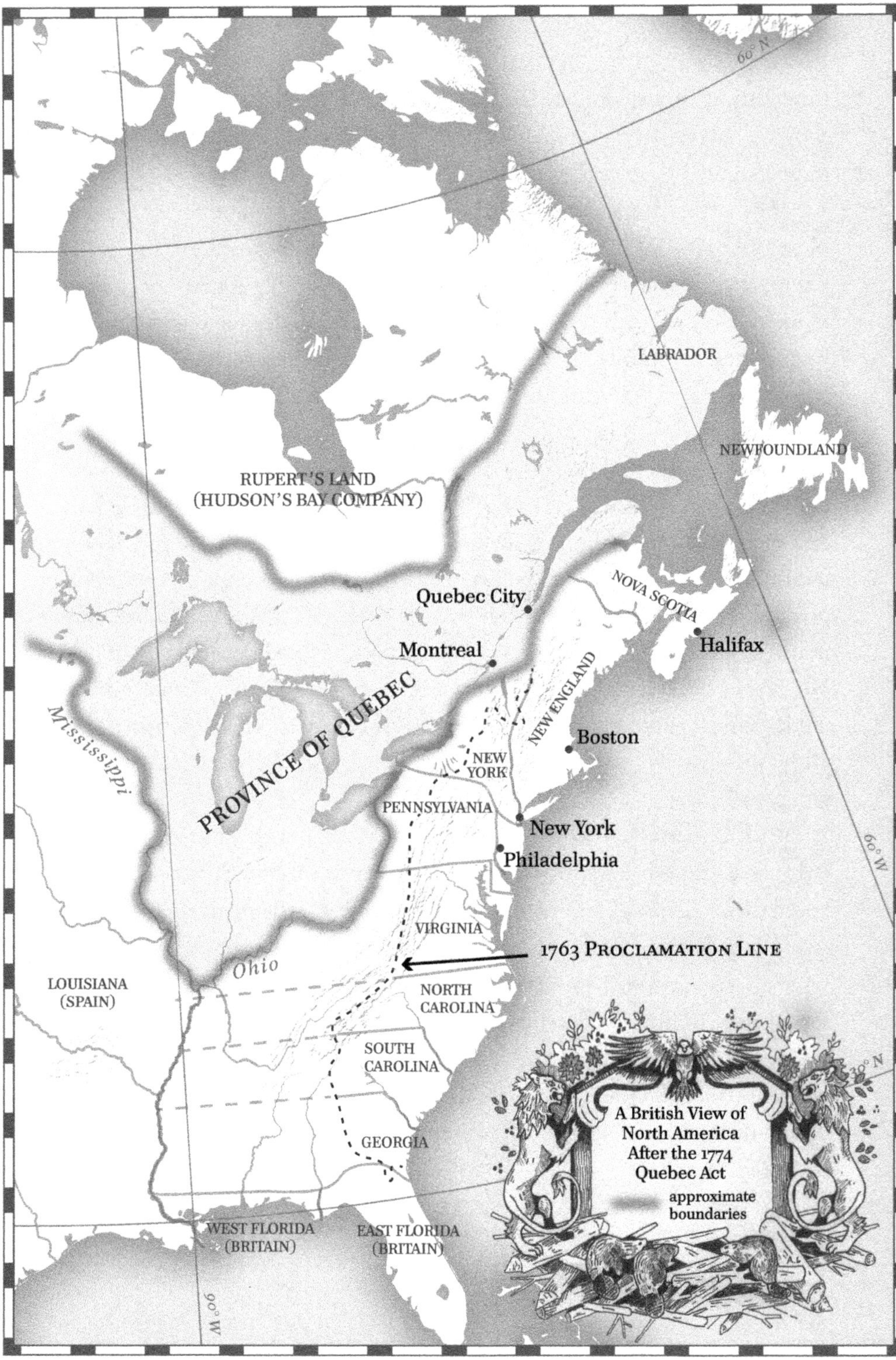
60° N
LABRADOR
NEWFOUNDLAND
RUPERT'S LAND
(HUDSON'S BAY COMPANY)
Quebec City
NOVA SCOTIA
Halifax
Montreal
NEW ENGLAND
PROVINCE OF QUEBEC
Mississippi
Boston
NEW YORK
PENNSYLVANIA
New York
Philadelphia
60° W
VIRGINIA
1763 Proclamation Line
Ohio
LOUISIANA
(SPAIN)
NORTH CAROLINA
SOUTH CAROLINA
30° N
GEORGIA
A British View of North America After the 1774 Quebec Act
approximate boundaries
WEST FLORIDA
(BRITAIN)
EAST FLORIDA
(BRITAIN)
90° W

CHAPTER 6

A New Papist Army: London 1774–1775

> We, having assisted in the conquest of Canada, at great expense of blood and treasure, had some right to be considered in the settlement of it.[1]
>
> — *Benjamin Franklin*

IN MAY 1774, THE BRITISH MINISTRY, LED BY FREDERICK NORTH, THE Earl of Guilford, introduced a bill in Parliament that completely undermined Franklin's notion of filling North America with British Americans. With the Quebec Act, more formally called An Act for making more effectual Provision for the Government of the Province of Quebec in North America, the British government acknowledged that the tens of thousands of French Canadians living in Canada (or the Province of Quebec, as it was now called) would not be deported or forced to assimilate, as Franklin had proposed in his 1760 *Canada Pamphlet*. Instead, Britain would recognize the Catholic religion and French civil law. The bill would remove explicit oaths against Catholic beliefs, although Canadians would still have to swear allegiance to the British king, and it would loosen the prohibition on Catholics holding public office. Far from becoming a place where Franklin's fellow American colonists would feel at home, Canada would remain a separate and distinct society, where foreign laws were used and the popish religion practised.

Equally upsetting to Franklin's idea of Americans settling the continent was that the act extended the borders of Canada back to about where they were under the French regime. It recreated New France in terms of its borders and its social, legal, and religious systems. And it reaffirmed, rather than erased, the 1763 proclamation line down the spine of the Appalachian Mountains that confined the American colonies to a strip along the Atlantic coast.

Franklin's letters from that time show he was in London, living in a set of rented rooms on Craven Street. He was now the London agent for the colonies of Georgia, Massachusetts, New Jersey, and Pennsylvania, and he regularly reported on events in London to the leaders of these colonial assemblies. And yet he did not appear unduly alarmed by the Quebec bill, mentioning it only in passing in his correspondence for several weeks after it was introduced. A diligent colonial agent, especially one with designs on Canada, should have caught wind of the bill while it was still in the planning stage and waged a fierce lobbying campaign to change its terms or prevent its passage. Public relations were, after all, Franklin's forte.

To be fair to Franklin, there was a lot going on at the time that required his urgent attention. In the spring of 1774, the North ministry was aggressively trying to subdue the rebellious colonists with a flurry of punitive legislation known collectively as the Coercive, or Intolerable, Acts. In May and June, the king gave royal assent to bills that closed the port of Boston to trade, replaced elected councillors with appointed ones in Massachusetts, sent those accused of a crime in the colonies to Britain for trial, and allowed British officers to demand better accommodation for their troops in the colonies. These were seen as far more consequential to the American colonists because they directly affected people and livelihoods at home. Franklin still harboured the illusion that the situation was salvageable and that good relations could be restored between Britain and the thirteen colonies.

The strength of emotions and depth of mutual incomprehension suggested otherwise. Neither Britain nor the colonies recognized that the circumstances and thus the attitudes of the other had changed significantly since the French threat had been forcibly removed from North America. Britain gazed on the colonies with an imperial eye, gauging how they fit in an empire that had massively expanded with the addition of Canada. British ideas on imperial governance were changing. So, too, were opinions on who should help pay off its huge war debts. North regarded the truculent colonists as ungrateful subjects. They regarded him and his ministers as tyrants trampling on their liberty. Having been left to largely govern themselves since their inception, the American colonists fiercely resented being taxed or told what to do. Even if this gap could be closed, Franklin was not the man to do it. For personal reasons, which will be described later, he was held in contempt by powerful ministers within the British government, which limited his usefulness in overturning any of the acts. Distracted, discouraged, and disdained, the best he could do once he realized the import of the Quebec Act was to mount a rearguard, and ultimately futile, campaign for its repeal.

What Came Before the Quebec Act in Britain

The British conquest of Canada in 1760 had presented the British ministry with a new set of problems. It added a vast new territory to an already sprawling empire, along with a sizeable population with a different culture, language, and religion. And it saddled Britain with debts. George Grenville, appointed prime minister in 1763, pushed for Britain to take a more hands-on approach to taxing and governing the colonies. He was given powerful support by the Earl of Halifax, a veteran minister in charge of colonial affairs. One of the arguments made by proponents of colonial taxation was that since the lion's share of the fighting in the war was done to remove the French threat to the American colonies, the colonists should help repay the debt. Another was that the American colonies either would not or could not defend their western frontier against Indigenous attacks, putting the burden on British taxpayers to fund a standing army to take on that task. That was not how the colonists viewed the situation. It was one thing for Britain to regulate their trade and impose minimal customs duties, quite another for the ministry in London to strictly enforce those duties, such as those covered by the Molasses Act of 1733, and impose new taxes, most notably under the Stamp Act of 1765. That now-notorious legislation required the colonists to pay a fee in hard currency, which was scarce, every time they used paper for most business and legal transactions. Everything from newspapers to college diplomas needed a stamp showing the tax had been paid to be legitimate. This provoked riots and boycotts of British goods in the thirteen colonies but not in colonies like Canada, Nova Scotia, and Jamaica, which entirely depended on funding from Britain to survive. And while Britain repealed the Stamp Act the following year because of the uproar, it made subsequent unpopular attempts to raise revenues by taxing glass, lead, paper, and tea and insisted on its right to tax the colonies.

These moves seem tone-deaf in retrospect. But they made eminent sense to a British government under financial pressure and unwilling to raise the already high tax burden on constituents at home. By one estimate, the British tax rate was 5–7 percent compared to 1–1.5 percent in the American colonies just prior to the revolution. The British national debt was estimated at almost £147 million in 1762. Paying the interest on that debt accounted for 22 percent of all government spending.[2] Ministers took as a given that the British Parliament was supreme throughout the empire and dismissed the colonial complaint that there should be no taxation without representation. They were confident that Britain had the right to do what it wanted with its colonies.

Colonists Held in Low Regard

Key to understanding British government actions at this time was a widespread attitude in Britain that colonials could not be regarded as equals. British attitudes toward colonists in general were growing more negative, even as their self-regard as custodians of a glorious empire increased. The writer Arthur Young expressed this sense of British exceptionalism in 1772, when he said that "in America, Spain, Portugal and France, have planted despotism; only Britain liberty."[3] But some at home found it increasingly difficult to reconcile the image of Britain as the most benevolent of the imperial powers with the reports of inhumane or corrupt actions by the British abroad. Accounts of slavery in the American colonies, plunder in Bengal by officers of the East India Company, and the slaughter and forced displacement of the Black Caribs of St. Vincent at the behest of British planters clouded the vision of imperial grandeur. There were plenty of voices raised in Britain against slavery. One of them, John Millar, a Scottish philosopher, had devoted considerable space to the topic in his 1771 tract, *Observations Concerning the Distinction of Ranks in Society*. He said slavery existed in barbarous nations. It was a "curious spectacle," he wrote, to see American colonists "talk in so high a strain of political liberty" when they had no scruples about depriving others of their rights. The solution for Britons stung by such words was to distance themselves from the perpetrators of these actions while conveniently ignoring any profits from such inhumane actions accruing to those at home.

What further sullied the reputation of the American colonies in British eyes was that they had long been a dumping ground for convicts and other undesirables. An estimated fifty thousand to fifty-five thousand convicts were transported to the American colonies before 1775.[4] In 1775 a member of Parliament cast doubt on whether the American colonists were in fact English because they were a collection of Scottish, Irish, French, Dutch, and German immigrants intermingled with felons, Indigenous Peoples, and enslaved Africans.[5] There was some truth to this observation on the mixed origins of colonists. The original Puritans numbered about 20,000, whereas more than 150,000 Scottish and Irish Presbyterians had settled in the colonies up to this point.

Franklin Fights Back

Throughout his time in London, Franklin drafted often prickly responses to such talk. He was sometimes joined by his colonial colleagues. For example, when Adam Smith wrote in his *Theory of Moral Sentiments* that the people of Africa were heroes, subjected to the refuse of the jails of Europe, Arthur Lee of Virginia responded with an essay of his own. Smith did not use the words "America" or "colonies" in the brief passage about midway through the 538-page book, but the reference was clear. It had been preceded by some glowing words about the "magnanimity and self-command" of the "savages in North America" and the assertion that "a negro from the coast of Africa" had more magnanimity than his "sordid master" was capable of conceiving. Lee, then a student in Edinburgh, retorted that "negro habitations" in the colonies were palaces compared with those of peasants in Scotland and Ireland and that far from being heroes, Black Africans were "dextrous rogues, prone to lying, frequently guilty of horrid murders, given to gross idolatry and honouring the devil." Yet in his *Essay in Vindication of the Continental Colonies of America, from A Censure of Mr Adam Smith, in his Theory of Moral Sentiments*, he seemed to be of two minds about slavery, concluding that it was "absolutely repugnant to justice" and that Europeans should abolish the slave trade.

Franklin adopted a slightly more measured tone in some of his attempts to set the record straight. "The first settlers of New England particularly, were English gentlemen of fortune, who, being Puritans, left this country with their families and followers, in times of persecution for the sake of enjoying, though in a wilderness, the blessings of civil and religious liberty," he'd huffed in an anonymous letter to *The Gazetteer* in 1765. He could not deny that slavery existed in the colonies. A contemporary estimate given by a Philadelphia Quaker suggested there were 850,000 enslaved Africans in the British colonies and islands at the time.[6] (The white population of the thirteen colonies was about 1.6 million in 1760 and about 2.5 million in 1776, according to estimates by the Census Bureau.) So he tried to minimize it. In a piece published in the *Public Advertiser* in January 1770, attributed to him, Franklin said there were few slaves in Pennsylvania and the northern colonies and that many Americans treated their slaves with great humanity. He went on to say that the majority of enslaved people "are of a plotting Disposition, dark, sullen, malicious, revengeful and cruel in the highest Degree." He added the Scots allowed slavery in the collieries and the English had it in the army and navy. He neglected to mention that he had at least two enslaved servants. Whataboutism and hypocrisy are not new inventions.

The ruling elite in Britain were not alone in regarding North American colonists as inferiors. There was a serious debate in European circles about whether those who moved across the Atlantic became morally and physically diminished with each generation. Cornelius de Pauw, a Dutch philosopher and diplomat, advanced this idea in 1768. It was taken up by others, including the French natural philosopher Georges-Louis Leclerc, comte de Buffon, and Abbé Raynal, who wrote a popular encyclopedia. Privately, Franklin dismissed such views as ignorance. Publicly, he attempted to fight them with facts and, when that failed, with satire.

Many of his earlier efforts to correct misperceptions were lighthearted. To poke fun at British ignorance, he wrote a satire in 1765 about Quebec starting a cod and whale fishery in the Great Lakes, which would lead to the sight of whales leaping Niagara Falls. The humour in his later satires is darker. For example, in "A Method of Humbling Rebellious American Vassals," which appeared in the *Public Advertiser* in May 1774, he suggested Britain could stop the colonies from growing too large and powerful by having a company of one hundred pig-gelders go from town to town, castrating colonial males. "It is true that blood will be shed, but Probably not many lives lost," he wrote. "Bleeding to a certain Degree is salutary."

Wounded by Privy Council Shaming

Franklin's ability to make a convincing case for the American colonies on any issue was blunted by an event in early 1774. The ill will toward Franklin was apparent at a January meeting of the Privy Council, whose members acted as advisors to George III. Franklin was there ostensibly to present a petition from the colony of Massachusetts, which he represented as agent, calling for the removal of their governor. Alexander Wedderburn, the sharp-tongued solicitor general, seized the chance to give him a dressing-down for almost an hour, attacking his character and questioning his motives. Franklin stood in silence while the privy councillors looked on and laughed. His crime in their eyes was to have obtained and then shared with contacts in Massachusetts the private correspondence between Thomas Hutchinson, the colony's governor, and Thomas Whately, Hutchinson's friend in Britain. Among other things, Hutchinson and Whately discussed the need for more British troops to subdue the rebellious colonists.

The publication of the letters in Massachusetts in June 1773 stoked public anger at a time when relations with Britain were already strained. Thomas Whately, who died before the letters came to light, had been Wedderburn's friend. This likely added to the solicitor general's anger. The Privy Council meeting took place just as news reached London of problems with tea shipments to the colonies. Angry Bostonians had the effrontery, in British eyes, to toss tea from the East India Company into the Boston harbour in December 1773, an event later celebrated as the Boston Tea Party. This deepened the ministers' thirst for retribution, coming as it did after other insurrections in Massachusetts by what the North ministry perceived as ungrateful and misguided colonists. Whom better to punish than their representative in London?

Franklin never revealed how he came to have the letters and only confessed his involvement in December 1773, after Whately's brother William had fought a duel with a man falsely accused of taking them. William Whately was lightly injured in the duel. A planned rematch was cancelled after Franklin admitted publicly that he was the culprit. Wedderburn said Franklin obtained the letters "by fraudulent or corrupt means for the most malignant of purposes" and had forfeited the respect of societies and men. In future men "will hide their papers from him and lock up their escritoires."[7]

These were serious charges at a time when a man's perceived honour determined whether he would be received or shunned by Britain's imperious elites. Franklin was already labouring under the twin burdens of being a colonial and a tradesman. News of his humiliation spread quickly through private letters, like those of Edmund Burke, and through newspapers and pamphlets, where caustic comments about his character became more frequent and venomous.

The *General Evening Post* published a verse just before the Privy Council meeting that called him a "base, ungrateful, cunning upstart thing" who was false to his country and to his king.[8] Burke confided to a friend that Wedderburn had delivered "a furious Philippic against poor Dr Franklin." Burke told another that the attack was "beyond all bounds and measure."[9] Franklin told friends afterward: "I was called an incendiary, and the papers were full of invectives against me."[10] There were rumours he would be charged with treason. That did not transpire, but he was dismissed from his post as deputy postmaster general for British North America.

Franklin did what he could to repair the damage, giving his version of events in anonymous letters to newspapers in London and the colonies. One such letter to the *Pennsylvania Gazette*, attributed to Franklin and published in April 1774, described his experience as akin to a "bull-baiting" and said the government ministry was out to "crucify" him. Another anonymous account, also attributed to him, appeared in the *Boston Gazette* that same month. It described Wedderburn as "virulent" and contended that Franklin had acquired the letters "honourably" and that his actions in transmitting them to Massachusetts were "virtuous." He brushed off the degrading encounter in his personal correspondence. When his friend Jan Ingenhousz sent commiserations, Franklin replied in March 1774 that "having myself been long engaged in public business, this treatment is not new to me." In a letter in March 1775 to his son, then governor of New Jersey, he called the dressing-down an "affront" and said he withstood it in "cool, sullen silence." Yet it clearly stung. And he knew there was truth in the saying he had published some years earlier in *Poor Richard's Almanack*: "Glass, China and Reputation are easily crack'd, and never well mended."

Wedderburn's aspersions and the negative comments in the press were bitter blows to a man who had struggled with humility his whole life. "In reality, there is perhaps no one of our natural Passions so hard to subdue as Pride," he had written in his autobiography. "Disguise it, struggle with it, beat it down, stifle it, mortify it as much as one pleases, it is still alive, and will every now and then peep out and show itself." Franklin was in the odd position of being lauded in scientific circles for his electrical experiments but damned in political ones. He was not welcome at gatherings where key decisions were made. "From the time of the affront given me at the Council Board, in January 1774, I had never attended the levee of any minister," he told his son in his March 1775 letter. "I made no justification of myself from the charges brought against me; I made no return of the injury by abusing my adversaries." Remaining aloof might have been balm to his wounded soul, but it left him ill-equipped to counter the Quebec Act and the series of punitive acts the North ministry pushed through Parliament in the spring of 1774.

What Came Before the Quebec Act in Canada

The Quebec Act, which received royal assent on June 22, 1774, was not primarily intended to punish the Americans. They thought it was aimed at them because it was introduced in the same period as the Coercive Acts, it reinforced the western limit to their expansion, and it allowed the practise of Catholicism and partial use of the French legal system in a hugely expanded Canada. The North ministry seemed happy enough to leave them with that impression. Yet the legislation had been in the works for at least two years before it was introduced in the House of Lords at the tail end of the parliamentary session. Guy Carleton, who had succeeded James Murray as governor of the Province of Quebec, had travelled to Britain as far back as 1770 to sort out the increasingly chaotic governance of the new colony. Wedderburn, the solicitor general, had given his views on what should be done in a December 1772 report. Edward Thurlow, the attorney general, followed with his report on governance in the new colony in January 1773. There were plenty of signs for Franklin, had he heeded them, that far-reaching changes affecting Canada and its relationship with the thirteen colonies were in the works.

For the first few years after the conquest of Canada in 1760, the British had left local laws in place and tolerated the practise of Roman Catholicism. There was no point in making massive changes when no one knew whether the French territories in North America would be traded back to France in the peace negotiations. That only became clear when the Treaty of Paris was signed in 1763. Franklin was among those who fervently pushed for Britain to retain Canada. Once that decision had been made, Britain forged ahead with a program to remake the French Canadians into loyal subjects of the British king. Under the terms of the treaty, Britain agreed its new subjects could continue to practise the Catholic religion. But the king was clear in his 1763 instructions to James Murray, the military governor who then became governor of the colony, that the inhabitants should be induced by degrees "to embrace the Protestant Religion, and their Children be brought up in the principles of it." Murray was also to replicate the English judicial system to the extent possible and to call a legislative assembly when he felt the time was right. This assembly would not include French Canadians. Only men who took the test oaths, which repudiated key concepts of the Catholic faith, could hold public office.

This governance plan looked good on paper but failed the test of reality. The French Canadians, who numbered between sixty-five thousand and one hundred thousand, vastly outnumbered English-speaking Protestants in the newly acquired colony. Carleton was exaggerating when he told the House of Commons in 1774 there were about 150,000 French Canadians and only about 360 male Protestants but not by a lot.[11] Many of the Protestants were army suppliers who had followed the troops north from the American colonies during the war and decided to stay. If each had a wife and four children, that would put the total Protestant population at about two thousand people. Yet this small group loudly insisted from the start that only English laws be recognized, including trial by jury and habeas corpus, and that only those who took specific oaths could hold a government post or sit in a legislative assembly, which they wanted convened as soon as possible. They pointed to the 1763 proclamation and Murray's instructions to justify their demands. But the governor knew he risked civil unrest if he enforced the official terms.

The ban on allowing Catholics to hold most government posts was never going to work. There were not enough English Protestants to fill available jobs.[12] Catholics did not sit on the governor's legislative council, but they did hold lower government posts, working as bailiffs, road officials, and court clerks, as well as notaries and lawyers. Strict adherence to English law was equally fraught because the French Canadians clung stubbornly to their old laws. They often settled disputes out of court rather than submit to the English legal system. Necessity forced the British rulers to adapt. Between 1764 and 1774, a mix of English common law and French civil law was used in the colony.[13] Trials were held in both languages. Murray, a Scot, resisted the most extreme demands of the English merchants, known as old subjects, whom he deplored. The French Canadians were known as the new subjects as they had only recently come under the British Crown. "Little, very little, will content the New Subjects but nothing will satisfy the Licentious Fanaticks Trading here, but the expulsion of the Canadians who are perhaps the bravest and best race upon the Globe," Murray said in a 1764 letter to the Board of Trade in London. The English-speaking agitators, however, had the ear of powerful people in London. They succeeded in having Murray recalled in 1768. Carleton, who replaced him, met with the same intractable problem posed by the small, vocal, and well-connected group of English-speaking malcontents who would not be satisfied until Canada resembled the American colonies.

Carleton seemed more promising to these merchants at first. But the military man from Ulster, who spoke French and German, bowed to numerical reality and denied their attempts to completely sideline French Canadians. Mindful of the growing unrest in the thirteen colonies, he tried to find a way to keep Canada peaceful. Old school and favouring the aristocracy, he made certain assumptions about the power of the clergy and the large landholders and their ability to sway the ordinary French Canadians that he would regret later.

The Quebec Act largely reflected Carleton's reading of the situation. It legalized what was already common practice in the colony. French law would be used in civil cases, with English law used in criminal courts. This division still exists in Quebec. The Catholic clergy were legally allowed to collect tithes from parishioners, as they did under the French regime and continued to do, with mixed success, after the conquest. The seigneurial system, where land was owned by a seigneur and worked by the habitants for an annual fee, was implicitly sanctioned by the act. Catholics could legally hold government positions if they swore a revised oath that was no longer explicitly anti-Catholic. There would be no legislative assembly for the time being. Catholics would be appointed to the governor's legislative council, although Protestants would hold the majority of places. This appearance of toleration by the British, remarkable at a time when draconian laws against Catholics were still in place in Britain, was slightly undercut by secret instructions to Carleton from the king that later came to light. The assimilation of the French Canadians was delayed for practical reasons but remained the ultimate goal.

American Reaction to the Quebec Act

Several provisions of the 1774 act alarmed American colonists and investors hoping to profit from territorial expansion. The act redrew the boundaries of the Province of Quebec to once again include the territory claimed by France around the Great Lakes and as far south and west as the rather amorphous borders of Louisiana (old maps did not agree on where Louisiana was located). This restored the massive territory that was severed from the province in the 1763 proclamation, including the *pays-d'en-haut*, the hinterland surrounding the Great Lakes that was essential for the fur trade. A swathe of land between this territory and the Appalachian Mountains was reserved for Indigenous Peoples and could not be settled without permission from the king. The 1763 proclamation line, which set the western boundaries of the thirteen colonies at the Appalachian Mountains, was not erased in the Quebec Act, as had been mooted, but drawn with a firmer hand. The claims of Virginia, Connecticut, and Massachusetts that their boundaries extended westward to the Pacific Ocean were denied. So, too, was New York's claim that its border extended north to the St. Lawrence River because the Six Nations, whose territory it was, were British subjects. The New York governor had already granted tracts in this area to disbanded officers and soldiers, some of whom had sold their claims to land speculators. The act ignored this and allocated a large slice of land south of the St. Lawrence to the Province of Quebec. It also extended Quebec's boundaries east to the Labrador coast, giving the colony control of the coastal seal fishery, previously overseen by a seasonal government in Newfoundland. Governance of this whole vast territory was made the responsibility of the governor of Quebec. This meant that a mix of French and English law and toleration of the Catholic faith would extend throughout the interior of the continent, around the backs of the thirteen colonies.

Land Speculators See Potential Profits Disappear

There was plenty here to anger the already irritated American colonists, especially the land speculators eager to profit from new settlements beyond the mountains and in the disputed territory to the north. These speculators included some of the leaders of the coming revolution, including George

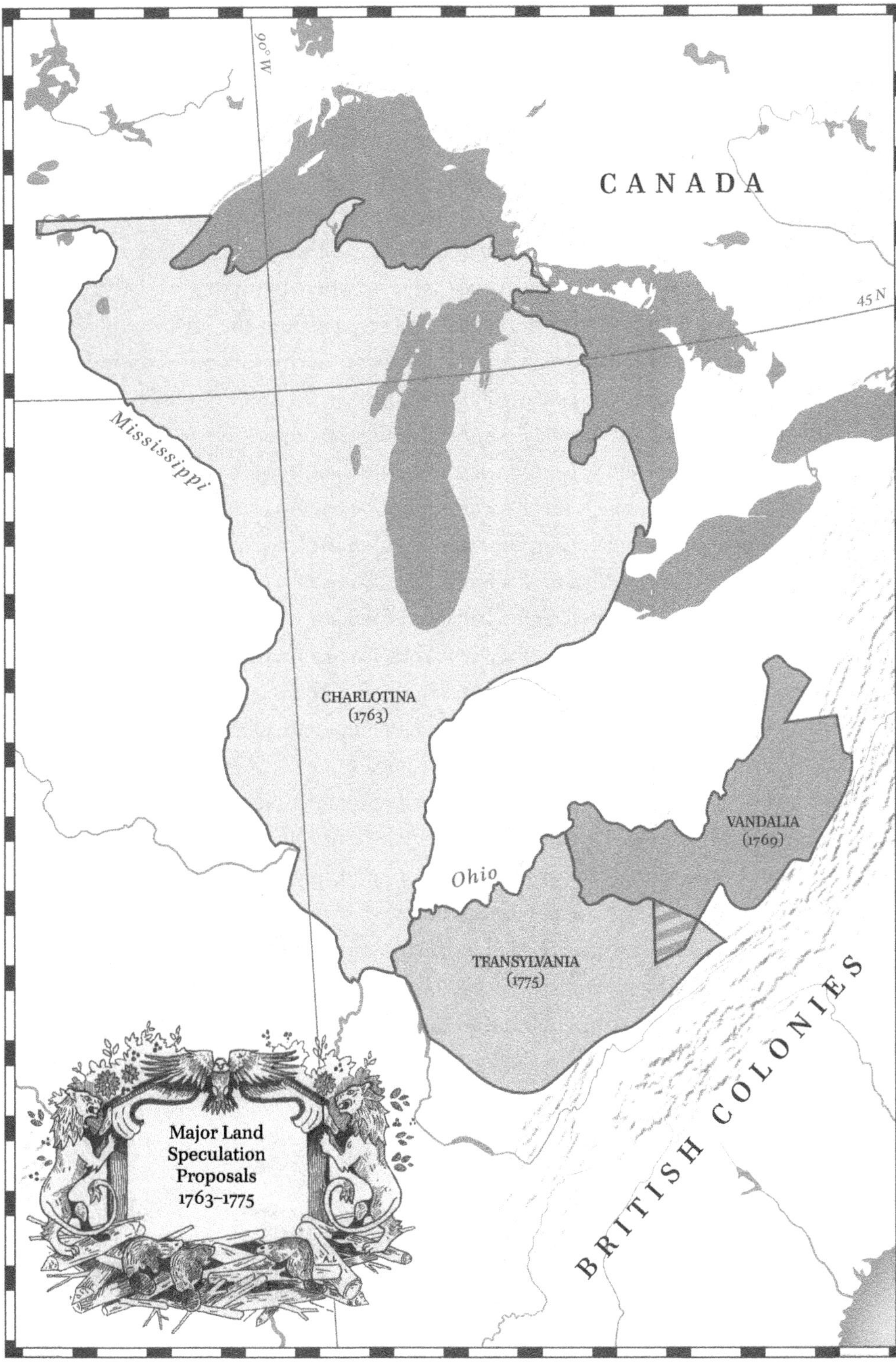

CANADA
90° W
45 N
Mississippi
CHARLOTINA (1763)
Ohio
VANDALIA (1769)
TRANSYLVANIA (1775)
BRITISH COLONIES
Major Land Speculation Proposals 1763–1775

Washington, Thomas Jefferson, Patrick Henry, George Mason, Richard Henry Lee — and Franklin.

Franklin was deeply involved with a request to the king by the Grand Ohio Company for a grant of nearly 1 million hectares (2.4 million acres), later increased to about 8 million hectares (20 million acres), in what is now West Virginia. He had a share in the company and helped woo wealthy English investors, including Thomas Walpole, Lord Camden, Lord Rochford, the Earl of Gower, and the Earl of Temple. The company wanted to set up a new colony called Vandalia on land west of the 1763 proclamation line, between the Appalachian Mountains and the Ohio River, which Britain acquired from the Haudenosaunee in the questionable 1768 Treaty of Fort Stanwix. That treaty, negotiated locally by the British Indian agent and the Six Nations, went against the wishes of the Board of Trade by opening lands for settlement far to the west of the proclamation line. It also angered the Indigenous inhabitants of the area because the Six Nations gave away their lands. The Quebec Act put Vandalia and other money-making ventures, including Transylvania, in jeopardy.

Franklin made a brief comment about the Quebec Act on June 1, telling Thomas Cushing, a Boston lawyer and speaker of the legislative assembly in Massachusetts, that the Quebec bill was among the papers he was sending. It came up again on July 25 in an "Extract of a Letter from London," which some experts dispute was written by Franklin, although its substance bears his hallmarks. The writer of the extract says the colonists risked becoming "eastern slaves" and that the British ministry had declared "open war" on the colonies with the punitive acts "and above all by the Quebec Bill." Franklin used the terms "bill" and "act" interchangeably, although technically bills become acts once they are given royal assent. In his personal correspondence, Franklin grumbled in a June 30 letter to his son, William, that the Quebec Revenue Act, a companion bill to the main act, treated the thirteen colonies as foreign countries in the trade of spirits and liquors. Imports to Quebec from the neighbouring colonies faced a stiffer duty than imports from Britain. "After all our expense in helping to conquer Canada for this Crown, we are put on the footing of foreigners, in our trade with It," he wrote.

It may be that no one could have swayed the North ministry once it had decided to clamp down on the rebellious colonies. But in 1774, Franklin was not the best man for this job. North and his ministers personally disliked him. He had been a thorn in the side of the ruling elite for some time because he held their policies up to ridicule in his writings and questioned their assumed superiority over the colonists. Franklin acknowledged this in an anonymous letter attributed to him published in the *Pennsylvania Gazette* in April 1774. The writer said Franklin was suspected of writing satirical pieces that "are thought to expose the late Measures too poignantly." Among the pieces the letter mentioned were "Rules by Which a Great Empire May Be Reduced to a Small One" and "An Edict by the King of Prussia." Both were published in September 1773 in the *Public Advertiser*, a London newspaper read by the elites. In *Rules* Franklin sardonically advised unnamed ministers in charge of the colonies to do things to enrage the colonists so that they would attempt to break free. Many of his points were things the North ministry was doing or contemplating, like taxing the colonists without their consent and sending unfit governors to the colonies. "Edict" was a hoax or fake news. In it he had Frederick II of Prussia provocatively proclaim that Britain was a colony of Prussia because parts of it had been settled by Anglo-Saxons, who had been governed by his ducal ancestors. This connection meant the British would have to start making payments to him so he could replenish his royal coffers. Franklin was delighted with these pieces. North and his ministers were not. In the spring of 1774, the ministry brought in legislation that incorporated into law many of the actions that Franklin had mocked in his writings.

Combatting that legislation prevented Franklin from reacting immediately to the Quebec Act when it was introduced. He was further distracted by legal woes. William Whately had brought a lawsuit against him in early 1774 to defend the honour of his late brother, Thomas. And Franklin was sidelined by illness for some time. He wrote his sister Jane Mecom in late March that he had a violent cold that affected his head and his eyesight.

Franklin thought the lawsuit launched by Whately was a stab in the back. Whately should be grateful to him, he decided, for admitting his involvement and thus preventing future duels. During this key period, he was also corresponding with friends in the colonies about starting a rival postal service to starve the British post office of funds. And he continued to write articles for publication to defend colonial interests.

Parliament Has Its Say

It was left to sympathetic supporters in Parliament to press the colonies' case when the Quebec bill was debated in May and June of 1774. They did their best, but it was hopeless. The North ministry had more than enough support to push the bill through Parliament. Among the most vocal critics of the ministry in the House of Commons were Edmund Burke, a member of Parliament and agent for the state of New York; John Dunning, a former solicitor general and Franklin's lawyer at the Privy Council hearing earlier in the year; and Isaac Barré, the son of French Huguenot refugees. Barré was one of the British soldiers wounded at the capture of Quebec City. Burke assured the New York assembly on May 30, 1774, that he would oppose the bill "with all my Might; but I apprehend with very little prospect of success."[14]

Barré declared the bill "carries in its breast something that squints and looks dangerous to the inhabitants of our other colonies in that country." He was not against allowing the French Canadians to practise their religion, he said, but not if the ministry intended to "raise a Popish army" against the American colonies. "The Americans will look on the Canadians as their task-masters, and, in the end, their executioners. I smelt this out from the beginning." Dunning and Burke fretted about allowing the use of French civil law without juries and its application throughout the newly expanded territory. "I would have English liberty carried into the French colonies, but I would not have French slavery brought into the English colonies," said Burke. The only way to make the French Canadians valuable and useful subjects was to give them English liberty and an English constitution, he said. If not, "Canada will become a dangerous instrument in the hands of those who wish to destroy English liberty in every part of our possessions."[15]

The idea was spreading through the thirteen colonies that popish Canada was once again a threat. This drew them together in a way that complaints about lost settlements or losing control of the fishery did not, because not all colonies shared these concerns. Objecting to the threat of tyrannical popery also sounded more high-minded than complaining about financial losses if the Quebec Act restricted land speculation.

The North ministry and its supporters easily parried opposition jabs. Those who objected to the use of French law were told British merchants travelling to Jersey, Guernsey, or Scotland dealt with the law of the land and did so by choice. It was the same thing for merchants travelling to Holland, the Baltic, or other parts of the world, according to North's solicitor general, Wedderburn. He viewed Canada as a foreign entity, separate and apart from the American colonies. As for the extension of French law over the vast territory around the Great Lakes that the British now considered part of Canada, North maintained there were few inhabitants except "beavers and bears." He added that there could be no legislative assembly in Canada for the time being because the French Canadians would not support one dominated by English residents and could not be trusted with one in which they formed the majority. "I think the sentiments of Canadians ought to be much attended to, in every regulation we make," said Wedderburn. He added, "This is the polar star to which all parts of the bill ought to be directed."

Parliamentarians Hazy on Canada's Borders

As the debate in the Commons continued, it became clear that North and his ministers were hazy on the particulars of Canada, conquered fourteen years previously. They did not know, or could not agree on, the borders of the colony, how many new subjects were acquired, and the attitude of those new subjects to all things British. The opposition critics were equally at sea and at times factually inaccurate in their charges. For example, William Burke, who with his distant relation Edmund Burke was critical of the bill, said the bill would "establish" popery and despotism in the province, something Britain had never done before.[16] This was untrue because Britain was not establishing Catholicism, merely tolerating its practice, as it had previously done in captured Catholic territories such as Acadia, Minorca, and parts of the West Indies.

The testimony of so-called expert witnesses did not improve matters. Carleton told Parliament that Louisiana had been part of Canada and had been cut off by the proclamation. Francis Masères, a French Huguenot in

British employ and the former attorney-general of Canada, said he was "ignorant of the bounds of what was anciently called Canada" but thought Canada extended south until it met Louisiana. Edmund Burke accused North of not knowing enough about the matter to fix the boundary in the act.[17] But Burke, too, was muddying the waters when he said New York extended north to the St. Lawrence, even though he knew the governors of Quebec and New York had already agreed that one point of that boundary lay south of the St. Lawrence where the forty-fifth parallel cuts through the top of Lake Champlain. There was equal fogginess on whether there were settlements in the territories that would be part of the extended colony. Thurlow, the attorney general, said he knew of no English settlements in the new territories. Edmund Burke said the fate of fifty thousand colonists was at stake. As for the newly acquired subjects in Canada, North agreed with Carleton's estimate of 150,000 Catholic souls and 360 Protestant males. Opposition critics said figures of sixty-five thousand Catholics and two thousand Protestants were more realistic.

There was surprising consensus among supporters and opponents of the bill, however, on the character of French Canadians, or new subjects, as they were called. The Canadians were variously described as docile, attentive, and obedient; quiet and submissive; orderly; and in perfect submission to the Crown. That did not mean they were the equals of the colonists. Burke contended that one English freeman was worth more than twenty "French slaves." The fearsome warriors, who with their Indigenous allies had terrorized the American colonies, had been replaced in British eyes by a peaceful, if somewhat ignorant, people who did not have the wisdom to see the benefit of superior English laws.[18] The existence of prosperous merchants and tradesmen among the French Canadians was ignored. Wedderburn, the solicitor general, said French Canadians should acquire the British mode of thinking and manners and even the use of juries in civil trials. But this would be "the work of time." Exactly how this would be achieved was unclear because Wedderburn also said he did not want to encourage emigration from Britain to Canada, nor did he want the English already there to settle.[19]

The Quebec bill, which decided the fate of an enormous territory, passed third reading in the Commons by a vote of 56 to 20. Most of the 558 members of the House of Commons had already left town for the summer recess. The bill was sent to the House of Lords, where it had speedy passage, and received royal assent by George III on June 22, 1774, despite a last-minute appeal to the king by the lord mayor of London and a group of aldermen worried about its impact on London merchants. The merchants decried the establishment of "idolatrous and bloody" Catholicism and reminded the king his family was only called to the throne because they were Protestant.[20] The king was unmoved and decreed the Quebec Act would come into force May 1, 1775.

Franklin Begins Belated Fight Against the Quebec Act

Faced with a *fait accompli*, Franklin began a rearguard action to have it and the punitive acts repealed. In the late summer of 1774, he met with William Pitt, now the Earl of Chatham and an opponent of the legislation. Pitt had won great acclaim for leading Britain as prime minister through the Seven Years' War. Franklin had tried to meet him in 1757 but was refused. But Pitt's power had since waned, along with his mental and physical health. Now he sought out Franklin for long discussions about the colonial grievances with which he sympathized, such as taxation without representation. Much of their conversation in those late summer meetings was about the punitive acts, but Franklin did seize the opportunity to bring up the "wrong politicks" that now prevented "extending our Western Empire adding Province to Province as far as the South Sea [Pacific Ocean]." In Franklin's telling, Pitt told him his idea "of extending our Empire in that manner was a sound one." Franklin said he hoped Pitt "and other great and wise Men of this nation" would unite to rescue this policy "out of the mangling Hands of the present Set of Blundering Ministers."[21]

Having laid the groundwork with Pitt, Franklin set about finding other allies who had the ear of powerful men. He was forced to act through intermediaries because he was *persona non grata* with the North ministry. Throughout the autumn and early winter, he sent reassuring letters about his progress to his contacts in the colonies and a group he called the Friends of America in Britain. In a September letter, he told Cushing in Massachusetts that "our Friends are increasing and endeavouring to unite." He did not want to go into details because he feared his letters were being intercepted, but he said, "I have reason to think a strong Push will be made at the very Beginning of the next Session to have all the late Acts revers'd, and a solemn Assurance given America that no future Attempts shall be made to tax us without our consent." Later that month, he wrote his close friend Jonathan Shipley, the bishop of St. Asaph, to say a coalition was forming of those who supported the American cause and its members would push for the repeal "of all the mischievous Acts that have of late almost dissolv'd our Union."

In December he held a series of meetings with two men who had the ears of ministers. They were David Barclay, a banker and former colonial agent with interests in the colonies, and John Fothergill, a doctor whose patients included Franklin and Lord Dartmouth, the minister responsible for the colonies. Barclay and Fothergill were Quakers. He worked with them on the terms required for peace, which he called "Hints for Conversation upon the Subject of Terms that might probably produce a durable Union between Britain and the Colonies." The first ten proposals or hints focused exclusively on the thirteen colonies, including that they pay for the tea they destroyed. In return Britain would repeal the Tea Act. The eleventh hint was that the Massachusetts and Quebec acts be repealed "and a free Government granted to Canada." Barclay and Fothergill suggested that this might be perceived as meddling in the affairs of another colony. "I reply'd that we, having assisted in the Conquest of Canada, at Great Expence of Blood and Treasure, had some Right to be considered in the Settlement of it. That establishing an arbitrary Government on the back of our Settlements might be dangerous to us all; and that loving Liberty ourselves, we wish'd it to be extended among Mankind, and to have no Foundation for future Slavery laid in America."[22] He insisted the hint be retained. Fothergill promised to show the suggested terms to Lord Dartmouth, the minister in charge of the colonies. Barclay said he would bring it to Thomas Villiers, Baron Hyde, a member of the Privy Council.

During this period, Franklin began playing chess with Caroline Howe, whom he called "the agreable Mrs. Howe." She happened to be the sister of Lord Richard Howe, a senior naval commander, and General William Howe, a senior army officer. Franklin took advantage of this new backdoor channel to the ministry, meeting several times over the next few months with Lord Howe. It would not be the first or last time he mixed business with pleasure. Howe told him at their first meeting it was unlikely the ministry would agree with his terms. He asked Franklin to make concessions that he could then show to various ministers. Barclay and Fothergill met with similar responses when they reported back on their meetings with government insiders. The North ministry refused to repeal the Quebec Act, they reported, but it might be possible to restore the borders of the province back to what they called "its ancient Limits."[23] They probably meant the borders drawn in 1763, when Canada was reduced to a rump of what it was under the French regime, and not the far older and far more expansive borders of 1760.

Franklin Loses Heart

Franklin continued his campaign to repeal the acts in early 1775, but his desire for further haggling was waning. North had treated a petition to the king from the American colonies with scorn. Sending a public petition directly to Parliament or the king had been a legal way for subjects to raise concerns since 1662, although some petitioners ended up in prison regardless of their rights. Members of Parliament had the option of ignoring petitions, and they often did. They did not have a high opinion of their constituents. Petitioning the king directly was seen as a way to circumvent Parliament. It was not a particularly effective route for petitioners to take because the king could not govern without the support of Parliament. It is unclear whether the American colonists, who submitted a steady stream of petitions to the king, realized this.

The petition North scorned emerged from the first continental congress, a meeting of delegates from most of the colonies in September and October of 1774. Among other things, the delegates complained to the king about the extension of Quebec's borders and about subjecting "British freemen" to French laws, an absolute government, and the Roman Catholic religion.

The petition was presented for consideration in the House of Commons in January 1775 amidst a jumble of other papers on American affairs, as if a message from colonists on the verge of revolt was not worthy of special attention. The ministry initially refused to discuss or debate it.[24] The same fate awaited a supportive statement made by Pitt in the House of Lords, which Franklin had helped craft.

If Franklin's spirits were not low enough with his failure to prevent, or at least repeal, the injurious acts, he received news early in 1775 that his wife, Deborah, had died in December. The two had lived apart for most of their married life. Deborah never joined her husband in London, despite his prolonged stay there from 1757 to 1762 and again from 1764 to 1775. Yet their correspondence was affectionate, and her death must have been unsettling. He was in a sour mood when, at the end of February, he wrote Joseph Galloway, a member of the Pennsylvania assembly. He complained about the "extream Corruption prevalent among all Orders of Men in this old rotten State" and the possibility that Britain would drag the colonies into "all the plundering Wars their desperate Circumstances, Injustice and Rapacity, may prompt them to undertake." His spirits were further depressed by a visit to the House of Lords to hear a debate on American affairs. "I was much disgusted from the ministerial Side, by many base Reflections on American Courage, Religion, Understanding, &c. in which we were treated with the utmost Contempt, as the lowest of Mankind, and almost of a different Species from the English of Britain," he told his son in a lengthy letter he wrote him toward the end of March.

By March 1775, Franklin could see that the hoped-for push to repeal the acts repugnant to the colonists had fizzled out. The North ministry was intent on forcing the American colonies to acknowledge the supremacy of the British Parliament, with violence if necessary. It was planning yet more punitive legislation to restrain the trade of New Hampshire, Connecticut, and Rhode Island and to prevent the American colonies from fishing off Newfoundland. North still believed that once the colonists felt the weight of Britain's power, "they would see they had been deceived by the leaders and would return to their duty." Parliament was debating a motion to repeal the Quebec Act, but it had little chance of passing. Indeed, when it was put to a vote several months later, it was soundly defeated.[25] Franklin had been unable to scupper a law that laid the groundwork for Canada to become a separate and distinct society from that of the American colonies. He abandoned his support for the British Empire and sailed for home at the end of March to join the budding revolution. But even as he worked to unite the colonies and win the fight with Britain, he retained his desire to possess Canada.

Part Three

CANADA IN PLAY

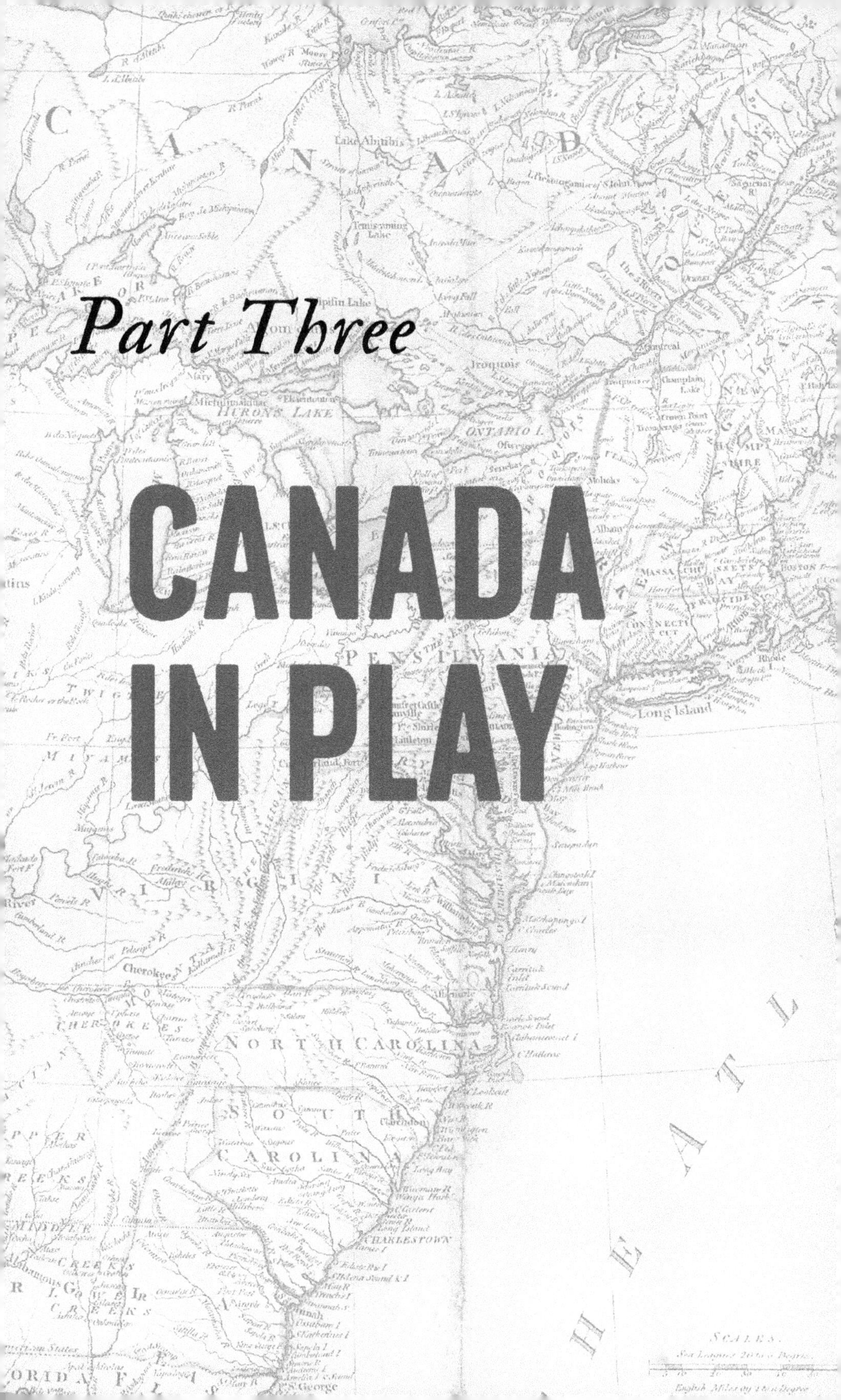

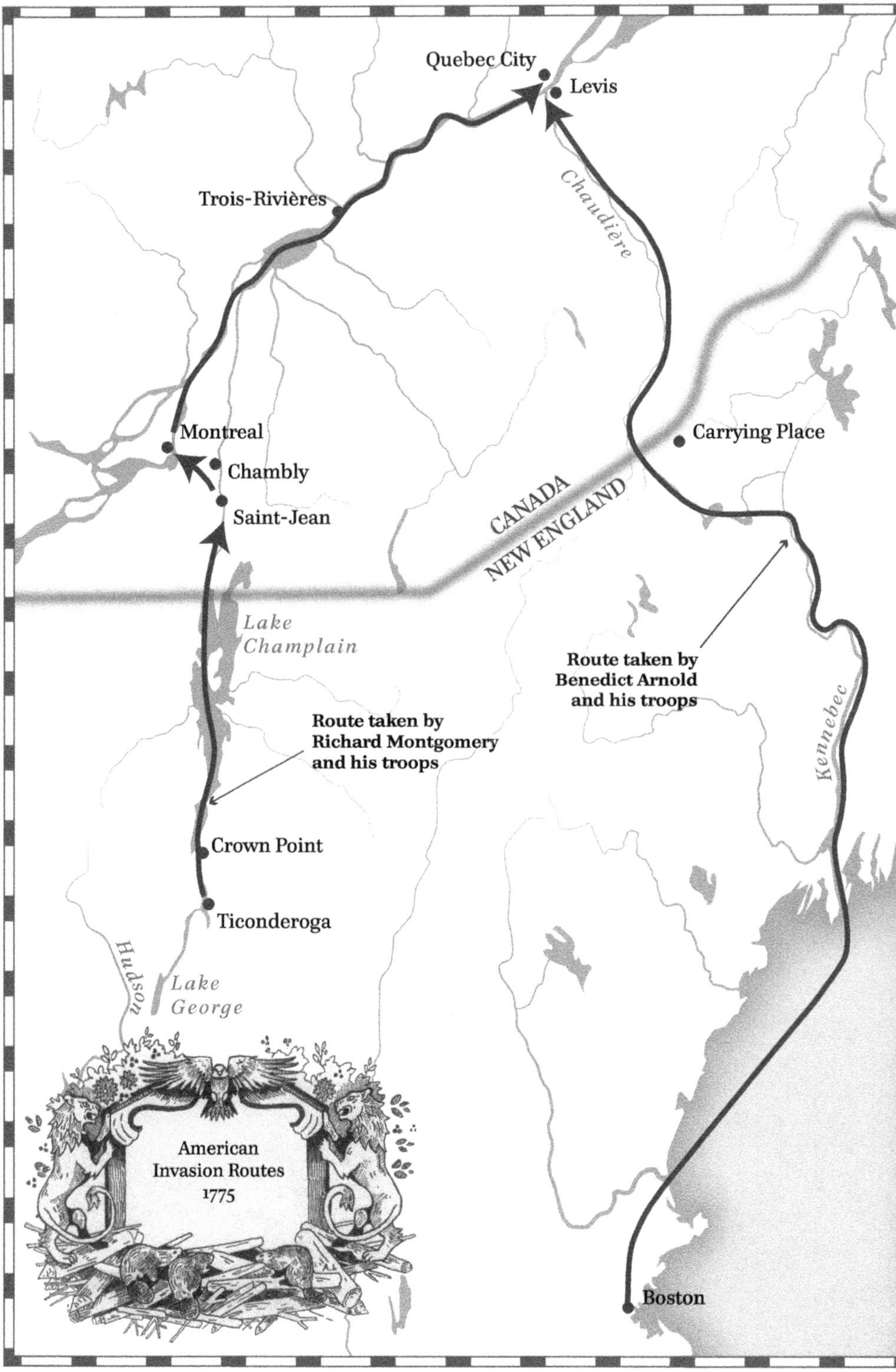

Quebec City
Levis
Chaudière
Trois-Rivières
Montreal
Chambly
Saint-Jean
Carrying Place
CANADA
NEW ENGLAND
Lake Champlain
Route taken by Benedict Arnold and his troops
Route taken by Richard Montgomery and his troops
Kennebec
Crown Point
Ticonderoga
Hudson
Lake George
American Invasion Routes 1775
Boston

CHAPTER 7

A Neighbourly Invasion: Philadelphia 1775

> It is a true old saying, that make yourself sheep and the wolves will eat you: to which I may add another, God helps them that help themselves.[1]
>
> — *Benjamin Franklin*

FRANKLIN DISEMBARKED FROM THE *PENNSYLVANIA* PACKET SHIP ON May 5, 1775, to find his fellow colonists in a warlike mood. There had been bloody engagements at Lexington and Concord between British troops seeking weapons stockpiles and colonial militia determined to hide them, which had fuelled public anger. The colonial propaganda machines were running full tilt, with newspapers and pamphlets blaming the British for firing the first shot in those clashes, which killed seventy-three British soldiers and forty-nine militia. In the story Americans tell themselves about how they came to be a nation, the battles in Massachusetts in April 1775 are portrayed as the turning point from peace to war. Soon after he landed, Franklin wrote David Hartley, a fellow inventor and a British member of Parliament, to tell him a civil war had begun. "I find here all Ranks of People in Arms, disciplining themselves Morning & Evening, and am informed that the firmest Union prevails throughout North America."

This was an exaggeration, both in terms of how much unity prevailed and the territory covered. There was a widening divide between royalists and those who wanted to end British rule. There was no unity within the thirteen colonies or in North America. It contained some twenty-three British colonies and territories, not to mention Spanish possessions in the south and southwest and vast Indigenous territories. The thirteen colonies were but a small slice of the continent. Franklin was neither the first nor the last American colonist to speak of a continental reach when none existed. For example, when the congress appointed George Washington as commander-in-chief of a newly formed army in June, Thomas Jefferson described him as the "Generalissimo of all the Provincial Troops in North America."[2] What Franklin might have said more truthfully was that some of the thirteen colonies, which had hitherto acted independently of each other, were leaning toward joint action against Britain in support of Massachusetts, the colony that had borne the brunt of the Coercive Acts of 1774. In the months ahead, Franklin would try to include Canada in that emerging union.

Anger at the Quebec Act Brings Diverse Groups Together

At this crucial point in the rebellion, the Quebec Act helped unite divergent factions chafing under British rule. Land speculators were angry at being walled in by the Appalachian Mountains. Protestants were appalled at the establishment of popery in a greatly enlarged Canada. And politicians fighting for something approximating democracy were astonished that the British established an authoritarian government in Canada. All could unite against what they saw as Britain's attempt to set up a tyrannical, Catholic colony on their doorstep; arm tens of thousands of Catholics; and then use them to subdue their troublesome, Protestant neighbours. "The Quebec Bill set fuel to the fire," Joseph Reed told the Earl of Dartmouth, minister in charge of the colonies, in September 1774. Reed, who would later become an aide to Washington, had begun an unofficial correspondence with Dartmouth to provide him with news unfiltered by the colonial governors. "The idea of bringing down the Canadians and Savages upon the English Colonies is so inconsistent, not only with mercy but justice and humanity of the Mother Country, that I cannot allow myself to think that your Lordship would promote the Quebec Bill or give it your suffrage with such intentions."[3]

Even without the threat of an invasion, the audacity of the British to sanction a government and a religion at odds with their own angered the American colonists. Some felt they had a right to interfere in the governance of Canada, regardless of what the French Canadians thought, because it was in their neighbourhood. (The Monroe Doctrine of 1823, in which then-president James Monroe warned European powers that the United States held sway in the Americas, has deep roots.) "Does not your blood run cold, to think that an English Parliament should pass an act for the establishment of arbitrary power and Popery in such an extensive country?" asked a young Alexander Hamilton in *A Full Vindication of the Measures of the Congress, &c.*, his 1774 pamphlet protesting British measures.

Franklin Re-enters Politics

This was where matters stood when Franklin returned to Philadelphia. It should not have been a triumphant homecoming. He had failed as the agent for the colonies in London to prevent the Coercive Acts and the Quebec Act from passing and was equally unsuccessful in obtaining their repeal. He had been humiliated before the Privy Council and ostracized by the ruling elite. Nonetheless, this had worked to his advantage in the colonies. "Nothing can exceed the veneration in which Dr. Franklin is now held, but the detestation we have of his enemies," Reed wrote another British correspondent in May 1774. But privately, Franklin was still stinging from the lash of British contempt and his inability to do anything about it. That might explain why he was so quick to write friends and acquaintances in London about the warmth of his reception back home. "I arrived here on Friday Evening, & the next morning was unanimously chosen by the General Assembly a Delegate for the ensuing Congress, which is to meet on Wednesday," he wrote Hartley on May 8. "I had not been here a Day before I was return'd as a Member," he told Edmund Burke on May 15. He repeated variations of this message in a letter to Jonathan Shipley that same day and in a May 16 letter to Joseph Priestly. He was still exclaiming about how quickly he had been chosen as a delegate to congress to his sister Jane Mecom in a letter on May 26, adding that this meant he would not have the repose he had wished for.[4]

Franklin had talked in the past about wanting more leisure time to read books and conduct scientific experiments. It is not certain whether he said that for effect or truly meant it. With Franklin it was never clear whether it was the man or the publicist wielding the pen. By the time he reached Philadelphia, he was almost seventy years old and could have argued that he had worked long enough for the colonies. But his time in London, especially the events of the last few years, made him despair of a reconciliation between Britain and the thirteen colonies and set him firmly on the path to American independence. He wanted to help shape that future by becoming a delegate to the next gathering of the colonies in congress. Franklin always maintained that he did not mix personal resentment with public business, but there may have been an element of revenge in his subsequent actions.

His time as an active delegate would be relatively short. It began when the second continental congress convened, on May 10, 1775, but would end on October 26, 1776, when he would leave for France to seek support for American independence. Despite his involvement during that period in the vast multitude of things necessary for the colonies to fight and eventually win their battle with Britain — he did everything from designing a better pike for the infantry, which could also be used as a tent pole, to arranging imports of arms and gunpowder, to editing the Declaration of Independence — Franklin found time to make two more attempts to promote the annexation of Canada to the American colonies. Neither would be successful. But still he persevered.

The First Congress Asks Canadians to Support Their Rebellion

Twelve of the thirteen colonies had sent delegates to the first general congress in Philadelphia in 1774, held while Franklin was still in London. Only Georgia was missing. The intent of the organizers was for delegates to discuss ways of countering mounting British aggression. That congress, which ran from September 5 to October 26, 1774, was popularly called the continental congress, although this was never its official title.[5] The frequent use of the words "continent," "continental," and "North America" by its members when talking about the thirteen colonies suggests delegates had far greater territorial ambitions than the narrow strip of land they occupied along the eastern seaboard. One of those ambitions was to persuade Canada and some of the other British colonies in North America to join the American revolt against the British ministry. Independence was not yet on the table, although it was whispered about in the corridors. Some colonists believed that once the king realized what his ministers had done, he would step in and reverse their policies. Franklin, a staunch imperialist until then, no longer shared that view.

In their initial dealings with Canada, the delegates assumed that if they were incensed about Britain's attempts to tax and control them, the Canadians must be too. This miscalculation was based on bad intelligence from agents and sympathetic merchants in the northern colony. There had been no violent reaction in Canada against earlier measures to raise revenues in the colonies to reduce the enormous debt from the Seven Years' War, notably the British Sugar Act of 1764 and the Stamp Act of 1765. The Coercive Acts, or Intolerable Acts, which followed a decade later, primarily targeted Massachusetts. The Quebec Act had the backing of the Canadian elites because it largely restored the previous borders of New France, which helped the fur traders, and established the rights of the clergy and seigneurs in British law. The habitants, or ordinary Canadians, may have been less enthused by a continuation of the semi-feudal seigneurial system and the reaffirmation of tithes for the church, but they lacked leaders who could give them a voice in the deliberations.

The first congress asked Thomas Cushing of Massachusetts, Richard Henry Lee of Virginia, and John Dickinson of Pennsylvania to write letters to the people of Canada, St. John's Island (now Prince Edward Island), Nova Scotia, Georgia, and East and West Florida, inviting them to join the Americans and send delegates to the next continental congress, scheduled for May 1775. The letter to the inhabitants of Quebec was a lengthy lecture on what rights they were entitled to as "English freemen," rights that villainous ministers in London were withholding from them. These included having a say in government through an assembly so they could approve laws instead of being ruled by edicts; trial by jury, so they would be judged by twelve of their peers in open court; habeas corpus, to ensure they could not be illegally detained; payment for land tenure through rents rather than services; and freedom of the press, so that oppressive government officers were shamed or intimidated into better conduct. There was no indication the letter writers were aware of the situation in Canada, where the tiny English minority wanted to deny some of these same rights to the French majority, and that the French Canadians might not want to become "English" freemen.

Having educated the Canadians on their rights, the letter went on to criticize the Quebec Act, saying everything it had granted could be taken away by the governor or the ministry and replaced with something far worse, including "the Inquisition." So insolent were the British ministers, the letter said, they were planning to have the Canadians "take up arms and render yourselves the ridicule and detestation of the world, by becoming tools, in their hands, to assist them in taking that freedom from us, which they have treacherously denied you." If this happened, there would be consequences, the letter implied ominously. "You are a small people, compared to those who with open arms invite you into a fellowship. A moment's reflection should convince you which will be most for your interest and happiness, to have all the rest of North-America your unalterable friends, or your inveterate enemies."

Conflicting Messages About Religious Toleration

Toward the end of the screed, the authors tackled the matter of religious differences between Catholic Canada and the mainly Protestant colonies. This did not have to be a problem, they said soothingly. The resulting union could be like the Swiss cantons, where Catholic and Protestant states lived in "the utmost concord and peace with one another" and jointly defended their freedom from tyrants. This declaration of religious toleration was undermined by a separate letter the congress prepared for the inhabitants of Britain, written several days earlier by John Jay of New York. This letter went through the long list of colonial grievances, including the Quebec Act, before addressing religion. But here, instead of pledging to overlook religious differences, Jay expressed astonishment that Parliament had established in Canada "a religion that has deluged your island in blood, and dispersed impiety, bigotry, persecution, murder and rebellion through every part of the world." The congress approved both letters before dissolving on October 26, 1774. It ordered the letter to Quebec to be translated into French and distributed in Canada.[6] Britain's supporters in Canada ensured the letter to the inhabitants of Britain was also translated into French so Canadians could see proof of American perfidy.

Franklin was still in London when the letter to Canadians was written. Yet it echoed his long-held belief that Canada should be joined to the American colonies. Security for the thirteen colonies figured in his thinking; so, too, did his belief that British colonists were destined to occupy the continent. He would have been aware of the letter's existence because he had arranged with a relative to send him colonial newspapers and pamphlets on a regular basis. This enabled him to keep on top of colonial news, albeit with a time lag. Even fast schooners took a month to cross the Atlantic to London. The journal of the proceedings of the congress, which also referred to the letter, was sent to him on November 1, time enough for it to reach London before he left the following March.

Rumours Spread About an Attack from the North

The rumour that Britain was planning to use the Canadians and their Indigenous allies to subdue the American colonists had gained credence among the delegates by the time Franklin reached Philadelphia in May. "We know the plan of ministry is to bring the Canadians and Indians down upon us," Richard Henry Lee wrote to his brother on May 21, 1775. But was this information accurate?

An invasion from the north was a live option for some British ministers, including Prime Minister North, and for Carleton, governor of the Province of Quebec. According to the *Parliamentary Register*, a summary of debates, North told the Commons on May 18, 1775, that if "the refractory colonies cannot be reduced to obedience by the present force, he should think it a right, proper, and necessary measure to arm the Roman Catholics of Canada, and to employ them on that service." Carleton mused as far back as 1767 about using Canadians or "new subjects" to supplement British troops in the province. "The new Subjects could send into the Field about eighteen thousand Men, well able to carry Arms; of which Number, above one half have already served, with as much Valor, with more Zeal, and more military Knowledge for America, than the regular Troops of France, that were joined with them," he wrote the minister in charge of the colonies. Such a show of British military superiority and strength would "curb and overawe" enemies of the Crown.[7] The only enemy he named at the time was France, but he was already keeping a watchful eye on unrest to the south.

Carleton still held this view as late as September 1774, when he sent two regiments of British regulars south to the thirteen colonies at the request of General Thomas Gage, the former governor of Massachusetts. Gage, then commander of the British forces in North America, told Carleton he was preparing for "the worst" in Boston. He asked whether Carleton could gather Canadians and their Indigenous allies to fight for Britain "should matters come to Extremities." Carleton assured Gage this was possible. "The Canadians have testified to me the strongest marks of Joy, and Gratitude, and Fidelity to the King, and to His Government, for the late Arrangements made at Home in their Favor," he wrote, referring to the Quebec Act. "A Canadian Regiment would compleat their Happiness, which in Time of Need might be augmented to two, three, or more Battalions."[8]

Carleton Mistaken About Canadian Zeal

Carleton, however, had been talking to the wrong people. The seigneurs he dealt with were keen to fight for the British to show their loyalty. The clergy were firmly on Britain's side. Beholden to the pope in Rome, they had nothing against arbitrary power. But he was mistaken in thinking the elites still held sway over the habitants. By February 1775, as this started to become apparent, he added caveats to his promises of support. There had been only loose government in Canada and no militia duty, since the militia was disbanded by the British in 1764, Carleton explained in a letter to Gage. As a result, the Canadians had "emancipated themselves," and it would take time and discreet management "to recall them to their ancient Habits of Obedience and Discipline."

By June 1775, when some American troops had briefly invaded Canadian territory before returning home, Carleton realized he had been mistaken in many of his assumptions. He wrote Dartmouth, the minister in charge of the colonies, in London to say the gentry and clergy were loyal but had lost much of their influence over the people. Jean-Olivier Briand, the Catholic bishop of Quebec, had helpfully issued a command to the faithful in May, telling them that it was their duty to defend their country and their king and that they should obey the commands of their "benevolent" governor. "Close your ears, dear Canadiens," Briand wrote, "and don't listen to those promoting sedition who want to make you unhappy, and fill your hearts with submission to your legitimate superiors."[9] Despite this show of support, Carleton told Dartmouth he had many doubts whether he could succeed in forming a militia and raising a battalion. The minds of the people had been tainted by "Cabals and Intrigues," he wrote, referring to propaganda being spread by American agents and their supporters in the colony. On June 9, he declared martial law, making militia duty compulsory.

American Agents Spread Propaganda

Like the congressional letter to Canadians, the American propaganda Carleton mentioned was a mixture of carrots and sticks. The Canadians were told that if they joined the Americans, they would be free of taxes and tithes and would enjoy American liberty. But they were also informed by one of the agents, John Brown of Massachusetts, that if they took up arms against the Bostonians, thirty thousand Americans would lay waste to Canada. William Hey, the chief justice in Quebec, said in a letter to London that the agents had persuaded Canadians they would be sent to Boston or sold to the Spanish. "Such a mixture of ignorance, fear, credulity, perverseness &

Prejudice never yet I believe took possession of the human mind," he wrote.[10] Aside from spreading conspiracy theories, Brown met with American sympathizers, including the discontented merchants in Montreal. They helped him spread his message. One of their number was suspected of defacing a statue of King George III on May 1, 1775, the day the Quebec Act went into force, although it was never proven. The bust, which the king had personally donated, was smeared with tar and given a necklace of potatoes. A crude sign proclaimed that the king was the "Pope of Canada and the Fool of England."

The evidence suggests that while the British wanted to use the Canadians against the thirteen colonies, they were incapable of doing so in the spring of 1775. Indeed, Carleton told Dartmouth in June of that year, "We are equally unprepared for Attack or Defence; Not six hundred Rank & File fit for Duty upon the whole Extent of this great River, not an armed Vessel, no Place of Strength; the ancient Provincial Force enervated and broke to Pieces." He desperately needed more British regulars. But Gage, who led the British occupation of Boston, could not afford to let a single man go. Boston was besieged by about five thousand Americans who formed part of the army newly approved by the congress. Dartmouth appeared not to have received Carleton's dismal news about the difficulty in raising the militia, because in early July he instructed Carleton to raise a force of three thousand Canadians, then doubled it to six thousand in a second letter.

The First Attack by American Colonists

American colonists had already mounted a limited attack on Canada when Carleton wrote Dartmouth in June. It started on May 10, the same day the congressional delegates convened in Philadelphia, although they had not sanctioned the offensive. Separate rebel groups in Connecticut and Massachusetts had decided to attack the string of British forts lining the traditional invasion route to Canada along Lake Champlain. There were three main forts, originally built by the French and then occupied by the British: Ticonderoga was the farthest south, Crown Point occupied a strategic point where the lake broadened to the north, and Fort Saint-Jean (also called St. John's) was on the Richelieu River, which connected Lake

Champlain to the St. Lawrence River. The forts contained cannons and other weaponry the American colonists coveted.

Brown, who had followed the Lake Champlain route to Montreal in March, recommended on his return to Massachusetts that if hostilities with the British broke out, Ticonderoga should be taken immediately. He was part of the colonial force that took it without bloodshed on May 10. The assault was led by Ethan Allen and his Green Mountain Boys, a militia that had been attacking New York colonists who had settled on land claimed by New Hampshire. They knew the local terrain and were happy to take a break from terrorizing their fellow colonists and be paid to fight the British instead. Crown Point fell shortly afterward. Benedict Arnold, who had persuaded the Massachusetts committee of safety to commission him for the same mission, showed up unexpectedly and joined forces with Allen.

The two fought over who should be in command. Arnold had previous military experience in the French and Indian War and had some knowledge of Canada because he had purchased rum and other goods there in peacetime. Allen won the tussle because he had the backing of his men. Arnold then decided to capitalize on the capture of Ticonderoga and Crown Point by sailing north up Lake Champlain to the fort at Saint-Jean on May 18. There he took an armed British sloop, four smaller boats, some military stores, and provisions. He then fled before British reinforcements arrived. Saint-Jean was the only one of the three forts within the acknowledged boundaries of Canada. Arnold did not make special mention of that fact in his May 19 report to the Massachusetts committee of safety. He did observe with satisfaction that "there is not left a single batteau for the King's Troops, *Canadians*, or Indians to cross the Lake in, if they have any such intention."[11]

When Allen and his men took Ticonderoga, he was reported to have declared he was doing so "in the name of the great Jehovah and of the continental congress."[12] Yet congressional delegates knew nothing about the assault until May 17 and did not hear of Arnold's attack on a fort within the bounds of Canada until some time after that. They reacted with a mixture of elation and alarm to the news that Americans were the aggressors in the attacks. It did not fit with their self-portrayal as victims of British aggression.

Franklin was in an unusually militant mood that May. In one of his first letters following news of the attacks, he told Humphry Marshall, a botanist friend in Pennsylvania, that as Britain had begun to use force, the colonists should do the same. "It is a true old saying, that make yourselves sheep and the wolves will eat you: to which I may add another, God helps them that help themselves."

Delegates Characterize Aggression as Self-Defence

Like Franklin, the delegates decided to cast the attacks as self-defence. After hearing from Brown, who had rushed to Philadelphia with the news of the fall of Ticonderoga and Crown Point, the delegates agreed on May 18 that there was "indubitable evidence" that the British ministry was planning "a cruel invasion from the province of Quebec, upon these colonies, for the purpose of destroying our lives and liberties." The British would have used the military stores and weapons in the forts in that invasion, the delegates decided, and so the attacks were justified. They were less certain about taking any further military action in Canada, fearing it might create unwanted hostility among the Canadians.

At this point, they decided another letter to Canadians was needed to explain their case and solicit support. John Jay, Samuel Adams, and Silas Deane were appointed to draft it. Jay had written the letter the previous year to the inhabitants of Britain, reminding them that Catholicism had drenched their islands in blood. Adams, a staunch Puritan from Boston and second cousin to John Adams, was on record as saying that Catholicism led to "anarchy and confusion, civil discord, war and bloodshed." Yet they managed to produce a letter that skated over religious differences. "We are your friends, not your enemies," said the letter addressed to "the oppressed inhabitants of Canada." The Canadians were to be pitied because they were now slaves of a tyrannical government and they had nothing they could call their own. As for the attacks on the forts, they were "dictated by the great law of self-preservation." The authors assured the Canadians that the thirteen colonies "will pursue no measures whatever, but such as friendship and a regard for our mutual safety and interest may suggest." They invited the northern neighbours once again to join with the Americans in alerting the king to the oppressive measures of the British ministry. Congress approved their work on May 29 and followed up with a resolution on June 1, 1775: "That no expedition or incursion ought to be undertaken or made by any colony, or body of colonists, against or into Canada." Less than a month later, the delegates would change their minds.

Franklin Sidelined by Suspicions About His Loyalty

The *Journals of the Continental Congress* note that Franklin was present as one of the delegates for Pennsylvania, starting May 10. The votes on the resolutions are not detailed enough to determine where he stood on the letter written by Jay, Adams, and Deane. His personal correspondence during that period yields no clues. At the end of May, he was appointed to a committee to establish a postal system, which made sense given that he had been deputy postmaster general of British North America. But in his first few weeks at the congress, he was not named to other committees, despite his extensive experience.

One possible explanation for not giving Franklin important tasks in those first few weeks is that some of his fellow delegates thought he was a British spy. Rumours were circulated by men who had reason to dislike Franklin because of previous dealings with him. William Bradford, for example, had been a printer in Philadelphia and New York, where Franklin had set up a former apprentice of Bradford's to compete with him for business. Bradford wrote James Madison of Virginia on June 2, 1775, telling him that some of the delegates had begun to "entertain a great Suspicion that Dr. Franklin came rather as a Spy than as a friend, & that he means to discover our weak side & make friends with the minister by discovering it to him." Bradford said he was told this by Richard Henry Lee of Virginia. According to Bradford, Lee said the delegates expected Franklin would have useful information for them about events in Britain "but hitherto he has been silent on that head & in every respect behaved more like a spectator than a member." Bradford did not mention, and perhaps did not know, that Lee's brother Arthur felt aggrieved that Franklin held on to the post of colonial agent for Massachusetts in London long after 1770, the year Arthur was appointed to succeed him. Franklin also promoted a land speculation scheme that conflicted with a proposal put forward by Lee, who was chagrined when Franklin succeeded and he did not. In his reply, Madison readily agreed with Bradford that sitting silent was suspicious behaviour. "Indeed it appears to me that the bare suspicion of his guilt amounts very nearly to a proof of its reality," he wrote on June 19.[13]

That suspicion should fall on Franklin during this period is not entirely surprising. It was a tumultuous time in the congress and in the colonies more generally. Opposition to Britain was mounting, but even its proponents disagreed on whether they were striving for independence or just a better deal within the empire. Lifelong friendships broke apart, as did families, when members took opposing positions on the question. Franklin grew increasingly estranged from his son, William, the governor of New Jersey, who continued in that post and sided with the British.

Franklin had been absent from the colonies for almost two decades and was an unknown quantity to most of the delegates, who knew him only by reputation. He was significantly older than most of his colleagues. His decades in London led many to believe he supported the British, as did his son's continued connection to Britain. Franklin had been too colonial to be accepted by the British as one of them. Back home, he was too British to be fully accepted by the colonists. In what was possibly an effort to still the rumours, he wrote a letter in July 1775 to Strahan, his long-time friend in London who was now a British member of Parliament, saying that Strahan's hands were stained with blood. "You and I were long Friends: You are now my Enemy, and I am, Yours," he wrote.[14] The letter was likely shared with Franklin's friends in Philadelphia, but it was never sent.

The letter and his dogged work in congress eventually helped dispel the rumours and improve his standing among the delegates. As the congressional sitting wore on, he was appointed postmaster general of the United Colonies and made a member of numerous committees, including the one tasked with writing a declaration for the newly appointed commander-in-chief of the United Colonies, Washington, to read at the rebels' camp outside Boston. In September he was one of the delegates sent to Cambridge to confer with Washington on how to regulate and support the new rebel army. Later that year, he was appointed to the committee of secret correspondence, a forerunner of the state department, created to sound out European support for the American rebellion.

Delegates Dither About Invading Canada

Despite everything that was happening in the busy spring of 1775, neither Franklin nor the delegates had forgotten about Canada or the Quebec Act. A complaint about its provisions appears in Washington's declaration at Boston, among the litany of colonial grievances. But, as the delegate John Adams told a friend on June 7, they were puzzled about what to do. Brown of Massachusetts and James Price, one of the English-speaking merchants in Montreal, had told the congress that the Canadians were not unfriendly to the colonists and that the Indigenous Peoples intended to stay neutral. (Price also asked the congress if Quebec could have an exemption from the trade barriers it was erecting against Britain, possibly the first example of similar requests for exemptions that continue to this day.) "But whether We should march into Canada with an Army Sufficient to break the Power of Governor Carlton, to overawe the Indians, and to protect the French has been a great Question," Adams wrote. "It Seems to be the general Conclusion that it is best to go, if We can be assured that the Canadians will be pleased with it, and join."[15] Adams wrote this letter less than a week after the congress had resolved there would be no invasion, which suggests that not everyone regarded the decision as final.

Beyond Philadelphia, other voices were calling for aggressive action. An anonymous writer from Fredericksburg, Virginia, wrote Adams that same week, proposing an invasion of Canada that would also serve to end southern fears of a slave insurrection and northern fears of an attack by Canadians and their Indigenous allies. The Fredericksburg writer suggested that slave owners lead an invading army of enslaved people into Canada. Following the conquest, which the writer assumed was foreordained, the owners would "bestow" liberty on the enslaved people as a reward for their bravery and fidelity. The victorious Americans would raise revenue to reimburse the slave owners for the cost of their enslaved people by taxing the Canadians.[16] Franklin had mentioned in a July letter to a friend that the British governors of Virginia and North Carolina were "exciting an Insurrection among the Blacks," while Carleton had been very industrious in "engaging the Indians to begin their horrid Work."[17]

Delegates were also being peppered with alarming letters from committees of correspondence, groups set up in each of the colonies by supporters of the rebellion, and from former and aspiring military men keen to strike a blow and win military glory. This was one of those times in Franklin's long pursuit of Canada that the idea of possessing the northern colony attracted growing support. Allen and Arnold, flush with their victories on Lake Champlain in early May, campaigned separately to lead a larger invasion. Allen told the governor of Connecticut, who supported the rebels, that he could have taken Canada with only the Green Mountain Boys if they had not just become part of the official army that congress created in June. Arnold wrote the congress, claiming he could "reduce the whole province" with two thousand men.[18]

Two more events pushed the delegates in that direction. The first was the Battle of Bunker Hill, fought between the rebels and British regular troops outside Boston on June 17. It was technically a victory for the British, but they lost significantly more men than the colonial forces. This emboldened the rebels. "All Europe will revere the fortitude, and stand surprised at the firmness and valour of this handful of brave, though undisciplined men," an anonymous American wrote in an open letter to the general who led the British troops. Another anonymous letter, supposedly from a British officer who took part in the battle but possibly a bit of fake news penned by an American, said: "The Americans are not those poltroons I myself was once taught to believe them to be … I tacitly admire their resolution and perseverance, against the present oppressive measures of the British government."

The second event was a letter sent to congress by the committee of correspondence in Albany, New York, saying they had information that Governor Carleton had encouraged "the French Caughnawaga Indians" to attack the American colonies and that six hundred British troops were building floating batteries and boats at Saint-Jean, a prelude to sailing down Lake

Champlain to attack the colonies. Arnold had already warned the congress that if the British retook the forts on Lake Champlain, they would use them as a base to destroy frontier towns, drive farmers from their fields, and "send distress and famine into the bowels of the country."[19]

Misinformation Fuelled Decision to Invade

The delegates discussed the Albany letter on June 27 and decided that same day to steal a march on Carleton by attacking Canada first. "General Carleton has been spiriting up the Canadian Indians to fall on our back settlements but this we hope will be prevented," Thomas Jefferson wrote to a friend.[20] The congress instructed Major General Philip Schuyler, who had only just been appointed to his position as commander of the northern troops, to take possession of Saint-Jean, the city of Montreal, "and any other parts of the country" if he thought it was practicable and would not be "disagreeable to the Canadians."[21] John Hancock, then president of the congress, repeated the same phrase on June 28 when he advised Washington about the change of heart. "The Alteration of the Sentiments of Congress since your Departure relative to making an Impression into Canada was Occasion'd by a Letter they Receiv'd from the Committee of Albany, a Copy of which you have Inclos'd," Hancock said.[22] Schuyler immediately set about assembling men, arms, and equipment. It would be some months before he received his marching orders from Washington and was ready to head north.

The idea that the French Canadians would not mind being invaded by their long-standing enemies to the south was based in part on information the delegates received from informants, most of whom were English speakers who supported the American cause. It is unlikely they had canvassed the full range of French Canadian opinion. In his appearance before congress on May 18, Brown of Massachusetts told the delegates the Canadians were resisting military duty under Carleton. Price, the Montreal merchant, told a committee in Connecticut that the Canadians found the idea of marching against the colonies repugnant. He likely repeated this information when he appeared before the congress on May 27. The French Canadians' reluctance to perform military duties was real. But it did not necessarily follow that this was because they did not want to fight for Britain or because they secretly favoured the American cause. The habitants had enjoyed a peaceful existence since the British conquest, during which their harvests and population had increased. It could well be that they did not want a return to war.

Nevertheless, some Americans jumped to the conclusion the French Canadians were secret allies, just waiting for the right time to join them. News supporting this idea filtered in from other colonists who had contact with Canada or knew someone who did. Jacob Bailey of Connecticut told a rebel group in New York that a dependable Indigenous man told him "the French and Indians will join us, and make no doubt but Quebeck will be taken."[23] Were the Canadians friendly? Or would they invade alongside the British? The delegates decided to attack the British in Canada, hoping the Canadians would join them or at least remain neutral.

Franklin Caught Up with the Fight Against the British

As a delegate, Franklin was involved in the congressional deliberations about Canada. But at this point, he was not leading the charge. His attention lay elsewhere. In June he became a member of the committee charged with finding saltpetre, a principal ingredient in gunpowder. The colonies were woefully short. Many of the letters exchanged between delegates and between military officials during this period dealt with how to obtain more, either by making it or importing it. Congress's decision to punish Britain by banning trade with Britain and British colonies, such as Quebec, Nova Scotia, and St. John's Island, made the shortages worse. Also in June, he became a member of the committee writing Washington's Boston declaration. And as president of the Pennsylvania committee of safety, Franklin helped organize the local troops. "My time was never more fully employed," he wrote a scientific friend in London in early July. "In the morning at 6, I am at the committee of safety, appointed by the assembly to put the province in a state of defence; which committee holds till near 9, when I am at the congress, and that sits till after 4 in the afternoon."[24]

Yet he made certain to include Canada when he reworked the plan for the union of the British colonies, which he first presented in 1754 at a meeting of some of the colonies in Albany. That plan required the colonies to band together for defence and security while retaining their separate constitutions and jurisdiction over more local matters. It called for a governor general, appointed by Britain, and a grand council to form a centralized government in limited areas. Franklin had initially wanted this union to cover all the British dominions on the continent. Canada was still under French rule when he first wrote it, but Acadia, renamed Nova Scotia, and Newfoundland had been in British hands since the 1713 Treaty of Utrecht. The final version of the 1754 plan named eleven of the thirteen colonies. It vaguely left some room for a more expansive membership by stating the plan was "for their mutual defence and security, and for extending the British Settlements in North America."

While the Albany Plan was stillborn because neither Britain nor the colonial assemblies gave the necessary approvals, Franklin's updated version was more explicit about hoped-for additions. It said: "Any and every colony from Great Britain upon the continent of North America not at present engaged in our association may upon application and joining the said association be received into this Confederation, viz. Quebec, Canada, St. John's, Nova Scotia, Bermudas, and the East and West Floridas: and shall thereupon be entitled to all the advantages and obligations of our union, mutual assistance and commerce."[25] If the Americans did not take Canada by force in the planned invasion, they might still be able to persuade the Canadians to join them peacefully.

Franklin read his proposal to the assembled members of congress on July 21, 1775. It was not officially debated. The delegates were not yet ready to contemplate such a step and were overwhelmed with more pressing matters, such as forming, equipping, feeding, and paying for an army to take on the British. "Such a vast Multitude of Objects, civil, political, commercial and military, press and croud upon Us So fast, that We know not what to do first," John Adams wrote an acquaintance that spring. "The state of fifteen or sixteen Colonies to be considered, Time must be taken."[26] Franklin's plan was set aside. Ever the publicist, he ensured it would see the light of day by being printed in *The Gentleman's Magazine* and *Scot's Magazine* in Britain in 1775 and in the *Pennsylvania Evening Post* in 1776.

Invasion Preparations Go Badly

The invasion sanctioned by the congress in late June had still not taken shape by mid-August. Schuyler was having difficulty finding men, money, and equipment. "The Troops here are destitute of Tents, they are crouded in vile Barracks, which with the Natural Inattention of the Soldiery to Cleanliness, has already been productive of Desease and Numbers are daily rendered Unfit for Duty," Schuyler complained to Washington in a letter dated August 6. He had no carriages for field artillery, less than a ton of gunpowder, and only twenty-four rounds of ammunition for each man. If the Canadians and their Indigenous allies were not as friendly as assumed, his troops would be in trouble.

Having approved the invasion, the delegates had left its organization in the hands of the army, headed by Washington. Communication difficulties meant there was a lag between events and when the congress heard about them. The delegates were on a break in August 1775. Franklin was caught up organizing the post office, which meant finding and appointing local postmasters. He was also preparing for a meeting with the Indigenous Peoples of the Ohio country. It is unclear whether he was even aware that Schuyler was having difficulties procuring troops and equipment.

Washington's reply on August 20 offered little comfort to Schuyler. The commander-in-chief mistakenly assumed that Schuyler had been joined by a significant number of troops from New York, when in fact only part of the promised regiment arrived. "I am sure you will not let Difficulties not insuperable damp your ardour," the commander-in-chief wrote bracingly. "Perseverance and Spirit have done Wonders in all ages." He did have a plan that he thought would help Schuyler: He would send a detachment of 1,000 to 1,200 men to Canada by way of the Kennebec River and then overland to Quebec City. They would divert Carleton's attention from Schuyler's advance. "He must either break up and follow this party to Quebec, by which he will leave you a free passage or suffer that important Place to fall into our Hands: an Event which would have a decisive Effect and Influence on the public Interests," wrote Washington. He conceded it was possible this incursion might alarm the Canadians and push them into the British camp. But with suitable precautions and strict discipline, this could be avoided. He ended by saying not a moment should be lost because "the Season will be considerably advanced," a reference to the approach of the harsh Canadian winter.[27]

The unhappy Schuyler replied on August 27 that he was on the brink of departure, although he only had about 1,700 men, a force "far short of what I would wish." The plan called for them to use the Lake Champlain route to Montreal, taking all the settlements along the way, and then move on to Trois-Rivières and Quebec City, the seat of government. Schuyler thought he had enough men to take the forts at Saint-Jean and Chambly and even Montreal. There were an estimated 650 British regulars spread between the forts and Montreal, he said, accompanied by about 300–500 Indigenous Peoples, Scots, and Canadians.[28] But he did not have enough to then take Quebec City. Although Schuyler could not have been aware of it at the time, a new phase in the hostilities had begun with the August 23 declaration by George III that subjects throughout the North American colonies, "misled by dangerous and ill-designing men," were in an "open and avowed rebellion." The king commanded all his officers, both civil and military, to "exert their utmost Endeavours to suppress such rebellion."[29]

Desertions, Illness, and Lack of Equipment Hamper the Invaders

In mounting a two-pronged attack on the northern colony, Washington adapted old battle plans used by the British and the colonists to attack Canada when it was still ruled by France. But in those plans, the force attacking Quebec City usually came by sea. This new plan called for Benedict Arnold to lead troops up the Kennebec River and then through the rough wilderness of what is now northern Maine. Arnold, keen for glory, readily agreed. Letters and memoirs from some of his men described a harrowing journey, with food running out and men eating dead dogs and even their shoes to survive. One congressional delegate later compared Arnold's march to that of Hannibal crossing the Alps.[30] By the time his tattered, ill-equipped troops reached the outskirts of Quebec City, illness, death, and desertion had reduced Arnold's force to about five hundred men.

Schuyler was supposed to lead the other prong but was sidelined by ill health. Rebel General Richard Montgomery, a former British officer, took over. His men captured the British-held forts north of Lake Champlain and marched into Montreal unopposed, having signed terms of surrender on November 12, 1775, with a representative group of French- and English-speaking Montrealers. Governor Carleton had fled for Quebec City just days before, taking the British regulars with him. Montgomery also had problems keeping men. Some headed home when their short enlistments expired, some deserted, some fell ill, and others were left behind to guard captured forts and towns. Of the 1,700 he set out with, only about 600 were left when Montgomery met with Arnold and his troops in mid-December at Pointe-aux-Trembles (now Neuville), about 32 kilometres (20 miles) west of Quebec City, to plan their assault on the fortified city. Montreal and Trois-Rivières were in American hands, but to complete the invasion, Quebec City had to fall. Too weak to attack the formidable fortifications, they settled into a siege.

Inside the walls of that city, Governor Carleton had done what he could to prepare for an attack. He had been bitterly disappointed by the lack of response from ordinary French Canadians to his call to arms. In some parishes, the men reacted violently, even attacking seigneurs as they attempted to organize a militia. This could be evidence of anti-British feeling, or it could be a reaction to the seigneurs, many of whom had made themselves unpopular by raising the fees paid by habitants. In Quebec City, the British authorities expelled anyone who refused to take up arms. That left Carleton with about 1,800 fighters made up of regular troops, marines from a British ship, some of the town's British merchants, and an estimated 543 French Canadians. Unlike the thousand or so rebels camped in the snow outside the walls, the defenders had shelter, warmth, and food. If they could hold out until spring, British reinforcements might arrive by sea to save them.

French Canadians and Indigenous Peoples Divided

At the start of the invasion, the French Canadians did not know how to react. Some joined the rebel regiments formed by Moses Hazen and James Livingston, who had both moved from the thirteen colonies to Quebec after the British conquest and volunteered to raise Canadian troops for the congressional army. Some, like those in Quebec City, joined the British side. But existing records indicate that the great body of ordinary French Canadians remained neutral. They, like many of the Indigenous Peoples in the colonies, regarded the rebellion as a family quarrel and did not want to get involved. Delegates to the congress had used those exact words when they sent a message to the Six Nations in the summer of 1775. "We don't wish you to take up the hatchet against the king's troops," they wrote. "We desire you to remain at home, and not join either side, but keep the hatchet buried deep."[31] For a time, the Six Nations were happy to follow this course. "We cannot intermeddle in this dispute between two brothers," the Oneida Chiefs told the governors of the New England colonies in June. "For these reasons possess your minds in peace and take no umbrage that we Indians refuse joining in the contest: we are for peace."[32]

For the French Canadians, neutrality did not mean they could not sell provisions and services to the rebels, especially in the early months of the invasion, when they were paid with hard currency. Dr. Isaac Senter, the army surgeon who accompanied Arnold, wrote of the "poor Canadian peasants" they met on their way to Quebec City. The peasants treated them with politeness and civility, he said, and served them "firkin butter and hot bread."[33] Arnold's account books from the siege of Quebec City contain numerous French Canadian names among those who provided food and fuel. But when the Americans ran out of money and tried to pay with paper script or promissory notes, the habitants grew far less accommodating. Those with long memories remembered the debacle after the British conquest, when France refused to fully honour the paper money it had used to pay for supplies and services prior to its defeat.

When the American invaders began to seize what they wanted, the attitude of the habitants soured further. "We no longer look on them as friends," the American sympathizer Hazen said in a letter to Schuyler, "but, on the contrary, as waiting an opportunity to join our enemies."[34] Some of the English-speaking merchants of Montreal sympathized openly with the Americans and were happy to petition the king to repeal the Quebec Act, but only a few of them dared to openly break with the British administration. They had their trade arrangements with London merchants to consider.

None of this was readily apparent to the congressional delegates back in Philadelphia, who received fleeting glimpses of the invasion through periodic dispatches sent by the generals. These often did not tell the whole story. The delegates were easily distracted by events closer to home and thus more important to their survival. They decided in early November to send a three-man commission — Robert Livingston, Robert Treat Paine, and John Langdon — to confer with Schuyler on what he needed to maintain an army of three thousand for six months in Canada. These commissioners were supposed to travel to Canada after meeting Schuyler, who was directing the invasion from Ticonderoga. The three were to use their utmost efforts to persuade the Canadians to become part of "the Association of the United Colonies" and to stress that "we hold sacred their rights of conscience and shall never molest them in the free enjoyment of their religion."[35] But the commissioners decided that they would get in Montgomery's way, and besides, winter was fast approaching. Livingston suggested sending another commission in the spring. The congress also resolved in November to send two agents to Nova Scotia to see whether the inhabitants there were friendly to their cause. If the answer was negative, congress wondered whether Washington would send a force to take away arms and ships and destroy the British dockyards in that colony.

Delegates Still Confident of American Victory

As 1775 drew to a close, expectations of victory in Canada ran high among the congressional delegates. They were told at least twice that Quebec City had fallen to their forces. When Jefferson heard that Montgomery had taken Montreal, he wrote on November 29 that the delegates expected to hear that Quebec had welcomed Arnold with open arms. "In a short time we have reason to hope the delegates of Canada will join us in Congress and complete the American Union as far as we wish to have it completed."[36] The congress drafted a letter to update its agents in London, telling them "the Canadians are much too liberal to be made instruments in the black design of enslaving their brethren and the Indians with their usual sagacity have by the firmest treaties accepted and pledged themselves to observe the neutrality which Congress desired."[37] Washington was hopeful. "We impatiently wait for accounts from Arnold," he wrote on December 15. "Would to God we may hear he is in Quebec — and that all Canada is in our possession."[38] That view was shared in London by at least two British parliamentarians. "You have lost all of Canada," David Hartley told the North ministry in parliamentary debates of December 21. His colleague, George Johnstone, observed that Britain probably no longer possessed "a foot of land in that province."[39]

The congressional delegates started making plans for what they would do with Canada, including repairing the fortifications at Quebec City to withstand any British attempt to retake it. They set up a committee, which included Franklin, to decide what to do with the merchant ships and their cargoes that had been spotted in the Quebec harbour. And they celebrated Montgomery's success by promoting him to major general, giving him a raise and backdating it to the day he entered Canada. The last news about the invasion that Franklin and the other congressional delegates received that year was a letter from Schuyler dated December 21, read in the congress on December 30. Schuyler said he had asked a messenger for news of Montgomery's progress and had been told "he was gone towards Quebeck."

Franklin was among those who thought it was only a matter of time before Canada would fall to the American colonies. Or at least that is what he said in a letter dated December 9 to Charles-Guillaume-Frédéric Dumas, a long-standing acquaintance and unofficial agent for the colonies in The Hague. In the letter, Franklin asked Dumas whether he knew any sources of arms, ammunition, and engineers in Europe and whether any European state would be willing to enter into a commercial agreement with the colonies. Franklin painted a bright picture for Dumas, saying the "whole continent was firmly united" and that an American army of twenty-five thousand men had been able to besiege the king's troops in Boston and invade Canada. "We have met with great success, as the printed papers sent herewith will inform you," he continued, "and have now reason to expect that whole province may be soon in our possession."

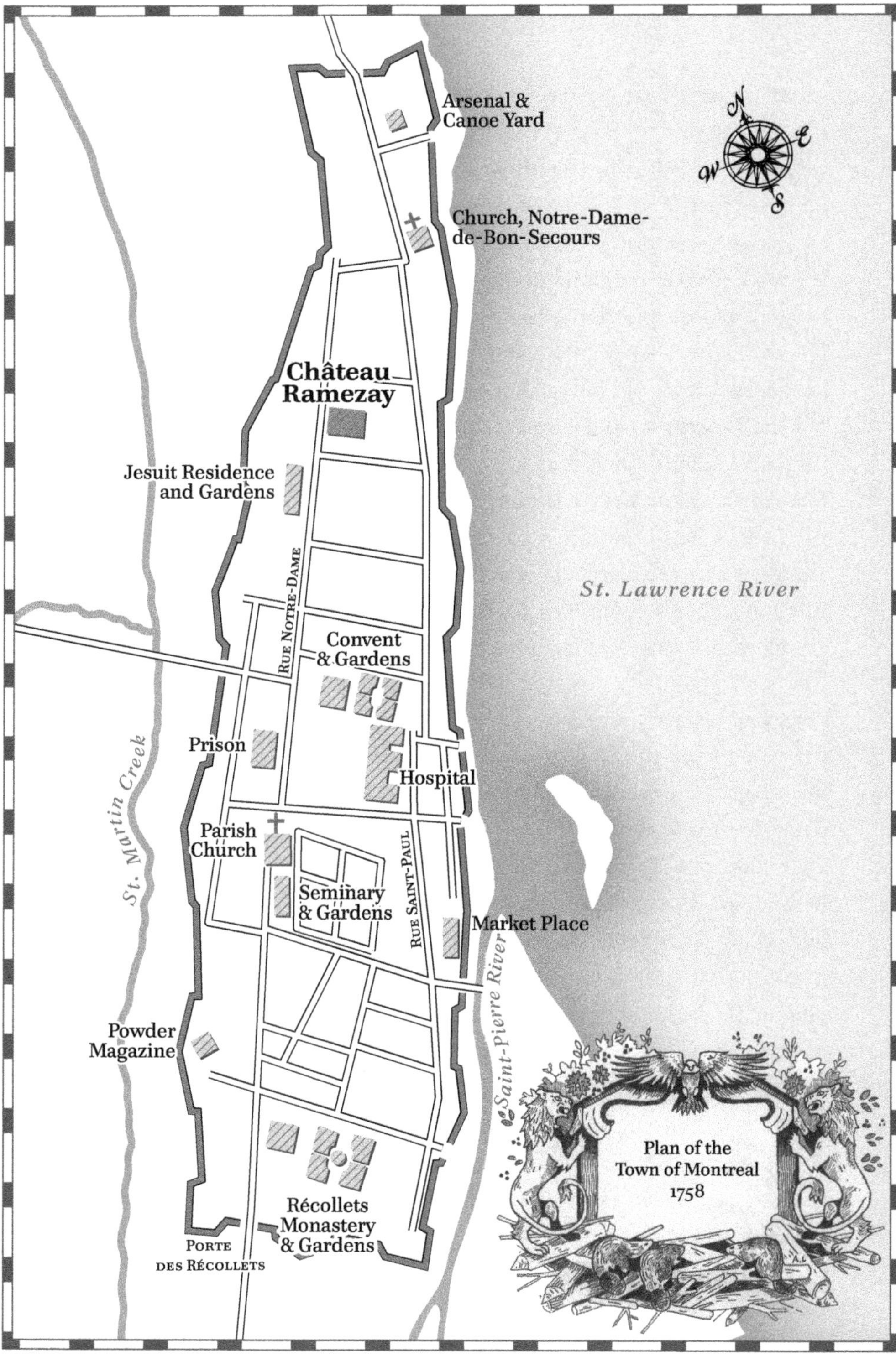
Arsenal &
Canoe Yard
N
E
W
S
Church, Notre-Dame-
de-Bon-Secours
Château
Ramezay
Jesuit Residence
and Gardens
Rue Notre-Dame
St. Lawrence River
Convent
& Gardens
Prison
Hospital
St. Martin Creek
Parish
Church
Rue Saint-Paul
Seminary
& Gardens
Market Place
Saint-Pierre River
Powder
Magazine
Plan of the
Town of Montreal
1758
Récollets
Monastery
& Gardens
Porte
des Récollets

CHAPTER 8

A Nest of Hornets: Montreal 1776

> [In Canada,] I was a Piece of a Governor, and I think a very good one, for a Fortnight; and might have been so till this time if your wicked Army, Enemies to all good Government, had not come and driven me out.[1]
>
> — *Benjamin Franklin*

THERE WERE FIFTEEN CENTIMETRES (SIX INCHES) OF SNOW ON THE ground and the lakes were still icebound when Benjamin Franklin and his travelling companions reached Saratoga in mid-April 1776. They were travelling through the colony of New York on their way north to Montreal. Something had gone terribly wrong with the American invasion of Canada. The congress dispatched Franklin, Samuel Chase, and Charles Carroll of Carrollton to fix it. Franklin was now seventy years old and suffering from gout, boils, and something he called scurf or scurviness, which may have been psoriasis. Although the three had brought their beds on the journey to avoid sleeping on the ground, it was still an arduous trek. Franklin morbidly admitted as much in a letter he sent from Saratoga to a friend, saying he "had undertaken a Fatigue that at my Time of Life may prove too much for me, so I sit down to write to a few Friends by way of Farewell."[2] And yet he continued northward by boat, cart, and carriage to the former French territory he had long wanted to annex to the thirteen colonies.

At the end of 1775, Franklin and his fellow delegates had been expecting to hear at any moment that Quebec City had fallen to the combined forces of the rebel generals Richard Montgomery and Benedict Arnold, leaving the Americans in possession of Canada. Montgomery had captured all the forts along the Lake Champlain route and the major population centres of Montreal and Trois-Rivières. All that was lacking was Quebec City. It was a shock for the delegates to learn on January 17 that the December 31 rebel attack on the fortified city had failed miserably. Montgomery had died in the attempt and Arnold had been badly wounded. Carleton, the British governor, and his mixed force of British regulars, sailors, merchants, and Canadians had prevailed.

The Americans thought the situation was still salvageable. "Our affairs may still be retrieved in Canada before the King's troops can get reinforced," Washington wrote rebel Colonel Joseph Reed in late January. The additional troops Washington was sending Arnold would be enough, he thought, to "complete the conquest of Canada this winter."[3] With this idea in mind, the congress decided on February 15 to send Franklin, Chase, and Carroll to Montreal. At least some of the delegates thought that if the men used the right words and spoke to the right people, they could convince the Canadians to join the budding rebellion against the British ministry.

The three commissioners were picked with an eye to what they could bring to the mission. Franklin had diplomatic expertise, scientific renown, and extensive experience in fixing problems for the Pennsylvania assembly and the continental congress. The delegates erroneously thought he was fluent in French, although he only had a smattering. Chase, a delegate from Maryland, strongly felt it was important to take Canada. "Quebec must at every Hazard be ours," he wrote John Adams in January, before the congress learned of the defeat at Quebec. He believed that once the Americans had explained their grievances against the British, the Canadians would be willing to join their fight. Chase suggested the addition of Carroll, thought to be the richest man in the colonies. Carroll was then asked to enlist John Carroll, a distant relative and a Catholic priest, to join the mission. Charles Carroll was a Catholic. Both he and his priestly relative had gone to school in France and were fluent in French. Fleury Mesplet, a French Huguenot printer who had moved to the colonies, was added some days later and asked to take his printing press. Neither John Carroll nor Mesplet were official commissioners.

"I must confess I have very great Confidence, in the Abilities and Integrity, the Political Principles and good Disposition of this Committee," John Adams wrote a fellow rebel leader. Adams also approved of the appointment of Charles Lee, an experienced general who spoke French, to command the northern troops. "The unanimous voice of the Continent is Canada must be ours and Quebec must be taken," he said.[4] Robert Morris, a fellow delegate and the banker who came to be known as the financier of the revolution, was of the same view. He approved of the commissioners and the necessity of conquering Canada: "Should it fall into the hands of The Enemy they will soon raise a Nest of Hornets on our backs that will Sting us to the quick."[5]

Congress Writes a Third Letter to Canadians

In late January, the congress sent a third letter to the inhabitants of Canada, addressing them as "friends and countrymen" and suggesting that their future happiness was intimately tied to that of the American colonists. This letter contained none of the pointed threats made in previous missives, although the congress did remark that two battalions of colonists had received their marching orders for Canada and another six battalions were being raised for this purpose. But the overall tone was friendly. "Your assistance in the support and preservation of American liberty affords us the most sensible satisfaction," it said, referring to the generally positive reception Montgomery received the previous year as he made his way up the Richelieu River to Montreal. The letter went on to say: "And we flatter ourselves that you will seize with zeal and eagerness the favourable moment to co-operate in the success of so glorious an enterprize."[6]

This optimistic take on events was reinforced by the testimony before a committee of congress of Prudent Lajeunesse, a Canadian militia captain from Montreal who joined Montgomery's forces early in the invasion and continued to fight alongside the Americans. He spoke to the committee of secret correspondence, a small group set up by the congress in 1775 to look for foreign support of the rebellion, among other things. Franklin was a member. Lajeunesse told the committee that there was popular support for the Americans among the habitants, but the clergy and the noblesse had undermined it. One way they did this was by reading the congressional letters to the largely illiterate country people, putting their own negative spin on the contents. Lajeunesse suggested the situation could be turned around if the congress sent representatives to Canada who could speak to the people face to face, explain their dispute with Britain, and reassure the clergy and noblesse that their interests would be protected. Franklin wrote up the committee report on what Lajeunesse said and presented it to the congress on February 14. He and the two other commissioners were appointed the next day.

The Congress Offers to Protect Canadians

The written instructions to the commissioners, approved by the congress on March 20, contained the same friendly message about mutual interests as the January letter. The American troops were in Canada "to frustrate the designs of the British court against our common liberties," the instructions said. The commissioners were to inform the Canadians that they could set up whatever form of government would bring them happiness. This freedom of choice was constrained by further instructions that the Canadians would have the same system of laws as the thirteen colonies, with some local differences, and that the commissioners should recommend the Canadians follow the American practice of setting up committees of safety and of observation and inspection in each colony and of holding a convention to elect delegates to congress. The implication was that the form of government the Canadians would be happiest with was the American one. Freedom of religion and freedom of the press should also be promised, the commissioners were told. The continued use of the French language was not mentioned. This was probably not an oversight. Language did not have the same importance to the British then as it does today. The educated class, including Carleton and Murray, spoke French. Perhaps the American colonists, like the British just after the conquest in 1760, assumed tens of thousands of French speakers would quickly adopt the culture of their conquerors. Should the Canadians agree to "put themselves under the protection of the 'United Colonies,'" the commissioners were to promise "that we will defend and protect the people of Canada against all enemies, in the same manner as we will defend and protect any of the United Colonies."[7]

Words used by the congress, such as "sister colony," suggested a merger of equals, but that idea was undermined by the statement that Canadians would be under the protection of the American colonies. Although the congress was no longer telling Canadians they were a "small people" it was clear the delegates regarded them as inferiors. The delegates had been emboldened by the British decision to withdraw from Boston on March 17, and congratulated each other on this propitious turn of events. They had the British on the run in at least one part of the thirteen colonies.

Commissioners Not Given the Full Picture of Disarray

Franklin, Chase, and Carroll did not have the complete picture of what was happening in Canada when they accepted the mission in February. They knew about the defeat at Quebec City and the death of Montgomery, who had been made into an instant hero by those pushing hardest for independence. The congress voted to erect a monument to him and gave Franklin £300 to find something suitable, preferably from Paris. Poems, plays, and pamphlets were written, including *A Dialogue Between the Ghost of General Montgomery, Just Arrived from the Elysian Fields; and an American Delegate in a Wood Near Philadelphia.* This pamphlet, attributed to Thomas Paine, author of *Common Sense*, had the ghostly Montgomery calling George III a "royal criminal" and urging the colonies not to waste any more time in declaring independence.

But the commissioners did not know of the disarray among the invading army, a significant factor in Montgomery's death. They only learned of it in the conversations they held on their way north with officers, soldiers, and civilians who had been in Canada or were familiar with what was happening there. What they heard disturbed them. After meeting General Schuyler in Saratoga, Franklin wrote John Hancock, then president of the congress, saying they planned to resume their journey the next day. "Tho' by the Advices from Canada communicated by him to us, and as we suppose sent forward to you, I am afraid we shall be able to effect but little there," Franklin wrote.[8]

Montgomery had been carrying a growing burden the day he decided to attack Quebec City. He had started the invasion with too few men, about 1,700 compared with the 3,000 Schuyler wanted. Even three thousand seemed inadequate compared with the numbers involved in previous attacks on Canada by the British and colonists. Planning for the 1709 attack inspired by Vetch stipulated more than double that number. The attack on the French fort at Louisbourg in 1745 involved four thousand colonists, backed by the British navy. Another 1745 plan by the governor of Massachusetts to invade Canada suggested raising twenty thousand men. British Major General James Wolfe had nine thousand men with him when he arrived by sea in 1759 to attack Quebec City. And his was only one part of a many-pronged assault by the British and the colonists on what was then New France.

One big difference between the 1775 invasion and calculations for previous assaults was the absence of French troops, who had been feared and respected by the American colonists. There had been as many as eight thousand French soldiers in the colony at certain points during the French regime. They were replaced after the conquest by a British military presence, albeit a feeble one by this time. But even against this weaker foe, Schuyler, who had fought with the British in the French and Indian War, insisted more men were needed to defeat any armed resistance the invaders might encounter and to impress the Canadians, especially those who had thrown in their lot with the invaders. "They were made to believe we had an army of 15,000 men going there," Jefferson wrote a friend in October 1775, referring to the Canadians. "This put them in high spirits. But when they saw Montgomery with but 2700 they were thunderstruck at the situation they had brought themselves into."[9] Jefferson was misinformed about how many colonial troops actually marched north.

Both the British and the Americans tried to persuade the Indigenous Peoples within their sphere of influence to join the fighting on their side. Some did. More would join later. But at this stage in the conflict, most were leery of involvement. Those in Canada had been told by the British after the conquest in 1760 that they should regard the American colonists as friends and brothers and forget past hatreds. Now they were being asked to fight them. An account in the *New-England Chronicle* in May 1776 of a meeting between Carleton and Indigenous representatives in December 1775 said that the Indigenous spokesman told the governor that his people believed both the British and Americans were their brethren. They did not want any part in the quarrel. After the last war, the Chief continued, "The war hatchet was buried forty fathoms deep," and they did not know where to find it. Carleton suggested they start digging, but the Chief informed him that the handle was rotten, and the hatchet could not be used.

The Congress Gives the Fight Closer to Home Priority

It was not just men that Montgomery was short of in the invasion of Canada. Clothing, provisions, weapons, and gunpowder were also required elsewhere in the thirteen colonies. The congress and Washington thought those demands trumped Montgomery's needs. When Schuyler asked the congress to send him gunpowder in August 1775, on the eve of the invasion, Franklin, who was answering congressional correspondence during the summer recess, replied they had sent all they had to Boston. He later persuaded Pennsylvania to send some to Schuyler. The buckskin breeches, felt caps, shoes, stockings, and waistcoats for three thousand men that the congress agreed in November to purchase for the troops in Canada were diverted in December to the army in Boston. Montgomery, the delegates reasoned, could probably get the winter clothing he needed in Montreal. Even Charles Lee, the general meant to accompany Franklin's salvage mission, was redirected. The congress told him at the beginning of March to go south instead of north. "My dear general," Lee wrote Washington on March 3, "my destination is altered. Instead of going to Canada, I am appointed to command to the southward." Lee noted it might have been more prudent to send him to Canada, given that he was the only general officer on the continent who could speak and think in French, "but I shall obey with alacrity, and hope, with success."

Montgomery was also dismayed at the quality of the men supplied by the colonies. In a letter he wrote in September 1775 from Île-aux-Noix south of Montreal, he told his wife, Janet Livingston Montgomery, about the panic and confusion he saw among the men he had sent to cut communication between Saint-Jean and Montreal. When one or two fired, they all started firing, even though there was nothing to shoot at, he said. "In short, such a set of pusillanimous wretches never were collected," he wrote. "Could I, with decency, leave the army in its present situation, I would not serve an hour longer."[10] He and other commanders complained the troops were reluctant to follow orders, especially when they were given by an officer from another colony. It might have been called the continental army, but the men remained stubbornly loyal to their home colonies. When his men balked at going to Montreal so late in the season, Montgomery was forced to promise they could go home once the city had fallen. The Green Mountain Boys did just that. Arnold suffered similar problems.

These problems did not end when Montgomery and Arnold met at Pointe-aux-Trembles in mid-November 1775 to plot what they hoped would be the final and decisive assault on the city. They found it increasingly difficult to buy food for the troops, given the locals' reluctance to accept paper continental currency as payment and constant pressure by the clergy not to aid the invaders. Smallpox began to spread among the poorly clad and underfed men camped in the snow outside the city walls. A rumour spread that Governor Carleton had sent an infected prostitute out to the Americans, although there was no proof he had done so. It was an appealing conspiracy theory, tailor-made to allocate blame elsewhere for their increasingly dire situation. The American soldiers began to inoculate themselves with the live virus from an infected person, giving themselves what they hoped would be milder symptoms. Sick, hungry, and disgruntled, the rebels wanted to go home. A significant number of them would be able to do that on January 1, 1776, when their enlistments expired. Montgomery had little choice but to launch an attack while he still had men. He did so in the early hours of December 31, in the midst of a snowstorm.

A Desperate Attack Fails but the Winter Siege Continues

The fortified part of Quebec City sits atop a cliff overlooking the St. Lawrence. All the important buildings of the town were within the walls. At the foot of the cliff was lower town, where the business of the port took place. Montgomery had meant to direct the bulk of his forces at upper town, but deserters from his camp told Carleton of his plan. He revised his plan and divided the rebel army in four, with two groups tasked with making feints toward the upper town to distract the defenders, while Montgomery and Arnold led separate attacks in a pincer movement on the lower town.

Price, the Montreal merchant who loaned money to the rebels and accompanied Montgomery to Quebec, told the congress later that the snow was one and a half metres (four feet) deep in places and the seven hundred men with Montgomery had to walk in single file in some areas. Montgomery, along with his aide, Major John McPherson, and Captain Jacob Cheeseman, were at the head of the line of men making their way along a narrow passage at the foot of a steep, rocky cliff. They were killed instantly when a post mostly manned by Canadians fired a cannon loaded with grapeshot. The blast was akin to that of a giant shotgun. Muskets and grapeshot from British and Canadian defenders "mowed them down like grass," observed Jacob Danford, a British artillery officer during the siege. A panicky retreat ensued. When a group of defenders surveyed the site the next morning, they found the bodies of Montgomery and his aides buried under snow.[11]

Arnold fared little better when he and about six hundred men attacked the lower town from the east. He was shot in the leg and was carried off the field. His men fought for a while and then surrendered. Carleton estimated that between forty and fifty American rebels were killed in the assault, including Montgomery, while the British side lost seven men. About three hundred Americans were taken prisoner.[12]

The gory details of Montgomery's end were glossed over in public commemorations. Mercy Otis Warren, wife of revolutionary leader James Warren and author of one of the first histories of the revolution, said Montgomery "fell at the gates by a random shot from the frozen walls of Quebec." She called him "an early martyr in the cause of freedom."[13] A 1786 painting by John Trumbull, *The Death of Montgomery*, further burnished this image of a martyr. It depicts a seemingly unscathed general dying in the arms of his men, with his equally unmarked aides lying at his feet. There is little snow. Everyone seems surprisingly well clothed and well fed.

The American besiegers hung on grimly after Montgomery's death, but their problems only worsened. "As soon as Montgomery was killed, the men being dispirited and dissatisfied, went away in droves," said Hector McNeal, who left Quebec City to fight with the rebels after Carleton ordered anyone who would not bear arms for the British to leave.[14] Moses Hazen, a rebel commander who lived near Saint-Jean, said Montgomery's demise added to the increasing hostility of the habitants. "The peasantry in general have been ill-used," he admitted in an April 1 letter to Schuyler. "They have, in some instances been dragooned with the point of a bayonet to supply wood for the garrison at a lower rate than the current price. For carriages and other articles furnished, illegible certificates have been given without signature, the one-half, of consequence, rejected by the quartermaster." As for what he called "the better sort of people," he described them as British supporters "who would wish to see our throats cut, and perhaps would readily assist in doing it."

Arnold took command of the depleted rebel army from his bed in a temporary military hospital outside Quebec City. He estimated he had between seven hundred and eight hundred men, including several hundred Canadians. "I shall endeavour to continue this blockade while there are any hopes of success," he wrote General David Wooster, the senior rebel commander in Canada who was then in Montreal.[15] Wooster then wrote Schuyler, begging for more men, money, and supplies. "Something must be done and that speedily, or I greatly fear we are ruined," he said. "There is but little confidence to be placed in the Canadians; they are but a small remove from the savages, and are fond of being of the strongest party."[16] Schuyler conveyed the message to Washington, who did what he could. But he was already begging the congress for more money and troops for use in the thirteen colonies and complaining that he was having trouble enlisting men.

He was also having trouble keeping those who did come forward. The same New England newspaper that carried the article about Carleton's meeting with local Indigenous leaders had seven separate advertisements for army deserters, offering a reward for their capture. Aside from the battle with the British, there were internal uprisings to deal with, including one in the New York colony where Sir John Johnson and about five hundred royalists were rumoured to be planning an attack on rebel forces. In Canada the two sides settled into a waiting game. Whoever managed to get reinforcements to Quebec City first would likely emerge the victor.

The Commissioners Arrive on a Salvage Mission

This was how matters stood when Franklin, Chase, and the two Carrolls arrived in Montreal on April 29, 1776. Arnold, who had been replaced by Wooster outside Quebec City, was on hand to greet them with as much ceremony as he could muster. John Carroll described their reception in a letter he wrote his mother on May 1. Arnold and his officers received them with military honours and fired a cannon salute, he wrote. "Being conducted to the general's house, we were served with a glass of wine, while people were crowding in to pay their compliments, which ceremony being over, we were shown into another apartment, and unexpectedly met in it a large assemblage of ladies, most of them French. After drinking tea, and sitting some time, we went to an elegant supper, which was followed with the singing of the ladies, which proved very agreeable, and would have been more so, if we had not been so much fatigued with our journey."[17] This took place at the Château Ramezay in Montreal, now a museum, then the headquarters for the rebel army. Charles Carroll wrote in his journal that after the festivities, the commissioners were taken to the nearby home of Thomas Walker, "the best built and perhaps the best furnished in this town."[18] Walker was one of the handful of merchants from the American colonies who had settled in Montreal after the British conquest. He was a leading agitator for the American cause.

What happened next in Montreal for Franklin and the commissioners can only be pieced together through the official letters they wrote to the congress. There is a gap in the existing personal correspondence of Franklin, Chase, and the two Carrolls. They appear to have stopped writing personal letters when they reached Montreal and then picked up again after Franklin left. It could be that life became so hectic they had no time for anything personal, even jotting in a private journal. That seems out of character for men who routinely dashed off notes to family and friends, even when life was exceptionally busy. They may have thought it would be difficult to send the letters, given the turmoil in the colony. Yet they were continually writing letters to the congress. And even when they reached places farther south, where they could be sure their missives would be delivered, they did not discuss in any detail what had happened in Montreal. This was another departure from their normal practice.

Perhaps their short-lived and ultimately unsuccessful mission was not something they wanted to remember. A related possibility is that the failure came at a sensitive time for the revolution and there was a tacit agreement among them not to publicize that America's first invasion had ended in disaster in case it sapped the willingness of colonists to continue fighting the British. And yet another is that the invasion of Canada, where they were the aggressors, did not fit with the story they wanted to tell the world of being victims of British tyranny.

Urgent Pleas for Money and Men — but Mostly Money

The commissioners' joint letter to the congress dated May 1 set the tone for what was to come. "It is impossible to give you a just idea of the lowness of the Continental credit here from the want of hard money, and the prejudice it is to our affairs," they wrote John Hancock, then president of the congress. They had to borrow silver from a supporter in Saint-Jean just to send a message to Arnold in Montreal and again when they needed to hire calèches (carriages) to take them to the city. The Canadians were beginning to think the congress was bankrupt and would be driven out of Canada as soon as the British arrived. Nothing but the immediate dispatch of £20,000 in hard currency would remedy the situation. As for the troops, they estimated there were about three thousand Americans in Canada, now that some reinforcements had arrived, but at least eight thousand were needed. This letter ended on a sombre note, saying smallpox was in the army and General Thomas, appointed commander when General Lee was reassigned, "has unfortunately never had it." Thomas died of the malady in June.

Five days later, they wrote Hancock again to say the lack of hard currency meant soldiers were not being paid and the Canadians were turning against them because commanders were resorting to violence in obtaining carriages and other provisions. "If hard money cannot be procured and forwarded with dispatch to Canada, it would be advisable, in our opinion to withdraw our army & fortify the passes on the lakes to prevent the enemy, & the Canadians, if so inclined, from making irruptions into & depredations on our frontiers." The one bright spot they noted was that seven Indigenous groups in Canada told them they intended to remain neutral in the fight. Two days later, they wrote again, begging for additional money over and above their original request because they had discovered the army was £14,000 in debt to its suppliers, who were reluctant to sell anything more on credit. (The colonists used a range of currencies at the time, including pounds and Spanish dollars.) The commissioners continually heard of plots to expel the Americans on the first news of the arrival of British reinforcements. "In short, if Money cannot be had to support your Army here with Honour, so as to be respected instead of being hated by the people, We repeat it as our firm and unanimous Opinion, that it is better immediately to withdraw it."[19] So desperate was the army for funds that Franklin had to dip into his own pocket repeatedly. He loaned Arnold $560, a significant amount at the time, and was later reimbursed by the congress for this and other loans made during the journey, totalling $1,221. The Canadians were not alone in their skepticism about the continental currency. There were reports from Philadelphia and New York of American colonists refusing to sell provisions to the army in exchange for the paper script.

The British Arrive, Forcing Americans to Flee

Unbeknownst to the commissioners when they wrote this letter, their situation was already untenable. On May 6, three British ships, led by the frigate

Surprise, appeared in the St. Lawrence before Quebec City. They carried about 150 soldiers, enough when combined with about 800 men from Quebec City to frighten the rebels into flight. More ships would follow, bringing an estimated nine thousand troops, including about two thousand mercenaries the king had hired from the state of Hesse-Kassel in what is now Germany. The British had won the race to supply reinforcements.

The rebels immediately fled their positions around Quebec City, leaving behind their cannons, about five hundred muskets, and two hundred sick soldiers. The snow and mud were knee-deep, according to rebel Major Samuel Blacken, and "there was not a pair of shoes to three men."[20] In a May 10 letter recounting this alarming state of affairs, the commissioners told Hancock: "We are afraid it will not be in our power to render our Country any farther services in this Colony." In a separate letter that day to Schuyler, they said it was likely the rebel army would have to abandon Canada and asked him to prepare boats and secure provisions to facilitate the retreat down Lake Champlain.[21]

The commissioners had little to show for their time in Montreal. They freed some Canadian militia officers that Wooster imprisoned after they refused to renounce their militia appointments that had been made by Carleton. And they issued passports allowing some fur traders to take goods to the *pays-d'en-haut* to exchange for furs. Wooster had tried to stop the fur traders from travelling to the interior because he thought they were secretly aiding the enemy. He had also ordered the churches be closed on Christmas Eve, no small thing in a colony where the overwhelming majority was Catholic. Wooster's arbitrary treatment of the citizens of Montreal had deepened resentment among the Canadians. Father Carroll made no inroads with the senior Catholic clergy, who reportedly gave him the cold shoulder. He told a friend that when he told a priest that Catholics would have freedom of religion under the Americans, he was informed that they had it already under the British. He was also advised that the American offer of religious toleration could not be trusted, given they had described Catholicism two years earlier as a religion that had "dispersed impiety, bigotry, persecution, murder and rebellion through every part of the world."[22] Those ill-chosen words in the letter the congress had written in 1774 to the inhabitants of

Britain made an impact on the clergy in Canada. And they had persuaded at least some Canadians it was best not to join the American cause.

Some French Canadians Supported the Rebels

Even retrospectively, it is difficult to get a fix on how many French Canadians supported the Americans and how many opposed them. There were vocal and active rebel supporters from the start, like Lajeunesse, who testified to congress, and Christophe Pélissier, co-owner of the forges at Saint Maurice, who wrote the congress a letter in January 1776 advising the delegates on how to conquer Canada. Pélissier also agreed to supply the rebels with shells and shot. There were a number of women in the countryside, known informally as "reines de Hongrie" (Queens of Hungary), who tried to whip up support for the invaders in their communities. This name was an allusion to Maria Theresa, the queen of Hungary, who was thought to have a masculine, warlike nature. The widow Gabourie, or Gaboury, of Saint-Vallier is mentioned more than once in this context. On the other side were French Canadians like Captain Bouchette, who quietly paddled a disguised Carleton past American sentries on the St. Lawrence in November 1775 and delivered him safely to Quebec City; Charles-Marie Charland, who played a decisive role in defeating Arnold's forces at Sault-au-Matelot outside the walls of Quebec City; and Simon Sanguinet, the notary who wrote an open letter in March 1776 chastising his fellow Canadians for bowing to the tyrannical *Bostonnais*. An investigation by the British later in 1776 found there had been widespread sympathy for the Americans among the habitants, even though most chose not to take an active part in the fighting. Historians would later conclude that while some French Canadians actively supported the British and others openly supported the Americans, most exhibited what was later described as a "benevolent" neutrality.[23]

Pierre Foretier, a Montreal merchant and Canadian militia colonel, is a good illustration of a French Canadian who played both sides for his own ends during the occupation. Foretier recounts in his memoirs how an American colonel, John Philip de Haas, was billeted in his house during the occupation. When Foretier was approached by British supporters to help steal American ammunition and deerskins, he agreed to help. He made sure that the dinner for de Haas and his aides was prolonged, giving his friends time to spirit away the stolen goods. De Haas, seemingly unaware of Foretier's role in this affair, bought eight hundred pairs of boots from Foretier and even warned him as he was leaving Montreal that Americans were planning to strip his shop the next morning. Foretier hid the gold and silver lace, ribbons, and fine cloth, replacing it with coarser goods, which the Americans plundered. The British then asked him to provide lodging for Carleton and his troops, and Foretier complied. But he also furnished a carriage to get Franklin and the wives of the merchants Walker and Price out of Montreal before the British forces arrived.[24]

In describing the attitude of Canadians to his superiors in London in September 1776, Carleton observed: "As to my opinion of the Canadians, I think there is nothing to fear from them when we are in a state of prosperity, and nothing to hope for when in distress." Some were guided by sentiments of honour, he continued, "but the multitude is influenced only by hopes of gain, or fear of punishment."[25] That might have been too harsh an assessment. Many Canadians saw the invasion as a family quarrel between two English-speaking enemies. Officers in both the British and rebel armies had been part of the British and colonial force that conquered Canada in 1760. Carleton and Montgomery had fought on the same side to drive the French out of Canada. Some Canadians were also aware that Franklin had urged the British to retain Canada after the conquest instead of giving it back to France. Regardless of who won, they would still be a conquered people. Henri Bourassa, an influential politician and journalist in Quebec in the late 1800s, would have another explanation for the behaviour of the French Canadians. "It was all very simple," he said. "We had to choose between the English of Boston and the English of London. The English of London were farther away and we hated them less."[26]

Franklin Leaves First, Pleading Ill Health

Franklin was the first of the commissioners to leave, departing early on May 11, apparently because of his health. Father John Carroll joined him the next day at Saint-Jean, which the Americans still held. They had the misfortune of accompanying for part of the way Martha Walker, the wife of American supporter Thomas Walker. She berated them for consorting with Tories (royalists) in Montreal and accomplishing little. Franklin said later that Mrs. Walker and her husband, the American supporter in Montreal who had joined the group farther south, "gave themselves such Liberties in taunting our Conduct in Canada that it almost came to a quarrel."[27]

Franklin wrote Schuyler from Saint-Jean, saying that he must send provisions to the army in Canada immediately; otherwise "they must starve, plunder, or surrender." Samuel Chase and Charles Carroll, who stayed behind in the belief the rebel army would make a stand, suggested that cannibalism was a possibility. "If further reinforcements are sent without pork to victual the whole army, our Soldiers must Perish or feed on each other," they wrote Schuyler. "Even plunder, the last resource of strong necessity, will not relieve their wants."[28] By May 16, they were begging Schuyler for provisions. "For God's sake, send powder & Pork," they wrote.[29] In their letter to the congress the next day, they grumbled about the chaos caused by food shortages. "Your generals are now obliged to be contractors and commissaries; and your commissioners, who have neither the abilities, nor the inclination, are constrained to act as Generals."[30] By the end of the month, they, too, had gone home and by July 1 all the invaders had left Canada. Arnold, who along with his men pillaged Montreal before leaving, was the last to depart. According to one historian, he reached Île-aux-Noix, shot his horse, stepped into a boat, and headed south.[31]

Carleton and his troops chased the rebels out of Canada but did not pursue them further. He was later criticized for his actions. There is speculation he still thought there was a chance of reconciliation with the American colonists and did not want to do anything to jeopardize that possibility. He was much tougher with the residents of Canada who had aided the invaders, seizing their goods and burning their houses. Walker, Price, and other American sympathizers later received compensation from the congress for their losses. Mesplet, the printer who arrived just before the commissioners left, decided to remain in Montreal. Several years later, he established the city's first independent newspaper, *La Gazette du commerce littéraire pour la ville et le district de Montréal*, a forerunner of today's *Montreal Gazette*.

Mismanagement Blamed for Failed Invasion

The congress set up a committee to determine what had gone wrong in Canada. It heard testimony from Canadians and Americans who had been in the colony at the time of the invasion. Chase and Carroll had delivered a report to the congress on June 11, but it does not appear in the *Journals of the Continental Congress* or in *American Archives*. Hancock summarized it in a letter to Washington written the same day, saying, "By their account there has been most shocking mismanagement in that quarter."[32] In a previous letter, Chase blamed the congress for the fiasco. "I am at a loss to express my Astonishment at the Conduct of Congress," he wrote fellow delegate Richard Henry Lee on May 17 from Montreal. "Almost two months ago they voted 4 Battalions, and since 6 more Battalions for this country, without the least provisions for their support. We have now 4,000 troops in Canada & not a Mouthful of food." He went on to say that the congress was not a fit body to act as a council of war, because it was too large and unwieldy. "Pray divide your business into different Departments, a War office, a Treasury board, et et," he wrote. Jefferson had his own ideas about why American affairs in Canada went "retrograde." He wrote a friend on July 1, saying, "The fatal sources of these misfortunes have been want of hard money with which to procure provisions, the ravages of the smallpox with which one half of our army is still down, and an unlucky choice of some officers."[33] He was likely referring to complaints about the conduct of General Wooster. The congressional committee's final report, dated July 30, replicated this list and added a further factor: short enlistments, which made the men disorderly and forced commanding officers to take actions that "their prudence might have postponed."[34]

Not mentioned in the congressional analysis was the role played by the Catholic clergy, who did everything they could to persuade their parishioners to stay loyal to the British, including refusing to marry or bury anyone who fought for the Americans. An even bigger omission, at least according to John Adams, was the delay in declaring independence. The Canadians had been asked to support the rebels in their fight against the British ministry or government, not to join forces with rebels wanting to establish an independent country and cut ties with the British king. "Had the Declaration of Independency been made seven months ago, it would have been attended with many great and glorious Effects," Adams wrote his wife, Abigail, on July 3, 1776. "We might before this Hour have formed Alliances with foreign states. We should have mastered Quebec and been in possession of Canada." Unfounded hopes of reconciliation with Britain made too many gentlemen "slow and languid" in pushing for measures to conquer Canada, he wrote. There were other delegates who shared Adams's opinion, but he felt the failure strongly. "Alas Canada," he lamented to Chase in a letter of July 1. "We have found Misfortune and disgrace in that Quarter." The next day, he told Samuel Cooper that the evacuation took place "with such a Complication of Circumstances, of Famine, Pestilence, Distress, Defeat, and Disgrace, as are sufficient to humble a prouder Heart than mine."

Franklin Distances Himself from the Failure

Franklin did not want to be associated with the failure. He retreated to his home in Philadelphia, telling acquaintances he was suffering from a severe attack of gout. When he emerged, he plunged into other congressional work. Even then, he slipped in references to Canada when he could. On June 5, he joined a congressional committee investigating how to set up a speedy mail service for the army. On June 11, he was named to a separate committee tasked with writing the Declaration of Independence. In the end, it was largely Jefferson's work, but Franklin provided editing comments. The Declaration cited some of the provisions of the Quebec Act as reasons why the thirteen colonies wanted to cut their ties with Britain, including establishing an "Arbitrary government" in a neighbouring province and enlarging that province's boundaries. On June 12, he was appointed to yet another committee to prepare a plan for treaties the yet-to-be-declared United States would sign with foreign powers, notably France.

On July 4, the day the congress authenticated the Declaration of Independence and ordered it to be printed, Franklin, Jefferson, and John Adams were appointed to a committee to design a great seal for the United States. Franklin wanted the American motto to be "Rebellion to Tyrants is Obedience to God," a line from a fictitious epitaph he had written and circulated earlier that year. He drew up proposed changes to state representation in the congress, meant to be included in the draft articles of confederation. He wanted representation based on population, which would have made Canada a junior colony, if and when it joined, subject to the will of the more populous American colonies, such as Virginia, Massachusetts, Pennsylvania, North Carolina, and New York. Both the draft articles of confederation and the final version adopted in 1781 left the door open for Canada to join the new union. Franklin also resumed his work on the secret committee of correspondence, which was busy trying to barter American goods for foreign weapons, gunpowder, and support. Although he did not attend many of the meetings in person, he must have been consulted because his name appears at the bottom of their decisions in June.

But he said little about his time in Canada publicly and only referred to his visit in passing in later private correspondence. Perhaps the experience of having Canada snatched by the British, when it lay within the Americans' grasp, made him bitter. There was certainly a sour tone to the remarks his sister Jane Mecom relayed to a friend. She said Franklin had returned from Canada dispirited by "the Raiseing the seige of Quebeck, the Ignorance of the Canadans, there Incapasity and Aversnes to have anything to do in the war."[35] In 1777, he struck a more upbeat tone in a letter to Emma Thompson, a British friend. He said that in Canada, he had been "a Piece of a Governor, and I think a very good one, for a Fortnight; and might have been so till this time if your wicked Army, Enemies to all good Government, had not come and driven me out."[36] This seems to be an exaggeration unless he had struck some kind of private and hitherto unknown deal to stay on in Canada if the invasion had succeeded. And in 1779, he told John Jay that congress's continuing lack of money was a good reason to defer a proposed attack on Canada. He wrote:

> The Canadians are afraid of Paper and would never take the Congress Money. To enter a Country which you mean to make a Friend of, with an Army that must have occasion every Day for fresh Provision, Horses, Carriages Labour of every kind; having no acceptable Money to pay those that serve you; and to be obliged therefore, from the Necessity of the Case, to take that Service by Force, is the sure Way to disgust, offend, and by Degrees make Enemies of the whole People, after which all your Operations will be more Difficult, all your Motions discovered, and every endeavour used to have you driven back out of their Country.[37]

Franklin might have expanded on his thoughts about the failed invasion had he completed his memoirs. The index he had drawn up had sections with titles like "Canada delenda est" (Canada must be destroyed) and "To Canada." He stopped writing before he got to those parts.

What if Montgomery Had Succeeded?

It is worth asking whether the Americans could have held on to Canada if Montgomery and Arnold had taken Quebec City. That depended on what the Americans, British, French Canadians, and Indigenous Peoples did next. The French Canadians were key in this calculation because there were so many of them. Would an American victory have persuaded a sufficient number to actively support the rebel cause and help the Americans withstand a British attempt to retake Quebec City? Would the Indigenous Peoples have joined what looked like the winning side? Would the British have sent their fleet to the captured city? Or would those ships and men have been redirected to New York City, which the British considered important? Would victory in Canada have encouraged the rebels in the thirteen colonies to redouble their efforts elsewhere in the colonies, thus forcing the British to send more ships and troops to those locations? Or would taking Quebec have given the rebel leaders the advantage they needed to press Britain to reconcile with the colonies on their terms, as some hoped? Would Washington have stuck with his plan to send north ten battalions, which at full strength would have numbered just over seven thousand men? Some were already heading to Canada in May and June. They turned around when they met the rebel army fleeing south. Washington admitted to John Hancock in late April 1776 that he was in a quandary. He wanted to reinforce the army in Canada, but he also needed an additional ten thousand men in New York because he feared the British would soon attack. With so many variables, it is impossible to guess whether the Americans could have retained control of a conquered Canada. Recapture by the British was a strong possibility but not a certainty.

Americans Had Not Given Up

Neither Franklin nor other rebel leaders discarded the idea of conquering Canada, even after the invasion failed. Some coveted it for security reasons alone. Franklin had a vision of the colonists peopling the continent and had made an economic argument to support that idea. In one of their last joint letters to the congress about Canada, Chase and Carroll picked up on that theme. "The importance of this colony will be made known to you by Dr. Franklin," they wrote. "It is a fine wheat country; it produced in 1771, for exportation, four hundred and sixty thousand bushels of wheat. The Indian [fur] trade is an object already sufficient to engage the attention of the Colonies; and growing yearly of more importance." As for the French Canadians, Chase and Carroll said they were "timorous and unsteady" and would only support the Americans if the army looked strong enough to cope with the British forces.[38]

Several more military invasions were planned over the next few years, including one under the Marquis de Lafayette, a young French noble eager for military glory who had joined the American army before France officially entered the war. All came to naught, largely because fighting closer to home took priority. Franklin continued to think of ways the United States could secure Canada through other means. He is thought to be the author of a document called "Sketch of Propositions for a Peace," found in his papers after his death. It is not clear whether it was sent to anyone or was just a summary of his latest musings on how to gain control of Canada. Written in the autumn of 1776, it called for Britain to cede to the United States the provinces or colonies of Quebec, St. John's Island (now Prince Edward Island), Nova Scotia, Bermuda, East and West Florida, and the Bahamas, with all adjoining territories that were claimed by Britain.[39] In return, the United States would pay Britain an undetermined amount of money per year (the space for the exact amount was left blank in the document) and guarantee free trade to British subjects throughout this expanded version of the United States. Further down, the document suggested the amount could be £100,000 per year for a hundred years. "It is worth our while to offer such a sum for the countries to be ceded," the author said, "since the vacant lands will in time sell for a great part of what we shall give, if not more; and if we are to obtain them by conquest, after perhaps a long war, they will probably cost us more than that sum." These peace proposals were not written in Franklin's hand but are attributed to him because he expressed similar ideas in other documents.

His ideas did not change, even as he set out for France on October 26, 1776, on the American sloop *Reprisal.* France seemed the most likely prospect for foreign support because of the size of its navy and its long-standing rivalry with Britain. That it was a Catholic power, an absolute monarchy, and a long-term adversary of the colonists in North America was deemed secondary to their urgent need for money, weapons, and men. The congress named Franklin, Silas Deane, and Thomas Jefferson as ambassadors to France on September 26, 1776. Jefferson declined because his wife was ill. He was replaced by Arthur Lee, who was in London.

Franklin had already given the matter of how to approach France considerable thought, having been on the committee tasked with drawing up foreign treaties, the first of which was to be with France. His initial instructions were to obtain the support of France for American independence. He was then asked to negotiate a peace agreement with Britain. Those negotiations presented him with what would be his last chance to annex Canada.

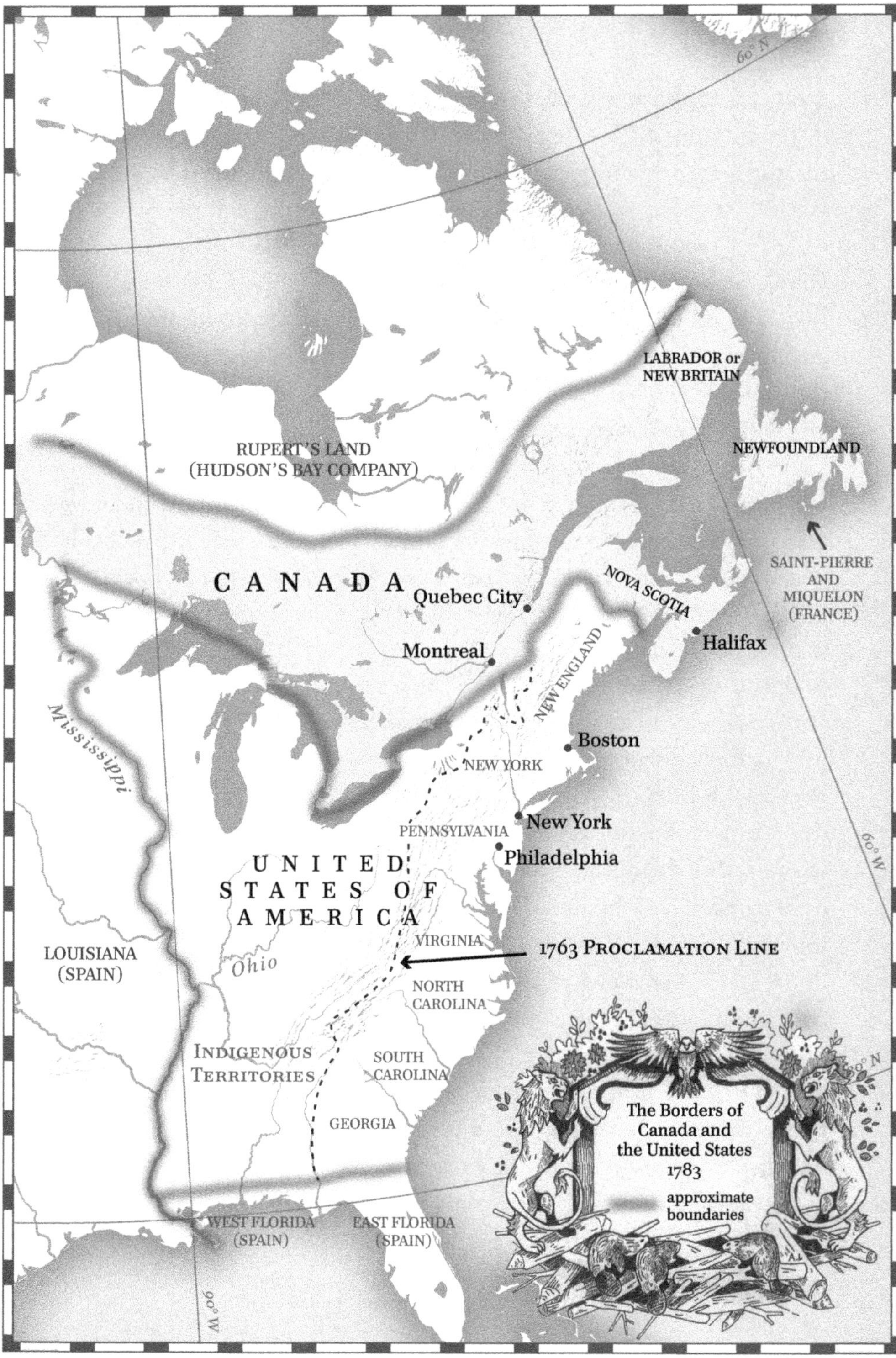

60° N
LABRADOR or NEW BRITAIN
NEWFOUNDLAND
RUPERT'S LAND (HUDSON'S BAY COMPANY)
SAINT-PIERRE AND MIQUELON (FRANCE)
NOVA SCOTIA
CANADA
Quebec City
Halifax
Montreal
NEW ENGLAND
Mississippi
Boston
NEW YORK
New York
PENNSYLVANIA
Philadelphia
60° W
UNITED STATES OF AMERICA
VIRGINIA
1763 PROCLAMATION LINE
LOUISIANA (SPAIN)
Ohio
NORTH CAROLINA
INDIGENOUS TERRITORIES
SOUTH CAROLINA
GEORGIA
The Borders of Canada and the United States 1783
approximate boundaries
WEST FLORIDA (SPAIN)
EAST FLORIDA (SPAIN)
90° W

CHAPTER 9

The Final Attempt: Paris 1776–1783

> After a Quarrel between Friends, nothing tended so much to conciliate, as Offers made by the Aggressor, of Reparation for Injuries done by him in his Passion. And I hinted that if England should make us a Voluntary Offer of Canada expressly for that purpose it might have a good Effect.[1]
>
> — *Benjamin Franklin*

FRANKLIN RECEIVED A RAPTUROUS WELCOME WHEN HE ARRIVED IN France in December 1776. From the moment the American envoy stepped off the boat in Auray, a small Atlantic port in Brittany, to his arrival in Paris, he was wined and dined by the notables on his route. His celebrity soared higher once he settled in the French capital. Admirers put engravings of him on their mantelpieces, struck medallions featuring his face, and put his image on everything from handkerchiefs to clocks. French women adopted a hairstyle *à la Franklin* that mimicked his marten fur cap, acquired on his trip to Canada and still worn for warmth and effect. "At his arrival he became an object of veneration to all enlightened men, and of curiosity to others," remarked French philosopher Marie-Jean-Antoine-Nicolas de Caritat, Marquis de Condorcet.[2] Franklin basked in the attention. He had not been in France a week when he wrote his sister Jane: "You can have no conception of the respect with which I am received and treated here by the first people, in my private character, for as yet I have assumed no public One."[3]

Franklin's fame was based mostly on his scientific accomplishments. His paper on electrical experiments had been translated and published in France in 1752. He was made a foreign associate of the prestigious Académie des sciences in 1772. A two-volume set of his works was published the next year. On the inside cover of these volumes was a portrait of Franklin, wearing a wig and holding a quill in his hand. The inscription read: "He stole the fire of Heavens and caused the arts to flourish in savage climes. America has placed him at the head of her sages. Greece would have set him among her gods."[4] That some mistakenly thought he was the instigator of the American revolution only enhanced his reputation. The Enlightenment was well underway in France, led by philosophers like Condorcet. Its adherents thought that progress in the natural and social sciences would improve human life. In a society that placed a high value on the arts, sciences, and knowledge, Franklin was the eighteenth-century equivalent of a rock star.

The warmth of his reception did not go unnoticed in London, where those paying attention to the strife in the thirteen colonies were keeping a watchful eye on his movements. "I hear that Dr Franklin had a most extraordinary reception in Paris from all ranks of People," Edmund Burke, the politician and former New York agent, observed in January 1777 to Charles Watson-Wentworth, the Marquess of Rockingham, who led the Whig political faction that opposed the war. Burke speculated that Franklin had travelled across the Atlantic to seek French support and was not fleeing the chaos in the colonies, as his critics had suggested. The Franklin he knew would not indulge in "so foul and so dishonourable a flight." Burke predicted the French would refuse to help and that Franklin would then try to negotiate a peace deal with the British ambassador to France, David Murray, the Viscount of Stormont. This, he suggested, provided an opportunity for Rockingham and his Whigs to act as mediators. It would be unnatural for the Americans to put themselves at the mercy of their "bitter, uniform, and systematik Enemies," Burke wrote, referring to the French, when they could turn to people like Rockingham, who had supported them all along.[5]

Franklin Seeks Money, Men, and Weapons in France

Unnatural or not, the congress had instructed Franklin to seek the aid of France. At the time of his departure, the rebellious colonists were still licking their wounds from the failed invasion of Canada and bracing for an anticipated attack from the north by the British forces, who had lifted the siege of Quebec City. They were desperately short of men, money, gunpowder, and ships. The Americans had suffered "manifold misfortunes," Robert Morris, the banker who was now chairman of the committee of secret correspondence, wrote Franklin in late December 1776. British troops had taken Fort Washington on the northern tip of Manhattan the previous month, capturing almost three thousand American prisoners. British warships prowled the coasts and blocked harbours, severely limiting much-needed trade. There were rumours Britain was gathering another eight thousand men, mostly mercenaries from the state of Hesse-Kassel, to invade Virginia and Maryland and that the enslaved people in those colonies would rise up, with British encouragement. Without support from France, the Americans would lose the war.[6]

Franklin carried with him a draft treaty for the French king to sign. Although he had been on the committee that created it, most of the writing had been done by John Adams. It largely focused on commercial relations, as Adams had wanted. However, one article in the draft stipulated that France would not invade or attempt to possess Canada, Nova Scotia, Labrador, Newfoundland, Cape Breton, or a host of other British possessions because the United States wanted to have "the Sole, exclusive undivided and perpetual Possession of all the Countries, Cities, and Towns, on the Said Continent."[7]

Franklin would spend the next six years in negotiations, first for French support for American independence and then for a peace agreement between the United States and Britain. He and a revolving cast of co-commissioners achieved both major goals. But throughout this time, he never completely took his eye off Canada. As peace talks with Britain neared their end in 1782, he would make his last, ultimately futile, effort to make Canada an American possession. His failure would create the conditions for the modern country of Canada to emerge and lay the foundations of future relations between the two political entities. The final deal would draw a line part-way across the continent, with the United States of America on one side and British North America on the other. Its terms would also drive tens of thousands of royalists (known as loyalists in Canada) northward, boosting Canada's population.

Why the Americans Turned to France

Burke, the British parliamentarian and friend to the American colonists, had a point when he questioned why the Americans would turn to France for support, given the long and bloody history of conflict in North America and the prevailing view in the colonies that Catholic France was an absolutist tyranny. But as David Ramsay, an American who wrote one of the first histories of the revolution, would explain in 1789: "Individuals are sometimes influenced by considerations of friendship and generosity, but interest is the pole star by which nations are universally governed." He added, "It was in the interest of the congress to apply to the court of France, and it was in the interest of France to listen to their application."[8]

In some ways, France was an attractive ally for the Americans. It had been plotting its revenge on Britain since it had signed a costly and humiliating peace treaty at the end of the Seven Years' War. In recent years, it had overhauled and streamlined its army, abolishing expensive units like the king's guards, including the Musketeers. It had rearmed the infantry with the Model 1777 Charleville musket, considered more reliable than the Brown Bess used by the British. The French army numbered about 140,000 in 1775, compared with about 45,000 in the British army. Britain's strength was in its navy. But here, too, the French had been busy. They had rebuilt their fleet since the last war. With the support of their ally, Spain, they could challenge Britain on the high seas.

France was the prize the delegates had in mind when they drafted the model foreign treaty in 1776, although they also solicited aid elsewhere, sending commissioners to Spain, the Netherlands, Russia, and Tuscany. The congressional delegates appointed Franklin, Silas Deane, and Arthur Lee to negotiate with the ministers of Louis XVI. They were to offer the French reciprocal free trade with the colonies, naval co-operation (although they did not have much of a navy), continued rights to a share of the fishery off Newfoundland, and an opportunity to have their revenge on Britain for territory lost in the 1763 peace treaty that ended the Seven Years' War.

There were potential pitfalls for the colonists in teaming up with their former enemy. It left them open, at home and abroad, to charges they had previously flung at Britain, such as encouraging popery in the colonies by tolerating the practice of Catholicism in Canada in the 1774 Quebec Act and using foreign mercenaries by signing contracts for Hessian troops for use in North America. There was also a lingering fear among the colonists that if France helped them drive British troops from Canada, it might be tempted to regain control of its former colony. That would leave the Americans back where they were before the last war, with the French on their doorstep, close enough to attack if an alliance struck to counter the British faltered. These were risks that the majority of congressional delegates were willing to take if independence was the result. They were not all of the same mind. Robert R. Livingston, a delegate from New York, proposed as early as January 1776 to offer "the quiet possession of Canada" to the French if they rerouted seven thousand French troops supposedly bound for the West Indies to the colonies to help the Americans fight the British. "It may indeed be objected that this would not be treating the Canadians as we promised them," said Livingston, who was a lawyer. "But it should be remembered that our promises were founded on their accession to the union & confederacy of these colonies, with which they have never yet complied."[9]

France Did Not Want Canada Back

The problem with this line of thinking was that official France did not want Canada back. It had been an expensive colony to maintain, and the senior

French ministers had been glad to be rid of it after the British conquest of 1760. France did not fight for it when the great powers traded territories prior to the final 1763 treaty, and they were not about to fight for it now. The policy pursued by the foreign minister, Charles Gravier, comte de Vergennes, but kept carefully hidden throughout the talks from Franklin and his co-commissioners was that Britain would keep Canada. Vergennes was a seasoned diplomat, having been ambassador in Constantinople and Stockholm. He wanted the newly independent thirteen colonies to remain anxious and dependent on France for support and trade. There were rumours that Britain was thinking of ceding Canada to France for similar reasons. Leaving the American colonies surrounded by French and Spanish territories would leave them dependent on Britain for support. Neither France nor Britain wanted Canada, but nor did they want the Americans to have it. For Vergennes, aiding the Americans was always about hindering Britain in what France perceived was the far more important fight for global supremacy.

French officials had begun musing along these lines shortly after the 1763 peace treaty was signed. Choiseul, foreign minister from 1758 to 1770, suggested to Louis XV in 1765 that a revolution in the thirteen colonies would work in France's favour as it would weaken Britain and increase the already sizeable British debt.[10] Were that to occur, Britain would no longer be feared in Europe. Choiseul wrote this at a time when the tensions between the colonies and the motherland were apparent, but the revolution was not yet in sight. He sent a series of agents to the American colonies, starting in 1764. They, like the agents he sent to Africa, India, and elsewhere in Europe, reported back on Britain's weaknesses and looked for ways to exploit them. That was doubtless what François-Marie Durand de Distroff had been doing in 1767 when he met Franklin, then a colonial representative in London. Franklin observed in a letter to his son that Durand "desired to have all my political writings, invited me to dine with him, was very inquisitive, treated me with great civility, makes me visits, &c. I fancy that intriguing nation would like very well to meddle on occasion, and blow up the coals between Britain and her colonies; but I hope we shall give them no opportunity."[11] Durand paved the way for Franklin's visit to France that year, providing letters of recommendation.

When Vergennes took over responsibility for foreign affairs in 1774, he had adopted many of Choiseul's views and policies. The alliance between France and Spain, both ruled by members of the House of Bourbon, was to be preserved. France would wage war with Britain only when there was a good chance of success. In the meantime, Vergennes would follow Choiseul's practice of using agents to keep an eye on British activities around the globe. He agreed with the suggestion of the French ambassador in London, Adrien-Louis de Bonnières, comte de Souastre, duc de Guînes, to send Julien Alexandre Achard de Bonvouloir, a retired military officer, as a secret agent to the thirteen colonies. Bonvouloir was to pretend to be a merchant looking for business. In this guise, he met with Franklin in Philadelphia in 1775 and discussed the possibility of a political and military relationship with France. Vergennes had told de Guînes that Bonvouloir had two main tasks: report back on the mood and events and reassure the Americans that France was not interested in recovering Canada.[12]

Vergennes Lays Out French Foreign Policy

After the American colonists invaded Canada in 1775, but before they declared independence, Vergennes wrote *Considérations*, a summary of French foreign policy that was printed in March 1776. His opinions were informed by reports from agents, including a February 1776 dispatch from Bonvouloir in Philadelphia, saying the colonists were on the verge of declaring independence. He also received multiple letters from a secret agent in London, the playwright Pierre-Augustin Caron de Beaumarchais, who urged France to secretly aid the Americans by supplying them with money and munitions. (Beaumarchais wrote *The Barber of Seville* and *The Marriage of Figaro.*) A continued war between Britain and her colonies would be "infinitely advantageous" to France and Spain, Vergennes wrote in *Considérations*, because it would "exhaust the victors and the vanquished." One way to encourage a prolonged conflict was to secretly aid the colonists while publicly assuring Britain that France and Spain wanted to maintain peaceful relations. There could be no treaty with the colonists until they were independent.[13]

Vergennes acknowledged there were potential downsides for France in siding with the colonists. The French were wary of Britain deciding to reconcile with the colonists, either because of a change of ministry in London or because the British would realize they were not capable of winning the war. A sudden reconciliation would leave France exposed and vulnerable. He feared that following a reconciliation, a combined British-colonial force might attack French possessions in the West Indies. Even if there were no reconciliation and the rebellious colonists won, a vengeful Britain might attack France in Europe, in the hope of distracting the British public from that defeat with a significant conquest closer to home. The newly independent colonies might themselves turn to conquests in the West Indies if their trade links with Britain were severed. Vergennes laid out all these possibilities and said it would be best not to make any precipitate move. Should Britain exhaust itself in the fight with the Americans, France could then strike a decisive blow. This, he hoped, would "return England to the order of secondary powers" and "deliver the Universe from a greedy Tyrant who wants to devour all the power and all the riches at one time."[14]

A second statement on foreign policy, *Refléxions*, written by Vergennes's secretary but possibly dictated by the minister, gave more details on how French support for the colonists could harm Britain and help France. One possible outcome was that France could recover some of the North American possessions it lost, such as Cape Breton, and fishing rights in the Gulf of St. Lawrence. Not included in this list of potential repossessions was New France. "We do not talk of Canada," the document said bluntly.[15]

The French king was uneasy about aiding rebellious subjects of any monarch but changed his mind when told that the British wanted to seize the French sugar islands. The royal reversal pleased Vergennes but angered the finance minister, Anne-Robert-Jacques Turgot, who resigned in protest. Turgot had argued, rightly it turned out, that the expense of a war with Britain, which would inevitably follow, would exhaust the French treasury. Its involvement in the war eventually cost France an estimated one billion livres. The resulting debt contributed to the financial crisis that helped prompt the French Revolution.

Yet in 1777, Vergennes was feeling optimistic. In a December 1777 letter to Armand Marc, comte de Montmorin Saint-Hérem, the French representative in Spain, he said that "the interest for separating the English Colonies from their mother country and preventing them from ever being re-identified in any manner whatever is so important that even if it had to be purchased at the price of a somewhat disadvantageous war, if the two Crowns [France and Spain] brought about that separation, it seems that they should not regret that war, whatever the issue may be."[16] He would try to limit the territorial growth of the United States to keep them from growing too large and too strong. "We do not desire that the new republic that is emerging become the exclusive master of this immense continent," Vergennes told Montmarin in a subsequent letter.[17]

The British Keep an Eye on Franklin in Paris

The French government had begun its clandestine support for the Americans before Franklin arrived. In the spring of 1776, it had given one million livres to Rodrigue Hortalez and Co., a dummy corporation set up by Beaumarchais to buy munitions and supplies in Europe and transport them across the Atlantic. The Spanish government provided a matching sum. None of this was a secret to the British ministers, who were kept informed by Stormont, their ambassador in France, of ships laden with supplies, arms, and French officers leaving for the thirteen colonies. Stormont wrote almost daily to his superiors in London, passing on court gossip and information about the comings and goings of the American representatives. He did not have a high opinion of Franklin, calling him "a subtle, artful man, and void of all truth." But he recognized that Franklin stood "high in the general opinion" and could use his connections to further the American cause. "I look upon him as a dangerous engine," Stormont wrote in one report, "and am very sorry that some English frigate did not meet with him on the way."[18] It delighted the ambassador that Franklin was frustrated by the seeming reluctance of the court and Vergennes to officially engage with him. It took almost a full year for the French foreign minister to signal he was ready to begin negotiations on a treaty that would recognize American independence.

Franklin was not idle while he waited. He kept up his contacts with the philosophers and scientists he had met on previous trips in 1767 and 1769. He got in touch with Voltaire when he learned the French scholar had returned to Paris in 1778 after a long period in exile. He also set about building a comfortable life at Passy, then a village outside Paris, and gaining an entree to French society to publicize the American cause.

A Luxurious Lifestyle for the "Homespun" Philosopher

Franklin lived a life of comparative luxury in a wing of the Hôtel de Valentinois, a mansion owned by Jacques-Donatien Le Ray de Chaumont. Chaumont was a rich entrepreneur who hoped to profit by selling weapons, ammunition, and supplies to the Americans. He was one of several Frenchmen whose aid to the Americans eventually led to their own financial ruin. At Passy, Franklin was able to stroll in the formal gardens and entertain guests. He was reported to have a wine collection of more than a thousand bottles. He told a friend that he dined out six days in seven and kept a coach and horses for such purposes. His lifestyle would eventually offend his co-commissioners John Adams and his old enemy, Arthur Lee. Adams was upset that Franklin rarely attended to business and instead slept late, dined out frequently, went to plays, and spent his evening with ladies, who sang and played pianofortes or played chess or checkers with him. "The Life of Dr. Franklin was a Scene of continual discipation," Adams wrote in his diary on May 27, 1778. Franklin was unrepentant. While he had preached frugality for decades, often under his assumed persona of Poor Richard, he later admitted privately that it was "a Virtue I never could acquire in my self."[19]

What scandalized the straitlaced Adams were Franklin's *amitié amoureuses*, intimate but not necessarily sexual relationships with women. In Passy, he spent two evenings a week drinking tea and playing chess with Anne-Louise Brillon de Jouy, a married composer. He also spent considerable time with Anne-Catherine de Ligniville Helvétius, the widow of a philosopher. He would later propose marriage to Madame Helvétius but in such a jocular manner that her refusal did not end their friendship. There is no doubt Franklin enjoyed the company of women. But there was a practical side to the relationships. The women introduced him to influential members of French society, whose support he needed for the American cause. "Every fête he consented to receive, every house where he consented to go, spread in society new admirers, who became so many partisans of the American Revolution," said Condorcet.[20]

On public occasions, Franklin presented a different image to the world. At a time when men wore colourful clothes, replete with ribbons and lace, and powdered wigs, he usually dressed plainly in sober colours and often wore his fur cap. It was a calculated pose. "Figure me in your mind as jolly as formerly, and as strong and hearty, only a few Years older, very plainly dress'd, wearing my thin grey strait Hair, that peeps out under my only Coiffure, a fine Fur Cap, which comes down my Forehead almost to my Spectacles," he wrote his British friend Emma Thompson. "Think how this must appear among the Powder'd Heads of Paris."[21] His style of dress entranced those philosophers who saw him as the living embodiment of the simple, virtuous, liberty-loving American, a frontier philosopher. One of his admirers, Louis Philippe, comte de Ségur, contrasted Franklin's appearance to the opulence of Versailles and the courtiers who gathered there. "His clothing was rustic, his bearing simple but dignified, his language direct, his hair unpowdered," said Ségur. "It was as though classic simplicity, the future of a thinker of the time of Plato, or a republican of the age of Cato or Fabius had suddenly been brought by magic into our effeminate and slavish age, the eighteenth century."[22] It was not received quite so well by those who still believed the colonists were inferior to Europeans. One anonymous pamphlet that was circulated in Paris called Franklin "the dean of all charlatans" and said that the senior French ministers "swallowed his humbug."[23]

France Waits to Go Public Until Americans Prove Themselves

Franklin had focused on making a splash in society until Vergennes finally agreed to talk about a treaty in December 1777, shortly after news reached the court in Versailles that the Americans had handed the British a stunning defeat at Saratoga, in the colony of New York. British General

John Burgoyne, who had led a large force south from Canada, as the Americans had anticipated, had been forced to surrender, along with an estimated six thousand British and Hessian troops. Vergennes sent his first secretary, Conrad Alexandre Gérard, to Passy to tell Franklin and his co-commissioners, Silas Deane and Arthur Lee, that it was now clear the colonies had the ability and the resolution to become independent. He invited them to resubmit the proposals they had sent to him months earlier for their proposed alliance with France.

Things moved quickly. On February 6, 1778, France and the United States signed two treaties. The first, the Treaty of Amity and Commerce between the United States of America and His Most Christian Majesty, focused on trade and mutual co-operation at sea. In making the treaty, France was acknowledging that it regarded the United States of America as a sovereign nation. The second, the Treaty of Alliance between the United States of America and His Most Christian Majesty, was a more political document. In it France and the United States pledged to join forces against Britain if it declared war on France. Both promised not to conclude a peace deal with Britain without the formal consent of the other, a promise Franklin would later break. The United States, as it now called itself, made clear its intentions for Canada in two articles of that treaty. Article 5 stated that if the United States decided to drive the British from northern North America and the Bermudas, "those Countries or Islands in case of Success, shall be confederated with or dependent upon the said United States." In article 6, the French king renounced forever possession of the Bermudas, as well as any part of the continent of North America that belonged to Britain or the United States.

The French and Americans tried to keep the second treaty secret, but the British knew about it almost immediately. Like France and the United States, Britain maintained a network of agents and spies. Edward Bancroft, secretary to the American delegation in Paris, was a secret agent for Britain throughout the negotiations. So, too, was William Carmichael, the secretary for Deane, and John Thornton, the secretary for Lee. Bancroft wrote hundreds of reports, often using invisible ink between the lines of fake love letters.[24]

Stormont, who also listened to court gossip and traded tidbits with his fellow ambassadors, had a good idea of what was in the treaties even before they were ratified by the congress in Philadelphia. In his letters to London, he agonized about whether to challenge the French openly on their "dark and treacherous machinations" or whether Britain might gain more "advantage, dignity, and the appearance of superior strength and vigor by striking the first blow."[25] The treaties forced the hand of George III, who declared war on France on March 17, 1778. The king would declare war on Spain in 1779 and on the Netherlands in 1780. Stormont was told to return to England. The king could pretend not to know about French covert aid to the Americans, but the open acknowledgement of American independence by France, accompanied by a pledge of military support against Britain, could not be ignored.

Franklin Presses for Annexation of Canada

The entry of France into the war started a new and ultimately decisive phase in the American Revolution. Britain and France were now openly fighting over their global possessions, chief among them the United States. Britain would have to fight on many fronts, rather than concentrating on its battle with the Americans. In this struggle, Canada was a mere pawn. The Americans wanted it. The French wanted the British to keep it but did not want the Americans to know. The British did not really want possession but thought that might be better than any other outcome. The rich fishing grounds off Newfoundland and in the Gulf of St. Lawrence were treated as separate issues, belonging as they did to the colonies of Newfoundland and Nova Scotia. In contrast to the territory of Canada, fishing rights elicited intense interest from all three parties, who fought over them to the end.

Throughout 1778 Franklin pressed his case with British friends for the annexation of Canada. He told James Hutton, a Scottish scientist, that if Britain wanted to show generosity and goodwill it could "throw in" Canada, Nova Scotia, and the two Floridas as part of any peace negotiations.[26] He sent the same suggestion to David Hartley, an English politician and inventor, and urged him to circulate it among his friends.[27] He wrote Hartley again in October 1778, saying it would be better for England to act nobly and generously and cede "all that remains in North America."[28]

The Americans were contemplating another invasion of Canada in 1778. For a while, it looked like a plan strongly backed by Lafayette, now a major general in the American army, would proceed. The congress sent a copy of the plan to Franklin on October 28, 1778, along with general instructions on its preferred relationship with France. He was told to present the invasion plan to the French ministers, telling them it was necessary "for the emancipation of Canada."[29] The plan called for an estimated 12,600 colonial troops, backed by another 4,000–5,000 men from France, to make multiple attacks all along the border between the United States and Canada, ranging from Detroit to Quebec City. If these attacks were successful, a French-American force would then attack the British naval base at Halifax, and eventually the British posts in Newfoundland. Military success would help France, the congress reasoned, because it would restore French control of the fur trade, protect its share of the fisheries, and open new markets for its manufactures. For the U.S., victory would eliminate the threat from the north, add new states to the union, and eliminate the British from the Newfoundland fishery, which would deprive them of fish and harm their ability to use the fishery as a training ground for sailors who could serve in the navy.

Washington Nixes New Invasion Plan

However, Washington, in his role as commander-in-chief, considered the plan impractical and overly dependent on luck. He said as much to the congress in November 1778. In a letter to Henry Laurens, then president of the congress, he went into detail about the poor state of the rebel army and the slim chance the plan would succeed. "I view the emancipation of Canada, as an Object very interesting to the future prosperity and tranquility of these States; but I am sorry to say — the plan proposed for the purpose does not appear to me to be eligible, under our present circumstances." He talked about the danger of the Americans not being able to fulfill their part of the plan, which might cause distrust and discontent on the French side, especially if they had a better use for their forces elsewhere in the world. He also thought the American colonists would not like to continue living in a state of insecurity while as many as 12,600 men were sent to pursue what he called "remote Objects." And he was by no means sure he would be able to find those men or transport the supplies they would need.

In a private letter to Laurens a few days later, Washington confessed he feared the French would not leave Canada if they had a hand in conquering it. The possession of Canada would give France seaports on the continent, the ability to monopolize the Newfoundland fishery, enhanced security for French islands in the West Indies, and the capability of dictating to the United States, which would be sandwiched between Catholic France in the north and Catholic Spain in the south, with Indigenous Peoples friendly to France to the west. He suspected that while Lafayette presented the plan as his own, it might have originated with the French ministry. "Canada would be a solid acquisition to France on all these accts and because of the Numerous inhabitants, subjects to her by inclination, who would aid in preserving it under her power against the attempt of every other," he wrote.[30] Washington's public and private objections proved persuasive. The congress set aside the invasion plan on January 1, 1779. It was not seriously considered again during the course of the war.

The Congress Grows Lukewarm About Canada

If Franklin were to win Canada, he would have to do it at the negotiating table. He was well placed to do so. The congress had made him minister plenipotentiary to the French court in September 1778 and recalled his colleagues Deane and Lee after the commissioners fell to arguing among themselves. At a congressional hearing into the causes of these "suspicions and animosities," Deane was accused of misappropriating funds, Lee of being unspeakably rude to the French, and Franklin of withholding information from the others, being haughty and self-sufficient, "and not guided by principles of virtue or honour."[31] There was some suspicion he had become too close to the French. Mercy Otis Warren, the historian and friend of John Adams, said Franklin remained attached to American interests but was "intoxicated by the warm caresses and unbounded applause of all ranks," which made him susceptible to French influence.[32] The congress held a vote on his recall but decided to leave him in place. However, the delegates decided to augment the negotiating team for peace talks with Britain to better reflect the views of the colonists. They added John Jay of New York, John Adams of Massachusetts, Thomas Jefferson of Virginia, and Henry Laurens of South Carolina. Only Jay and Adams made it to France in time to participate in the negotiations.

Franklin's room for manoeuvre, however, was shrinking. Canada had slipped well down the list of congressional priorities by the time a committee began writing instructions for its peace negotiators. The committee's first report, delivered in February 1779, dealt at length with the Newfoundland fisheries and the possible cession of Nova Scotia but did not mention the British ceding Canada to the United States. Its final report, approved by the congress in August 1779, raised the question of Canada but linked its fate to that of Nova Scotia and the fisheries. The report said that "although it is of the utmost importance to the peace and Commerce of the United States that Canada and Nova Scotia should be ceded, and more particularly that their equal common right to the Fisheries should be guarantied to them, yet a desire of terminating the war hath induced us not to make the acquisition of these objects an ultimatum on the present occasion."[33] Gérard, now the representative of France in the colonies, had warned the delegates not to make excessive demands if they wanted peace. This approach fit with France's covert policy of leaving Canada in British hands.

According to these instructions, Franklin could still make a play for Canada, but he could not make its annexation a condition of any peace agreement. He had a few years to mull over how he would approach this problem because negotiations did not start in earnest until the hawkish North ministry in Britain fell in March 1782. It was replaced by a ministry led by Rockingham, whose leading members wanted to end the war and were sympathetic to the American cause. Among them was Shelburne, who had known Franklin since at least 1766. Franklin had lobbied Shelburne on behalf of his son, William, about securing land in the contested area west of the Appalachians when Franklin was a colonial agent in London. The two had subsequent conversations about American affairs.

Franklin Renews His Quest for Canada

Franklin wasted no time in renewing their acquaintance. He wrote Shelburne on March 22, 1782, relating news of their mutual friends Abbé Morellet and Madame Helvétius. Shelburne responded on April 6. He was home secretary in the new ministry, a position that made him partly responsible for the colonies. He told Franklin he was sending Richard Oswald to France for informal talks. Oswald was a former slave trader, who had acquired estates in the West Indies and America through marriage and made money as an army contractor during the Seven Years' War.[34] Shelburne described him as an honest, practical man who knew Shelburne's thoughts.[35] The home secretary would later be criticized for selecting for this important mission a man who, while loyal to Shelburne, was inexperienced as a diplomat and intellectually outmatched by the American negotiators.

Oswald had barely arrived in France in mid-April 1782 when Franklin raised the idea with him of Britain making a gift of Canada to the United States. If Britain wanted reconciliation, they should offer reparations to the Americans, including those who had suffered from British "scalping and burning parties," Franklin wrote in a journal, recounting the conversation. "I spoke of the occasions of future quarrel that might be produced by her continuing to hold it; hinting at the same time, but not expressing too plainly, that such a situation, to us so dangerous, would necessarily oblige us to cultivate and strengthen our union with France." He also suggested that money raised by selling "vacant lands" in Canada would be used to compensate Americans whose homes were burned by the British and royalists whose estates had been confiscated. He sent Adams, then in the Netherlands, a partial summary of the April 19 meeting, saying Oswald liked the idea and said he would try to persuade the British ministry.[36]

It was about this time that Franklin produced another one of his hoaxes, this one designed to bolster his claim that Britain owed the Americans reparations. Using the private printing press he had set up at Passy, he published what looked like a special, two-page supplement to the Boston *Independent Chronicle.* To add authenticity, he made up advertisements. The first page carried a letter supposedly written by a militia captain from New England, who described capturing what he thought were bales of furs from the enemy, only to find that eight of the bales contained scalps of "our unhappy country-folks." The American scalps, the letter said, had been taken by the Seneca and were being sent as a gift to the British governor of Canada, Frederick Haldimand, who had succeeded Carleton. The militia captain brought them to Boston, where there was talk of shaming Britain by sending scalps taken from women and children to the queen, with the rest distributed to the king, members of Parliament, and bishops.[37] Franklin sent copies of his hoax to Adams, Jay, and several European and British friends. It was printed in the British press several months later.

Franklin knew, of course, that the British, the French, and the American colonists had offered scalp bounties to their Indigenous allies for some time, encouraging a practice that predated the European arrival in North America. Franklin himself had written a captain under his command on the frontier in 1756, reminding him that the colonial government paid a bounty for scalps. After attacks by the French and their Indigenous allies on the Pennsylvania frontier during the Seven Years' War, angry settlers demanded the Pennsylvania assembly pay a bounty for Indigenous scalps they brought in. The colonies of Virginia and Maryland had done the same at the request of their colonists. The Europeans whom Franklin was targeting with his hoax probably were not aware of these details. He hoped their gullibility might play to his advantage as he painted the British as brutal oppressors.

Franklin Makes Inroads with the British Negotiator

Oswald returned to Paris in early May after conferring with the British ministry. According to Franklin's journal, Oswald said he had reason to believe that Franklin's suggestions on how Britain could achieve reconciliation "might be settled to our satisfaction towards the end of the treaty; but in his own mind he wished it might not be mentioned at the beginning."[38] It is unclear why Oswald would have raised Franklin's hopes about Canada in this way. Shelburne had written him a note just prior to the meeting, in which he rejected Franklin's reasons for why the British might hand over Canada. And yet Oswald was still making optimistic noises in June, when he told Franklin he was not without hope that it would be agreed.

In July Oswald asked Franklin to lay out clearly which points needed to be settled between Britain and the United States for peace to be achieved. Franklin gave him a list of eight items: four that were necessary for peace and four that were advisable. The necessary items were recognition of American independence and complete withdrawal of British troops, a settlement of the boundaries of the thirteen states, a reduction in the boundaries of Canada to what they were before the Quebec Act, and freedom to fish off Newfoundland and elsewhere. His advisable conditions were compensation for Americans whose properties were damaged by the British during the war, an acknowledgement by the British Parliament that it had made an error "in distressing the Colonies," an agreement that American ships and trade would have the same privileges in Britain and Ireland as British ships and trade, and the cession of Canada and Nova Scotia.[39]

In keeping with his instructions from the congress, Franklin could not insist that Britain give Canada to the Americans, which was why he described it as advisable rather than necessary. Shelburne, who became prime minister after Rockingham died in late June, wrote Oswald at the end of July to say he hoped Franklin's advisable conditions would be dropped. Yet Franklin raised Canada again when he met with Oswald in August. "The Doctor at last touched upon Canada, as he generally does upon the like occasions," Oswald wrote in a report to Thomas Townshend, Shelburne's replacement as home secretary. "He said there could be no dependence on peace and good neighbourhood while that country continued under a different government, as it touched their states in so great a stretch of frontier." Oswald told Franklin he had no orders about Canada and suggested that the matter be raised at a later date.[40]

On September 1, Oswald received definite negotiating orders. Townshend said he had shown Oswald's reports to George III, and the king authorized Oswald to agree only to the conditions Franklin had identified as necessary: America would have its independence, British troops would be withdrawn, the boundaries would be settled, and Americans would be free to fish on the Grand Banks and elsewhere. But they would not get Canada. The British might agree to reduce its borders, hugely expanded by the Quebec Act in 1774, back to the limits set in the 1763 treaty.[41] That the 1763 borders bore no relationship to the vast extent of Canada or New France at the time of the British conquest was not mentioned. Oswald duly showed Townshend's letter to Franklin.

Franklin Falls Ill at Crucial Stage in the Talks

It is unclear whether Franklin would have continued his quest for Canada had he not been sidelined by severe illness at this critical point in the negotiations. He stopped writing in his journal of the negotiations at the beginning of July. Laid low by gout and kidney stones, he handed negotiating responsibilities to Jay in September. Jay had arrived in June from Madrid, where he had been unsuccessful in negotiating a treaty with Spain. Adams, who had more luck with the Netherlands, arrived in late October. Henry Laurens, also appointed by the congress as a negotiator, had been captured by the British on his way to Europe and only weighed in at the very end. Jefferson did not go to France at this time. Franklin had suffered from gout, kidney stones, and psoriasis for many years. He may have made his problems worse by trying treatments such as Belloste's pills. These were a mixture of mercury and purgatives that their inventor, Augustin Belloste, said "expels out of the Body all that is foul, malignant, and extraneous, and that it averts the Infirmities of Old Age."[42] In Franklin's case, the pills expelled three teeth. He stopped taking them when he found the rest of his teeth were loose.

It was Jay who presented a preliminary draft of a peace treaty to Oswald on October 5. It contained Franklin's four necessary conditions, on which the two sides were generally agreed. The idea of ceding Canada to the United States had been dropped. Still to be negotiated were the exact borders, the extent of the shared fishery, and whether royalists whose properties had been confiscated by the Americans would receive compensation. The balance of the war between Britain and France had shifted with a British naval victory over the French in the West Indies in April and then another victory in September at Gibraltar, where Britain defeated the combined navies of France and Spain. The British were prepared to take a harder line in the negotiations.

Borders Are Drawn and Redrawn at the Talks

Oswald initially agreed to borders that restricted Canada to its 1763 extent and gave the Americans the lands between the western boundaries of the colonies and the Mississippi River. This was territory that both France and Britain had claimed previously and that Britain still felt belonged to the Crown, not the colonies. He also initially agreed to a northern border that would have given the United States all the Great Lakes and the area that is now southern Ontario. After Oswald sent him a draft treaty in October, Shelburne chastised him for giving in on points that were diametrically opposed to British interests. The charters the colonists said gave them traditional rights from sea to sea were "nonsense," said Shelburne, adding that "the soil is, and has always been acknowledged to be the king's."[43] He sent a home office official, Henry Strachey, to Paris to stiffen Oswald's spine. Vergennes was equally opposed when he learned how much territory the Americans were claiming. "I do not see by what title the Americans can form pretensions on Lake Ontario," he wrote in mid-October to the French agent in Philadelphia. "These lands belong to the savages, or are a dependancy of Canada. In either case, the United States have no right to them whatever."[44]

Strachey negotiated a compromise that still favoured the Americans but left more territory in British hands. The map he sent Shelburne in early November established a northern border broadly similar to the one that exists today in eastern North America. From west to east, a line was drawn through the middle of Lakes Superior, Huron, Erie, and Ontario and the St. Lawrence River to forty-five degrees latitude. It then went straight east through Lake Champlain until it hit the highlands that divide the watersheds of rivers flowing into the St. Lawrence River from those that flow into the Atlantic Ocean. The border followed this divide around the bump of what is now Maine. (Disputes about the eastern end of the border between

Maine and Nova Scotia lingered until the Webster-Ashburton Treaty of 1842). Strachey's proposed map confined the original thirteen colonies to the eastern seaboard and made the Mississippi River the western border of the United States. The land between the Appalachian Mountains and the Mississippi River was part of the United States but was meant to be reserved for the Indigenous Peoples.

Strachey and Oswald were wholly unsuccessful in persuading the Americans to compensate royalists whose properties had been confiscated during the war. The Americans portrayed themselves as the wronged party. They were entitled to compensation. The royalists were not. Franklin was still ill during this period but was frequently consulted by Jay and Adams. He had hinted royalist compensation was possible in his earliest conversation with Oswald when he suggested the Americans would get Canada, but then he reversed course and became adamantly opposed. The fact that his son, William, former governor of New Jersey, had sided with the British in the revolution might have fuelled his growing opposition to the idea that those who remained loyal to the British Crown be compensated for lost property and land. Adams observed that "Dr. Franklin is very staunch against them [the royalists], more decided a great deal on this point than Mr. Jay or myself."[45]

Britain Buys Peace by Ceding Canadian Territory

The preliminary articles of peace, signed by representatives of the United States and Britain on November 30, 1782, at the Grand Hôtel Muscovite in Paris, acknowledged American independence and used the boundaries Strachey had outlined to Shelburne. At the stroke of a pen, Britain agreed to cede an estimated 910,000 square kilometres (351,000 square miles) of territory that the French Canadians considered their hinterland. It has since become the states of Kentucky, Tennessee, Alabama, Ohio, Michigan, Indiana, Illinois, Wisconsin, and part of Minnesota. The Americans would also get unrestricted fishing rights off Newfoundland and in the Gulf of St. Lawrence, much to the joy of Adams, who had pushed hard for this concession. In return they agreed to a vague promise that the congress would "recommend" that the individual states compensate royalists whose estates, rights, or properties had been seized. Laurens arrived at the last minute, just in time to have a clause inserted to the effect that the British promised not to carry away any enslaved people.

Franklin was not quite ready to give up on Canada. Within days of signing the provisional agreement, he and John Adams drew up a list of nine more articles they would like to include before the treaty was finalized. Number seven on that list was "the concession of Canada & Nova Scotia, to join the Confederation."[46] Yet this article did not appear in the final or definitive treaty, signed September 3, 1783. That same day, France, Britain, and Spain signed a separate final peace treaty at Versailles. Britain and the Netherlands had signed a preliminary peace treaty the day before.

Franklin, Adams, and Jay later explained to the congress why they had failed to secure Canada. "The court of Great Britain insisted on retaining all the territories comprehended within the Province of Quebec by the act of Parliament respecting it," they wrote in a joint letter. "They contended that Nova Scotia should extend to the river Kennebec; and they claimed not only all the lands in the western country and on the Mississippi which were not expressly included in our charters and government, but also all such lands within them as remained ungranted by the King of Great Britain. It would be endless to enumerate all the discussions and arguments on the subject." The American negotiators decided it was more important to gain secure title to the lands between the Appalachian Mountains and the Mississippi River and retain access to the east coast fisheries than it was to insist on Canada.[47]

Vergennes was unpleasantly surprised by the terms, when he first heard of the preliminary deal. He wrote Franklin a terse, two-paragraph letter pointing out that Franklin, Adams, and Jay had ignored the explicit instructions from the congress and had sidelined the French foreign minister during the final round of negotiations. He commented to his secretary that "the English buy the peace, more than they make it. Their concessions, in fact, as much as to the boundaries, as to the fisheries, and the royalists, exceed all that I should have thought possible."[48] Vergennes saw the deal as "a kind of surrender" by the British and wondered at the motives behind such generosity. Franklin attempted to mollify him by saying the peace deal between the United States and Britain would not be finalized until France, Spain, and Britain completed their separate negotiations. That did not stop Vergennes from expressing his displeasure to the French representative in Philadelphia, who duly passed it on to the congress.

Britain Makes Continued Trade a Priority

Shelburne had a rough ride when the provisional treaty was debated in the House of Lords in February 1783. Critics accused him of destroying the fur trade, deserting the royalists, betraying the Indigenous Peoples who had fought for Britain by giving away their land, ceding land and access to the fisheries unnecessarily, leaving Canada defenceless by abandoning forts throughout the ceded territory, and sending Oswald to negotiate. Oswald had shown "shameful ignorance," said Stormont from his seat in Parliament. "What reason could be given for sending out such a man as Mr. Oswald to treat with the four American commissioners? He was far over-matched by any one of them." Shelburne replied to his critics that the fur trade was tiny, amounting to no more than £50,000 a year in imports to Britain. "Suppose the entire fur trade sunk into the sea, where is the detriment to this country?" He admitted he was not happy about the section of the treaty on the royalists, but he relied on "the wisdom, the honour, and the temper of the congress" to ensure the royalists were compensated. As for the Indigenous Peoples, they were not "abandoned to their enemies; they were remitted to the care of neighbours." Britain did not need reciprocity in fishing rights, he maintained, because it had enough already. The generous land boundaries showed the Americans "that we desired to live with them in communion of benefits, and in the sincerity of friendship." It was clear he was prepared to make any number of sacrifices to renew Britain's trade with the Americans. This would not be the last time the British went against Canadian interests to curry American favour.

Townshend, the home secretary, focused on the commercial benefits of peace when he defended the treaty in the House of Commons. He said that "it was obviously the interest of Great Britain to establish as close a commercial connection as possible between this country and the United States."

To settle the treaty, government ministers did not want "to keep back any thing the United States might justly expect." If Britain had insisted on keeping the 1774 boundary of Canada, it would have irritated the Americans, Townshend said. "It had been thought better to fix a new boundary, fair, just, and liberal, and such as the Americans themselves approved."[49]

The Americans back home very much approved of the terms when they finally received official notice of the provisional treaty on March 12, more than three months after it had been signed. There had been rumours of a possible settlement in February, brought by a merchant ship that had been in the West Indies. But it was another month before the official dispatches arrived in Philadelphia, courtesy of Captain Joshua Barney of the *Washington* packet. The treaty was read to the assembled delegates, who communicated them to family and friends the same day. "The Articles respecting the Boundaries of the United States & that respecting the right of Fishery, are Ample & I believe Equal to the most Sanguine Expectation," wrote John Taylor Gilman of New Hampshire. William Floyd of New York thought the northwest boundary was not quite right, but in general the boundaries "are as Extensive as we had any Reason to Expect, Considering our Circumstances."[50] In his notes of the debates that day, James Madison of Virginia summed up the mood: "The terms granted to America appeared to Congs. on the whole extremely liberal."[51]

Two weeks later came news that France, Britain, Spain, and the Netherlands had signed a separate provisional peace pact on January 21, 1783, following long sessions of horse-trading about who would keep what of their various global possessions. Now that all the belligerent powers had settled their differences, peace was finally at hand. The delegates to congress once more sat down at their writing desks to spread the news. In his letter of March 24, Gunning Bedford Jr. of Delaware went through the long list of islands in the Caribbean, settlements on the coast of Africa or in the East Indies, and islands in the Mediterranean that were either being restored to or retained by one of the imperial powers. North America was mentioned with respect to the east coast fisheries, where Britain and France agreed to largely maintain the terms of the 1763 treaty, and with respect to the far south, where Spain would have both East and West

Florida and a strip of land below the thirty-second parallel that included the mouth of the Mississippi.

Canada Forgotten in the First Flush of Independence

Yet in the existing letters written immediately after they received news of the provisional treaty, no delegate expressed alarm or even disappointment that it did not forcibly join Canada to the United States. Men who had backed the failed invasion of 1775–1776 or who had loudly proclaimed that Canada in British hands was an existential threat to the American colonies had nothing to say on the matter. Hamilton waited until the autumn of 1783, after he had given up his seat in the congress, to mention that the United States might want to strengthen its garrisons on the northern frontier in case the British decided to annoy them. It was not a call for another attempt at annexation. Canada was no longer a congressional priority.

This was understandable, given the perilous position of the new country. The thirteen colonies had won their independence, the single most important thing they wanted. But the United States was broke, the army was on the brink of mutiny, and delegates to the congress could not agree on how to raise money to pay bills and repay estimated debts of more than $40 million. The mood of the army was particularly concerning. The officers and enlisted men seemed likely to keep their weapons until they received their back pay and to use them if money was not forthcoming. In the weeks leading up to and following the official announcement of the provisional peace deals, the congress was consumed by debates on taxes and debt. Arthur Lee, now back in congress, complained to Samuel Adams about the mounting pressure on delegates to impose permanent taxes. "The terror of a mutinying Army is playd off with considerable efficacy," he wrote.[52]

It is possible that those who seemed to share Franklin's desire for Canada only did so when invading Canada served a military purpose in their fight with Britain. An invasion at the start of the revolution had the potential of forestalling a British attack on the thirteen colonies and tying up British soldiers, ships, and weapons that might otherwise have been used against the Americans. Once the fighting stopped, the desire may have ebbed. The overly generous terms Britain granted the United States in the peace agreement, clearly marking its intention to restore good relations, especially commercial trade, also made a future threat from the north less likely.

Lafayette was among the few to express qualified regret. He wrote the congress from Cádiz, Spain, within days of the signing of the final peace treaty. He was there, he said, with the French vice-admiral Charles Henri D'Estaing, who had forty-nine ships and twenty thousand men poised to attack the British in the West Indies and Canada. Instead, he had to offer his congratulations on the news of a general peace. "So far as respects me, I have no regret," he wrote. "But, independent of personal gratifications, it is known that I ever was bent upon the addition of Canada to the United States."[53] Franklin remained in France as the American representative until 1785, when the congress agreed to his request to return home. He was almost eighty years old and in so much pain from gout and kidney stones that Marie-Antoinette, the French queen, loaned him an enclosed litter to travel to Le Havre to board the ship.[54] He may have dressed like a frontier philosopher, but he enjoyed the trappings of luxury. He carried with him a farewell gift from Louis XVI, a small portrait of the king surrounded by diamonds. The congress later allowed him to keep it.[55]

Once home and rested, he returned to the congress and weighed in on matters, such as the creation of a constitution. But much of his time was spent in bed at home, taking laudanum (opium) to control his pain.[56] He made no further attempts to annex Canada.

The Dream of Conquering Canada Lived On

And yet the idea that the British colony should belong to the United States did not die away entirely. It flared up again in 1812, when tensions arose between Britain and the United States. Adams, who as one of the American negotiators in Paris had decided to drop the idea of acquiring Canada, had a change of heart. "Canada must be ours, to be sure, and will be ours," he wrote a friend in March 1812. "We should be dunces indeed, to leave such a nest for Conspiracies against us, in the hands of England."[57] He wrote Jefferson in June that year, saying he remembered a time "when Indian murder, scalping, depredations and conflagrations, were as frequent on the Eastern and Northern frontier of Massachusetts, as they are now in Indiana, and spread as much terror." Another conquest of Canada would "quiet the Indians forever."[58]

The United States declared war on Britain in July 1812 and promptly invaded Canada. The official reasons for war were British interference with American trade, the impressment of men on American vessels into the British navy, and alleged British efforts to inflame the Indigenous Peoples on the Americans' western frontier. But the British, and even some congressional critics of the war, thought President James Madison and his administration also meant to capture and keep Canada as part of what one British diplomat described as a system of conquest and aggrandizement that included land in the Indigenous territories, the two Floridas, and Louisiana. "It is notorious to the whole world that the conquest of Canada and its permanent annexation to the United States was the declared object of the American Government," the British negotiators wrote their American counterparts when they assembled at Ghent for peace talks.[59] They attached to their September 14, 1814, letter the proclamations made in 1812 by the American generals William Hull and Alexander Smyth. "The United States are sufficiently powerful to afford you every security, consistent with their rights, & your expectations," Hull said to Canadians after his troops had crossed the river to Sandwich (now Windsor) in Canada. "You will be emancipated from Tyranny and oppression and restored to the dignified station of freemen."[60] Smyth was even more direct when he addressed his troops in Buffalo, New York. "Companions in Arms! The time is at hand when you will cross the stream of Niagara, to conquer Canada, and secure the peace of the American frontier. You will enter a country that is to be one of the United States."[61]

The American negotiators protested that the government had not approved the words of their generals and so this was not official policy. The British team scoffed that the government had not disavowed the words. It is unclear whether the British knew that James Monroe, acting secretary of state for the U.S., had instructed his negotiators to ask for Canada. In a letter written June 23, 1813, Monroe said: "And altho' Governments and Nations are apt on such occasions, to consult, rather the pride of dominion, than their true interest, it may be worth while to bring to view, the advantages to both Countries which is promised, by a transfer of the upper parts and even the whole of Canada to the United States." He raised the matter again in a letter dated January 1, 1814, saying: "The reasons given in my letter of the 23rd June, and of the first of this Month, in favour of a cession of the Canadas to the United States, have also gained much additional force from further reflection."

It was not until the balance of the war shifted decisively in Britain's favour — and after British and Canadian troops burned the White House in Washington — that Monroe abandoned this plan and instructed the negotiators to seek a peace deal in which both parties gave back what they had taken in the fighting.[62] He was likely swayed by the anticipated end of the Napoleonic Wars in Europe. Peace in Europe would free up forces Britain could use against the Americans.

In the final year of the war, delegates to the congress were sharply divided about whether to continue. Canadians, who now included tens of thousands of royalists who had left the United States, had not rallied to the American cause, disproving the widespread assumption that they were friendly to the Americans and would offer little resistance. Jefferson had famously told a friend the acquisition of Canada would be "a mere matter of marching."[63] Once again, the Americans had misjudged local opinion. They did not overcome the British and Canadians by force, despite a huge numerical advantage in population. By one contemporary estimate, there were five hundred thousand Canadians and seven million Americans. Congressman Morris Miller of New York said his constituents and those of a colleague in New Hampshire were opposed to "this war of ambition and conquest." He wanted to end what he called "the crusade against Canada." Charles Ingersoll of Pennsylvania strongly disagreed. He reminded colleagues that Britain had suffered many defeats before it finally wrested Canada from France. "They failed, year after year, till Wolfe achieved it at last," he said. The current situation was no reason to abandon the effort to secure Canada, he said. That would only postpone it to the next generation and perhaps the one after that.[64] The implication was that eventually the Americans would succeed.

Why Franklin's Quest Mattered

While others frequently shared Franklin's belief that Canada should be American, he differed from his contemporaries in that he had the skills and means to publicize his views, as he did with the *Canada Pamphlet* in 1760, and held positions that allowed him to pursue his goal, whether it was being sent to Montreal, when it was occupied by American troops in 1776, to ask the Canadians to join the American rebellion, or inserting a clause in the Articles of Confederation in 1775 that left the door open for Canada to join. He was able to press influential friends along the way to support his quest for Canada, and he used his position as chief negotiator in Paris to repeatedly demand that Britain make a gift of Canada to the Americans. He used his celebrity, intelligence, and cunning to full effect and was not overly burdened by principles, which allowed him to indulge in hoaxes or fake news and conspiracy theories if they served his ends. He had drive, focus, and seemingly limitless curiosity well into old age.

Yet the man powerful enough to "snatch lightning from the sky and the sceptre from tyrants," as one of his French admirers said, was stymied at every turn when it came to Canada. Bad luck, bad timing, poor planning, faulty intelligence, and the whims and interests of American politicians and European powers prevented him from achieving his goal of possession. The story of his failure is also a timely reminder to Canadians that Franklin's reasons for wanting Canada — enhanced security and better access to land and resources — continue to resonate in the United States today. Understanding the deep-seated nature of these concerns is critical to the construction of a successful Canadian response to American actions.

There is a portrait of Franklin tucked away in a corner of the Château Ramezay in Montreal, now a museum. An older, sombre Franklin gazes out from the gilt frame. The plaque beside the picture has a brief description of his visit in 1776 and a quote attributed to him that it would have been easier to buy Canada than to take it by force. He had tried in so many ways to make Canada American. With apologies to Julius Caesar, the outcome of Franklin's quest can be summed up in eight words: He came, he saw, he did not conquer.

Canada
United States Bicentennial
Bicentenaire des Etats-Unis
QUEBEC
Trois Rivières
MONTREAL
Lake Champlain
ALBANY
BOSTON
Hudson
NEW YORK
Philadelphia
10

CANADA
250 ANS DE SERVICES POSTAUX
YEARS OF POSTAL HISTORY

EPILOGUE

Letting the Losers Write Canada's History

> Seeing one thing is not seeing another. Recounting one drama is forgetting another.[1]
>
> — *Paul Ricoeur*, Memory, History, Forgetting

TWO HUNDRED YEARS AFTER THE EVENTS IN THIS BOOK, CANADIAN postal officials were casting about for a way to commemorate the anniversary of the American Declaration of Independence and lit on the unlikely idea of honouring Franklin with a stamp. The choice made sense to the U.S. Postal Service, which had agreed to jointly issue a bicentennial stamp. Americans revere Franklin as a founding father, a scientific inventor, a homespun philosopher, and the diplomat who helped wrest independence from a reluctant Britain. But his connection to Canada is not so glorious. He spent decades trying — in big ways and small — to annex it to the American colonies. Why would Canadian officials want to celebrate someone who did not want Canada to exist as a separate entity?

The reason they gave was that post offices were opened in Montreal, Quebec City, and Trois-Rivières during Franklin's time as deputy postmaster general for British North America, a royal appointment he held from 1753 to 1775. It is not clear from their archived correspondence when it was that they realized that Franklin had far more than postal matters in mind with regards to Canada. By the time the Franklin stamps were sent to collectors, the information package acknowledged that Franklin visited Montreal in 1776 "to proclaim the gospel of liberty" and had asked the British to give Canada to the Americans during the Paris peace negotiations. Still, all anyone who was not a collector saw was a stamp with Franklin's face and a map from that era in the background.

It may seem quaint to talk about postage in this age of digital communication. But choosing whom or what to put on stamps was a big deal in the pre-internet days of 1976, when people corresponded with each other on paper. Ordinary Canadians cared enough about stamps to pepper the postmaster general with suggestions of appropriate subjects. Newspapers, then still a powerful medium, ran columns dedicated to stamp collectors. Governments used stamps to present their view of their country and the world and as a means of raising significant amounts of money. A Franklin stamp in 1976 would be good business for the post offices on both sides of the border.

Implicit in the choice of Franklin was the assumption that Canadians had the same view of him as Americans and either did not know or did not care that he had been part of an American occupying force in 1776 or that he had made multiple attempts over several decades to make Canada an American territory. A thin, tattered file in the post office archives, labelled "Comments, Complaints U.S. Bicentennial," suggests that was the case. It contains just three letters, only one of which complained about the stamp, saying that Canada should be celebrating its own bicentennial rather than that of the United States.[2]

If that last line seems jarring it is because the idea of celebrating the outcome of the American Revolution as a foundational moment for modern Canada is not part of mainstream thinking north of the border. Yet the British and American peace negotiators in Paris, including Franklin, created not one political entity but two when they drew a line through eastern North America in 1783. To the south lay the United States of America, which extended to the Mississippi River but did not include the separate colonies of East and West Florida. To the north lay colonies that did not join the revolt. Critics will argue there was no thought at the time that the remnants of British North America would become an independent country or that the terms of the treaty would be respected. But without the groundwork laid in the 1783 treaty, in which the Americans grudgingly acknowledged that the lands north of the border did not belong to them, modern Canada would not exist. The American Revolution created a new concept of British North America, out of which the idea gradually emerged of tying the various northern colonies together in a federation.

Why Franklin's Failure Is Overlooked

In the hands of a determined mythmaker, Franklin's failure to acquire Canada and its consequences would be a highlight in the much longer tale of who Canadians are and how they came to be. That Canadians eluded the grasp of such a powerful and prominent man, by both passive and active resistance, might have been and perhaps still could be the basis of a stirring episode in Canada's origin story. And yet the events of 1776 and 1783, not to mention Franklin's earlier attempts to make Canada American, are footnotes at best in the more widely accepted versions of Canada's creation.

They are overlooked in Canada for three main reasons: the memory of what happened was so divisive, embarrassing, or inconvenient for the main groups involved that they preferred to forget; the events were eclipsed by others seen to be far more consequential to each group; and no individual or group in Canada has found a way to put Franklin's failure to use in the present. But not acknowledging or recalling the key events that occurred at the dawn of bilateral relations between the newborn United States and embryonic Canada does not erase their impact on the present and perhaps the future. A better understanding of what happened 250 years ago would help Canada shape relations with its powerful — and increasingly unstable — neighbour.

To take one example of how divisive events can lead to collective memory loss, everyone involved in the invasion that drew Franklin to Montreal in 1776 had good reasons to forget. French Canadians fought on both sides, although the majority remained neutral. The memory of fathers fighting sons was painful. Those who openly supported the invaders were punished. Some were driven from their lands afterward by a vengeful occupying power. Those who fought alongside the British were often seen as traitors to the French Canadian cause. Indigenous Peoples were similarly divided, as were the small number of English-speaking merchants who had made Canada their home following the conquest. Some merchants openly aided the Americans both before and during the invasion, spreading propaganda throughout the province and passing on intelligence. Others fought on the ramparts of Quebec City alongside British troops and Canadian militia.

The Americans themselves were split between those who wanted to teach the British a lesson and those who wanted independence. They had additional reasons to suppress memories of the failed invasion. The Americans portrayed themselves as victims of British tyranny. Yet they were the aggressors. Despite superior numbers and a string of early victories, the congress botched its first foreign invasion. The ragtag army camped in the snow outside the walls of Quebec City through the winter of 1775–1776 lacked food, clothing, and money. The inglorious details of the military and intelligence failures at the start of their revolution were best not recalled.

Other events loomed larger in the consciousness of each group, which aided this collective forgetting. For French Canadians, it was the British conquest, which upended their world in 1760. Many saw the American Revolution as a family quarrel with no upside for them. No matter which side won, they still would be ruled by English-speaking foreigners. The defining event for the Indigenous Peoples was when Europeans first made contact and decided to stay in North America. They, too, saw the revolution as a fratricidal fight. The result would not reverse the European invasion. As for English-speaking Canadians, there were so few of them at the time of the invasion that it made little impression on the group's collective memory. History for many in English-speaking Canada only started after the revolution, with the arrival of tens of thousands of royalists fleeing the republican hordes. They preferred to cite the War of 1812, when they were present in greater numbers, as a milestone in Canada's history. For Franklin and his fellow Americans, the failure of the invasion was quickly obscured by the crowning achievement of the Declaration of Independence, made even as the last military stragglers were arriving home. The British were focused all along on retaining the thirteen American colonies, whose loss would have far more impact on their treasury, merchants, and sense of imperial well-being than the successful defence of an unloved colony.

You could go through each of the times Franklin made a play for Canada and find many of the same dynamics. In all of them, Canada was a pawn in the hands of the main actors, who were pursuing other goals. This came out clearly in the Paris peace negotiations when the question of Canada arose. Britain wanted to preserve commercial ties with the Americans. France wanted to weaken Britain. The Americans wanted independence. No one particularly cared what effect their actions would have on the French Canadians. They had other goals in mind. "Seeing one thing is not seeing another," said the French philosopher Paul Ricoeur. "Recounting one drama is forgetting another."

This need not have meant the invasion or indeed any of Franklin's other annexation efforts would be forgotten forever. There are plenty of events in history that are plucked from obscurity, dusted off, and then put to new uses in the present. But for that to happen, someone has to recognize their worth in the service of a cause and have the power and skill to weave them into a sustainable myth.

Why Past Attempts Failed

There were at least two attempts to promote the importance to modern Canada of the failed invasion, one of the more consequential American efforts that Franklin was involved in. Both were swept away by shifting political and demographic currents within the province of Quebec and the country. One hundred years after the successful repulse of the American invaders, the Institut canadien de Québec, a group representing the social, economic, and cultural elite of Quebec City, held a gala attended by seven hundred people to pay homage to what its secretary and archivist, Honoré Julien Jean Baptiste Chouinard, called "the glorious defenders of

Quebec." The names of Governor Carleton and a host of English and French Canadians were painted on banners that lined the room. The military band played "God Save the Queen" (Victoria was on the throne), a funeral march for Montgomery, and a "quadrille canadien."[3] The poet laureate read a poem in honour of Montgomery, whom Chouinard called one of the "illustrious vanquished." At the time and for some decades afterward, members of the French Canadian elite, like Chouinard, talked of Quebec as the cradle of Canada.[4] The defeat of Montgomery and Arnold in December 1775 was used to bolster the importance of these events in Canada's origin story. As late as 1943, the Quebec premier, Adélard Godbout, still echoed this narrative.[5] But the idea fell out of use and disappeared with the rise of the Quebec independence movement in the 1960s. The memory of siding with the British to resist American overtures and incursions was no longer popular among French Canadians, and English Canadians were increasingly imposing their own version of history on the country.

The second effort, also involving Chouinard, occurred in 1908, when Quebec City celebrated its tercentenary. Here was another opportunity to weave the events of 1775–1776 into the broader story of modern Canada. But competing versions of history ran afoul of each other, producing a confusing and not terribly accurate portrayal of how Canada came to be. Earl Grey, the British governor general of Canada, was part of the problem. He thought Canada's history began with the British conquest in 1760 and wanted the pageant to feature the battle of the Plains of Abraham, where the British defeated the French. Sir Wilfrid Laurier, the Liberal prime minister, thought commemorating a French defeat would be divisive. He wanted to tell a tale of the French and English peoples coming together to live peacefully. Keeping the country together was more important to the French Canadian prime minister than emphasizing Quebec's role in its creation. Chouinard, who had suggested the public celebration, wanted to highlight Samuel de Champlain, who founded Quebec City in 1608 and planted the seeds of Christianity in that part of North America. No one got what they wanted. In the actual battle on the Plains of Abraham, the British and French generals died. In the 1908 pageant, they politely greeted each other and marched off together at the head of a combined army, while the band played "God Save the King" and "O Canada." In another historical mishmash, the actors portraying the French Canadians who helped defeat Montgomery in 1775 marched alongside those representing soldiers from the War of 1812.[6]

The Dominant Group Decides What Is Important

English speakers were a tiny minority of the local population at the time Franklin made his final attempt to possess Canada. But by the mid-1800s, they outnumbered French Canadians, their ranks swelled by the large number of royalists who fled north after American independence and other, more recent immigrants. The tercentenary celebrations demonstrated the power of the dominant group to decide what should be commemorated and how it should be portrayed. Early English-language history books often began the story of Canada with the royalist arrival, discounting what had come before. Later ones sometimes started the story in 1867, when the Dominion of Canada was formed. Neither version gave much importance to Franklin's relations with Canada because they occurred before the bulk of the royalists arrived. Even supposedly federal bodies, like the Historical Sites and Monuments Board of Canada, created in 1919, tended toward this Anglocentric view of Canada's past. In the first ten years of its operations, the monuments board selected 240 monument sites, of which only 47 were in Quebec.[7] The board's bigoted story of Canada was that French civilization tamed Indigenous "savagery," only to be supplanted by superior British civilization. (By 2024, the total number of national historic sites had grown to 1,004, of which 201 were in Quebec and 271 in Ontario.)

A smaller example of English Canadian history dominating that of French Canada can be found in Toronto, where the ruins of Fort Toronto, established in 1750 under the French regime, were obliterated in the late 1800s.[8] The fort and nearby village have since been marked with paving stones, an obelisk, and a plaque. Meanwhile, Fort York, built by the British in 1793, was made a national historical site because of a battle fought there in the War of 1812. Fort York claims to be "the birthplace of urban Toronto," elevating its importance far above the pre-existing Indigenous and French settlements on that site.

French Canadians can be similarly selective in the province of Quebec, where they are the dominant group. In a recent example, François Legault, Quebec premier at the time of writing, announced the creation of a new history museum in April 2024, which he said would focus on the last four hundred years. He dismissed complaints by prominent Indigenous groups that he was ignoring their history. A historian and consultant to the project asserted that the Indigenous Peoples belonged to Quebec's "prehistory."[9]

American Cultural Dominance Skews Canadian Views

Within North America, there is no more dominant group than the Americans. They have shaped how Franklin is remembered in the United States and in Canada through movies, books, television series, and social media. Canadians reading the major biographies of Franklin, mostly written by American authors, or watching films and television shows about the American icon produced in the United States are unlikely to learn much, if anything, about his enduring interest in acquiring Canada. For example, a four-hour documentary by American filmmaker Ken Burns, which aired in 2022, devotes about forty seconds to Franklin's trip to Canada in 1776. He was there, the narrator says, "to convince the Canadians to join the colonial cause." There is no mention that American troops had already invaded and were occupying Montreal when he arrived, nor that he made another play for Canada during the peace negotiations in Paris. It received more attention in the 2024 television series on Franklin starring Michael Douglas, although the larger context of his longstanding interest was not given. The narrator in the Burns documentary talks of the four nonnegotiable demands Franklin made in Paris but not the four demands he termed advisable, which included that Britain give Canada to the United States. When a CBC journalist interviewed Burns about his documentary, none of these points of interest to Canadians was mentioned.[10] What Franklin did or thought about Canada was seen as irrelevant by the American filmmaker and thus became irrelevant to his Canadian interviewer.

This is not a gripe about American views of Canada. It makes perfect sense that American authors and filmmakers focus on the aspects of Franklin's life that had the most impact on the United States. Every country is the star in its own movie. It is an observation that viewing Canada's past through an American lens produces an incomplete and distorted image of history. This is a constant risk for Canadians, who happily consume vast amounts of American cultural output. Yet in absorbing and repeating American views, Canadians are unconsciously letting the losers in the contest for the northern half of the continent tell — or not tell — the tale.

The Absence of a Founding Myth

One of the biggest impediments to giving Franklin's quest the treatment it deserves in the story of Canada is that Canadians, unlike Americans, have yet to agree on a single origin story or myth. Depending on whom you ask, the story of Canada starts as early as five thousand years ago, when the Sivullirmiut began moving east from the north shore of Alaska; in 1534, when the French explorer Jacques Cartier sailed the lower reaches of the St. Lawrence River in search of gold, spices, and a northern passage to Asia for the king of France; or, for the purists, as late as 1982, when Canada gained control over its constitution from Britain and became a fully independent country. The most widely accepted origin narratives are that Canada made a steady progression from colony to nation and the related story that the country was negotiated into being by the Fathers of Confederation. Canada had thousands of years of history before the Fathers of Confederation put on their frock coats and trundled off to Charlottetown and then Quebec City in 1864. Starting the national story at this point ignores millennia of Indigenous history and centuries of French Canadian history. Yet no one has come up with a more sweeping origin story that would seize the public imagination and win widespread support.

Origin stories do not arise naturally. They are created and promoted by political parties, religious groups, artists, writers, publishers, and others, who select aspects of the past that serve their present purposes. If enough people agree on a set of facts, real or imagined, the story becomes part of a society's collective memory, a term invented by the French philosopher Maurice Halbwachs. Collective memory is not the same as history, which is a record of events that occurred. Collective memory is a selection of events, some of which can be wildly exaggerated or even untrue, that fit an agreed narrative. Events that do not fit, because they are sensitive, inconvenient, or contradict the main narrative, are purposely ignored — silenced in authoritarian states. Historians talk about this in terms of groups trying to create a useable past or groups inventing traditions to tie a nation together. British historian Eric Hobsbawm, who studied invented traditions, said such stories only catch hold if the public are in a mood to hear them, or, as he put it, they are broadcast on a wavelength the people are ready to receive. Timing and context matter.[11]

The founding myth of the United States, replete with exaggerations and deliberately forgotten events, is a good example. After a violent split with Britain, Americans needed a new story of who they were and where they came from. Harkening back to British roots no longer served the purpose. They came up with an inspiring tale of beleaguered colonists rising as one to defend their liberty against British tyranny. Like many origin myths, it has been challenged in recent years but remains widely accepted, despite its holes and inconsistencies. The colonists were far from united. John Adams estimated that a third were for independence, a third wanted to remain loyal to Britain, and the rest were undecided. It is in the eye of the beholder whether Britain was being tyrannical when it wanted the colonists to help pay for their own defence and reduce the massive debt Britain accumulated during the fight against the French in North America. In British eyes, the Americans were trying to get something for nothing and were exaggerating British oppression. And how could the right to liberty be central to the revolution when the colonies contained an estimated one million enslaved people? William Pulteney, a British member of Parliament, pointed out this contradiction in 1778 when he wrote: "To those who dare think for themselves, it will appear impossible that a rebellion can have liberty for its object, which has the proprietors of slaves for its leaders."[12] Americans created a commonly accepted version of their beginnings by setting aside such awkward and contradictory facts.

Canadians Yet to Agree on a National Story

Canadians have been less adept at crafting a national story. "We have no myths and no successful myth-makers," Ramsay Cook complained in

1966. He blamed Canada's "orderly growth from colony to nation," which deprived it of heroic events.[13] His was a fairly typical English Canadian view. Provinces have had some success, particularly Quebec and Alberta. They have jurisdiction over education, which gives them an advantage in selecting how history is portrayed in school textbooks. There have been attempts over the years to write a national history, a necessary step in creating a national identity. But stepping outside the bounds of an accepted provincial view has its dangers. Following the Second World War, Athanase David, a senator from Quebec, pushed for a single national history book to be taught across Canada. He was called a traitor by his critics and received an official reprimand from the archbishop of Quebec. Arthur Maheux, a Quebec historian, published a book in 1941 that he hoped would promote a national history. Intellectuals in English Canada praised it. Quebec intellectuals attacked him.

Most prime ministers try to sum up the country in a way that supports their government's policies. John A. Macdonald, the first prime minister, was fighting a Liberal push for trade reciprocity with the Americans in 1891 when he proclaimed, "A British subject I was born, and a British subject I will die."[14] But when rising immigration and political reality made clinging to British roots untenable, prime ministers tried to create a new national identity. Justin Trudeau, the Liberal prime minister who presided over a sharp rise in immigration, used "diversity is our strength" as a unifying theme after the 2015 election.[15] More worryingly to some, he has also said that Canada might be a postnational state, with no core identity, tied together by shared values.[16] In contrast, Stephen Harper, Conservative prime minister from 2006 to 2015, mounted at least two serious attempts to reshape the national narrative and the country's self-image. He focused on the Arctic as a unifying factor. "This is the frontier," he asserted. "This is the place that defines our country."[17] Harper made annual forays to the far north, often timed to coincide with military exercises. "We either use it or lose it," was the catchphrase in one of his government's early strategy papers.[18] He announced the construction of a new, polar-class icebreaker called the *John G. Diefenbaker* (cancelled by the succeeding Liberal government). It was on his watch that construction began on the Inuvik-to-Tuktoyaktuk highway, Canada's first all-weather road to the Arctic Ocean. Stories need heroes and Harper did his best to supply them. He became personally involved in the discovery of the wreck of the *Erebus*, one of the ships lost during the search for the Northwest Passage by John Franklin, a British naval officer. To this tragic hero Harper added a hardy, French Canadian mariner, Joseph-Elzéar Bernier, who made eight government-sponsored voyages in the early 1900s to assert Canadian sovereignty in the Arctic.[19] Harper's efforts were dismissed by some critics as trying to put a Conservative stamp on an identity that had been mostly fashioned by Liberal governments. There was some of that. But it was also a concerted attempt to promote an origin story that supported his government's policies.

The portrayal of Canadians as people of the north, prepared to defend their territory, had some promise as a national story. It had heroes, drama, a reference via John Franklin to Canada's roots as a British colony, and positive roles for French Canadians and the Indigenous Peoples of the Arctic. It even appealed to the tendency of Canadians to define themselves in opposition to the Americans. It was the Americans who were challenging Canada's sovereignty over the Northwest Passage at the time.

The Americans were also the enemy in the Harper government's campaign to promote the War of 1812 as a nation-defining experience. The government made the war a central theme in the Canada Day celebrations of 2012, even hiring a theatrical producer to help stage events. It commissioned a new monument on Parliament Hill and named the war "The Fight for Canada." While this raised the profile of the war in the public consciousness, the campaign did not catch fire because the fighting largely took place in central Canada. It meant nothing to westerners and little to the residents of Quebec.

Both the Arctic narrative and the focus on the War of 1812 required some deliberate forgetting of inconvenient facts. The vast majority of Canadians live as far south as they can go along the Canada-U.S. border. Canada was still a British colony, defended by British troops as well as local militia, when the "Fight for Canada" took place. The discrepancy between reality and the myth need not have been fatal. However, the Conservative government was replaced by a Liberal one in 2015. The Arctic focus was dropped, leaving Canada with the same hodgepodge of tales that varied by region or language group.

Why We Need a National Story

Not everyone agrees that Canadians need a story that the majority could embrace. Some argue that the country has managed to hang together until now without one. None of the competing regional versions has grown strong enough to disrupt the country, although the Quebec independence referendums in 1980 and 1995 came close. Yet can we count on that steady state to last? My editor at *The Economist* once described Canada as fissiparous, or something inclined to fall apart (I had to look it up). Would it not be better to counter this tendency by finding a story that pulls Canadians together? Something that could give groups enticed by the idea of their own nationhood — Quebec in the past, and potentially Quebec or Alberta in the future — additional reasons to stay? Something that would explain to new immigrants what kind of country they are joining?

This is not impossible. It could build on the story that the Harper government had begun to shape. Or it could take a totally different direction, emphasizing the complexity of Canada in a coherent and compelling way. What is needed is a willingness to take on the task, the clout to see it through, and an element of luck with the timing. Franklin's great failure to annex Canada, along with other overlooked milestones, could be placed within this broader structure. Putting more emphasis on the revolutionary period would have the added advantage of showing that anti-Americanism, often seen as a knee-jerk reaction to our powerful neighbour, has deep roots. Canada's three founding peoples all had good cause to dislike and even fear the Americans of their era.

Having a clearer explanation of who they are and where they came from would help Canadians deal with the problems they face today, including a new and more challenging relationship with the United States. Increasing political and social instability in the U.S. is a potential threat to cross-border relations that have long been predicated on the idea, most memorably expressed by John F. Kennedy in 1961, that "geography has made us neighbours. History has made us friends."

This idea was still in fashion when the Franklin stamp was issued in 1976 as part of a government-wide effort to celebrate the American bicentennial. A committee of senior bureaucrats, convened to oversee the effort, decided its central theme would be "The Neighbour."[20] Departments mostly fell into line and turned a blind eye to events that did not fit a determinedly upbeat treatment of 1776. The Department of External Affairs (now Global Affairs Canada) published a special issue of its journal, *International Perspectives*, "Sharing the Continent, Our Common Heritage, Canada's Neighbour." The invasion of 1775–1776 was not mentioned, although the War of 1812, a subsequent failed invasion, made an appearance. Prime Minister Pierre Elliott Trudeau took a similar approach in the foreword to *Between Friends/Entre Amis*, the commemorative book he gave President Gerald Ford on June 16, 1976, at the White House. He made a fleeting reference to past conflicts in the book of photographs of the border. "Long ago we even fought each other, usually in relation to the very boundary which this book illustrates," he wrote. But the bulk of his one-page introduction was about the "peace and friendship" between the two nations. That comforting thought has made it easy for Canadians to forget that countries have interests, not friends, and that the lengthy period of peaceful coexistence Kennedy referred to came after an even longer period of unfriendly relations.

A Long History of Unfriendly Relations

American colonists, often but not always led by the British, made serious attempts to seize all or part of what now constitutes Canada in 1690, 1711, 1745, and 1759, when it was under the French regime, and in 1775 and 1812, when it was under British control. There were invasion fears in Canada in the 1840s, when an expansionist United States annexed the short-lived Republic of Texas against the wishes of Mexico, and American newspapers trumpeted their country's manifest destiny to control the continent. New bouts of invasion jitters occurred during the American Civil War and with the American purchase of Alaska from Russia in 1867. In the parliamentary debates of 1865 leading up to Confederation, an estimated sixty speakers referred to the American menace or the prospect of American violence. Those fears subsided temporarily with the creation of the Dominion of Canada in 1867 and the departure of most British troops from Canadian soil in 1871. Yet the spectre of invasion loomed again in 1895, when a dispute between Britain and the United States over the boundary between Venezuela and British Guiana briefly threatened to become an armed confrontation on Canadian soil. Even after that, planning for a possible invasion continued on both sides of the border. A 1921 plan put together by Canadian Brigadier James "Buster" Sutherland Brown, called Defence Scheme No. 1, had Canada resisting an American invasion by a pre-emptive seizure of territory in the northern states. The United States and Britain had plans for conflict between Canada and the United States right up to the eve of the Second World War.[21]

Ignoring the Elephant in the Room

Not remembering, or deliberately forgetting, this history allows Canadians to ignore the possibility, however remote it might seem, that the United States could once again see Canada as a direct or indirect threat and take aggressive action. Critics of this thinking will scoff and say it has been more than two hundred years since the Americans last invaded Canada and that in many of the earlier instances, the target of American aggression was a European power, with physical security of the American colonists as the main motivation. Land and resources, especially the rich fishing grounds off Newfoundland, were usually secondary considerations.

The world and the bilateral relationship have changed significantly in 250 years, yet there are some uncomfortable similarities between then and now that bear thinking about. In 1776 the Americans were bitterly divided, uncertain about their place in the world, and fearful of external enemies. Fake news and conspiracy theories were rampant. No one knew whom to trust. They believed they had a right to take territory claimed by others because they were an exceptional people. A powerful minority pushed for radical change to the accepted order. That could equally describe the United States in 2025.

The list of potential security threats has lengthened considerably since 1776, and it includes not just state actors, as was the case in the past, but also more amorphous threats like migration, health security, terrorism, trade, cyber warfare, and climate change, to name a few. There is more scope for Canada to be perceived as a danger to the United States and vice versa.

The issue of access to resources has not gone away. The idea that Americans had a right to resources in Canada was expressed openly in the revolutionary era. John Adams was prepared to scupper the Paris peace treaty if the British did not guarantee American access to the rich fishing grounds off Canada's east coast and those around Newfoundland. A modern version of that extraterritorial reach was Donald Trump's assertion during the 2024 presidential election campaign that water from Canada should be piped to drought-stricken California. Trump's bizarre description of a giant faucet that controlled the flow and his penchant for making wild statements made it easy to dismiss this as the raving of a mad politician. And yet at about the same time, a seemingly sane academic from the southern states published an opinion piece in the *New York Times* about tapping the Great Lakes and piping the water south (he was against the idea).[22] The piece did not mention once that the water in the Great Lakes is a shared resource (the international boundary runs through the middle of them) or that Canada might want to have a say. The implicit assumption was that if the Americans wanted the water, they would have it. While still president-elect, Trump suggested to the Canadian prime minister that Canada might want to become the fifty-first state. Canadian officials dismissed it as a joke.[23] Underlying such thinking is the old idea that it is the manifest destiny of Americans to control the continent. It is unclear how many Americans share this view. Just a handful in positions of power would be enough to wreak havoc in the bilateral relationship. The United States has overwhelming superiority in political, economic, and military matters. It might be easier for Canadian policy-makers to stick with the fiction that the two countries are friends than contemplate what actions would be required if the relationship turns hostile. That approach leaves Canadians vulnerable.

A Second Franklin Stamp

Knowledge of the past sheds light on possible futures and leads to better-informed decisions in the present. At least that is the theory. It did not seem to work that way for the Canadian post office. By the time the 1976 stamp came out, officials knew Franklin was no friend to Canada. Yet in 2013, they issued another stamp with his face on it. This one commemorated 250 years of postal service. It had a familiar etching of Franklin, set against a painting of the harbour at Quebec City. There is unintentional irony in the choice of background. It was at Quebec City in December 1775 that the American invaders came closest to conquering Canada and where a combined force of British, French Canadians, English-speaking merchants, and Indigenous warriors helped turn Franklin's dream of possessing Canada into dust. Franklin may well have been a genius, as many of his biographers maintain, but even geniuses suffer the occasional failure. Canada remained the prize that eluded him.

Acknowledgements

THERE WERE MANY TIMES IN THE LAST FOUR YEARS WHEN THIS BOOK project would have come to an abrupt halt without the help of certain people. My late mother, Joan Drohan, helped finance my studies at the University of Ottawa, where I began the research for this book. Serge Durflinger, then head of the history department, made my dream of returning to school come true when he accepted me into the master of arts in history program. I could not have asked for a more knowledgeable and supportive supervisor than Damien-Claude Bélanger, himself an author of many books. He steered me away from some rocky shoals in both my university memoir and in this book, which he kindly read. Any mistakes that remain are mine. A legacy from my late sister, Joyce Drohan, meant I could spend two years after graduation researching and writing without the worry of unpaid bills. I wish she and my mother were alive to see the finished work.

I did much of the research during the Covid-19 pandemic, when travel and physical access to libraries were limited. It would have been impossible without the Internet Archive, a digital library, and its immense collection of books and documents.

My friends Nic Baer and Edison Stewart and my husband, David Lord, now know more than they probably ever wanted to know about Benjamin Franklin and Canada. They read, reread, and commented on each chapter, giving me valuable feedback on what readers might want to know. I salute their perseverance.

I was fortunate that David Johnston, my agent, was up to the challenge of finding a publisher for a book on history. Thankfully, Kathryn Lane and Elena Radic at Dundurn Press still believe that readers are interested in what happened in the past. They welcomed me into the Dundurn fold and put me into the competent hands of editor Jess Shulman. Her questions and comments forced me to sharpen my thinking and my copy. She was a joy to work with. Janna Green, the copy editor, gave everything a final polish.

I like maps because they help the reader understand things that cannot easily be described in words. Cartographer Julie Witmer performed the difficult task of transcribing borders drawn on old maps, whose creators had an uncertain grasp of geography, onto modern versions. My talented granddaughter, Agnes Lord, created the elegant cartouche seen on each map and the device at the end of the book. The production and design team, Rudi Garcia, Laura Boyle, and Karen Alexiou, produced a striking cover and layout. The sales and marketing team, Kendra Martin, Ankit Pahwa, Eden Boudreau, Sara Ibrahim, and Mylène Bouilly, then worked their magic.

Without the help of all these people, my book would not have found a way into your hands or onto your screen. I am especially indebted to my husband, David, who had to live with my frequently querulous requests for peace and quiet and yet still summoned the energy and enthusiasm to read and comment on what I had written. That's true love.

Madelaine Drohan
Ottawa
January 2025

APPENDIX

Wars and Treaties Mentioned in This Book

Queen Anne's War in North America (1702–1713)

Part of the larger War of the Spanish Succession in Europe (1701–1714).
Main belligerents in North America: Britain, France, and their Indigenous allies.
Ended by: Treaty of Utrecht, 1713.

King George's War in North America (1744–1748)

Part of the War of the Austrian Succession in Europe (1740–1748).
Main belligerents in North America: Britain, France, and their Indigenous allies.
Ended by: Treaty of Aix-la-Chapelle, 1748.

French and Indian War in North America (1754–1763)

Part of the Seven Years' War (1756–1763).
Main belligerents in North America: Britain, France, and their Indigenous allies.
Ended by: Treaty of Paris, 1763.

Pontiac's War (1763–1766)

Main belligerents in North America: Chippewa, Delaware, Miami, Odawa, Ojibwe, Potawatomi, Seneca, Shawnee, and Wendat versus Britain.
Ended by: Treaty of Fort Ontario, 1766.

American Revolution/War of Independence (1775–1783)

Main belligerents in North America: Britain versus the thirteen colonies, France, Spain, and their Indigenous allies.
Ended by: Treaty of Paris, 1783 (signed by the United States and Britain) and the Treaty of Versailles, 1783 (signed by Britain, France, Spain, and the Netherlands).

War of 1812 (1812–1815)

Main belligerents: Britain, the United States, and their Indigenous allies.
Ended by: Treaty of Ghent, 1814.

Notes

INTRODUCTION

1 Mark R. Anderson, *Invasion of Canada by the Americans, 1775–1776, As Told Through Jean-Baptiste Badeaux's Three Rivers Journal and New York Captain William Goforth's Letters* (SUNY Press, 2016), 32.

2 Angus Brown, review of "Buster: A Canadian Patriot and Imperialist," by Atholl Sunderland Brown, *Journal of Military History* 70, no. 1 (January 1970): 257–58; and Roger F. Swanson, "The United States as a National Security Threat to Canada," *Behind the Headlines* XXIX (July 1970): 9–16.

3 "From Benjamin Franklin to John Jay, 2 June 1779," *Founders Online*, National Archives and Records Administration (hereafter NARA).

4 Albert Henry Smyth, ed., *Writings of Benjamin Franklin*, vol. 9 (Macmillan, 1906), 612–13.

5 Max Farrand, ed., *Benjamin Franklin's Memoirs* (University of California Press, 1949), 416, 421, 422.

6 "From Benjamin Franklin to Emma Thompson, 8 February, 1777," *Founders Online*, NARA.

CHAPTER 1: THE THREAT FROM THE NORTH: BOSTON 1706–1723

1 Benjamin Franklin, "*The Interest of Great Britain Considered*, [17 April 1760]," *Founders Online*, NARA.

2 John Williams, *The Redeemed Captive Returns to Zion*, March 3, 1707 (Evans Early American Imprint Collection, University of Michigan), 49; and Francis Parkman, *A Half-Century of Conflict: France and England in North America*, vol. 1 (Little, Brown, 1907), 88–89.

3 John Williams, "God in the Camp," Sermon, March 6, 1707 (Evans Early American Imprint Collection, University of Michigan).

4 Parkman, *Half-Century*, vol. 1, 55.

5 Parkman, *Half-Century*, vol. 1, 103.

6 James D. Alsop, "Samuel Vetch's 'Canada Survey'd': The Formation of a Colonial Strategy, 1706–1710," *Acadiensis* 12, no. 1 (Autumn 1982): 39–58.

7 "Instructions of Queen Anne to Col. Samuel Vetch, for the Organization of a Colonial Contingent for the Conquest of Canada, 1708," *Pennsylvania Magazine of History and Biography* 38, no. 3 (1914): 335–45.

8 Pierre-Georges Roy, "Un project d'expedition de M. D'Iberville contre Boston," *Bulletin des recherches historiques* 29, no. 10 (October 1923): 289–94.

9 Williams, *Redeemed*, 87.

10 Mark Van Doren, ed., *Samuel Sewall's Diary* (Macy-Masius, 1927), 103, 135, 172.

11 *New-England Courant: A Selection of Certain Issues Containing the Writings of Benjamin Franklin* (American Academy of Arts and Sciences, 1956), 5–6.

12 Walter Isaacson, *Benjamin Franklin: An American Life* (Simon & Schuster, 2004), 38.

13 Arthur Bernon Tourtellot, *Benjamin Franklin: The Shaping of Genius, the Boston Years* (Doubleday, 1977), 155.

14 Isaacson, *Franklin*, 19.

15 *New-England Courant*, Issues 28, 42, 47, 51, 54, 58, 80–113.

16 *New-England Courant*, Issues 80, 89, 91, 94, 95, 98, 101–11, 113.

CHAPTER 2: PAPIST CONSPIRACIES: LONDON 1724–1726

1 "*A Narrative of the Late Massacres*, [30 January? 1764]," *Founders Online*, NARA.

2 Jerry White, *London in the Eighteenth Century: A Great and Monstrous Thing* (Random House, 2012), xx–xxi, 1–3, 7–11, 24–25, 44, 47, 307; and Walter Thornbury, "Lincoln's Inn Fields," in *Old and New London*, vol. 3 (London, 1878), 44–50.

3 John Partridge, *Merlinus liberatus: an almanack for the year of our redemption 1724* (J. Roberts, 1724).
4 John Trenchard and Thomas Gordon, *Cato's Letters*, vol. 2 (Wilkins, Woodward, Walthoe, and Peele, 1737).

CHAPTER 3: A DANGEROUS MAN: PHILADELPHIA 1726–1748

1 Carl Van Doren, *Benjamin Franklin* (Penguin Books, 1991), 73, 74, 105, 258, 260; and Isaacson, *Franklin*, 3.
2 Dr. Alexander Hamilton, *Hamilton's Itinerarium* (William K. Bixby, 1744).
3 Charles Henry Lincoln, ed., *Correspondence of William Shirley: Governor of Massachusetts and Military Commander in America, 1731–1760* (Macmillan, 1912), 162–63.
4 John A. Schutz, "Imperialism in Massachusetts During the Governorship of William Shirley, 1741–1756," *Huntington Library Quarterly* 23, no. 3 (May 1960): 219, 223–24, 243.
5 Francis Parkman, *A Half-Century of Conflict: France and England in North America*, vol. 2 (Little, Brown, and Co., 1899), 77, 80.
6 Samuel G. Drake, ed., *Narrative of the Capture and Burning of Fort Massachusetts by the French and Indians, written at the time by one of the captives, Rev. Mr. John Norton, Chaplain at the Fort* (Joel Munsell, 1870), 10, 16.
7 *Minutes of the Provincial Council of Pennsylvania*, vol. 5 (Theo Fenn, 1851), 89, 92, 96, 99, 101, 103.
8 *Minutes*, vol 5, 229, 231.
9 Sally F. Griffith, "'Order, Discipline, and a Few Cannon': Benjamin Franklin, the Association, and the Rhetoric and Practice of Boosterism," *Pennsylvania Magazine of History and Biography* 116, no. 2 (April 1992): 137–38.

CHAPTER 4: CASTING A COVETOUS EYE: PHILADELPHIA 1749–1756

1 François Barbé-Marbois, *Histoire de la Louisiane et de la cession de cette colonie par la France aux États-Unis de l'Amérique Septentrionale* (Firmin Didot, 1829), 139.
2 "Thomas Lloyd to ———, 30 [31?] January 1756," *Founders Online*, NARA.
3 Benjamin Franklin to John Van Etten, "The Organization of John Van Etten's Company, 12 January 1756," *Founders Online*, NARA.
4 Gerald Stourzh, *Benjamin Franklin and American Foreign Policy*, 2nd ed. (University of Chicago Press, 1969), 59.

5 Carl Van Doren, ed., *Indian Treaties Printed by Benjamin Franklin, 1736–1762* (Historical Society of Pennsylvania, 1938), x.
6 Alfred P. James, "Benjamin Franklin's Ohio Valley Lands," *Proceedings of the American Philosophical Society* 98, no. 4 (August 16, 1954): 255; and Sheila L. Skemp, *Benjamin and William Franklin: Father and Son, Patriot and Loyalist* (St. Martin's Press, 1994), 15.
7 Étienne Silhouette, *Mémoires des commissaires du roi et de ceux de Sa Majesté britannique sur les possessions & les droits respectifs des deux couronnes en Amérique — avec les actes publics & pièces justificatives*, vol. 4 (l'Imprimerie royale, 1755–1757), 460; and Silhouette, *Mémoires*, vol. 1, 10–11.
8 E. B. O'Callaghan, ed., *Documents Relative to the Colonial History of the State of New York*, vol. 10 (Weed, Parsons, 1858), 223–24.
9 Marcel Trudel, "The Jumonville Affair," *Quarterly Journal of the Pennsylvania Historical and Museum Commission* XXI, no. 4 (October 1954): 25.
10 Fred Anderson, *Crucible of War* (Vintage Books, 2001), 45, 50, 52, 54–55, 64.
11 Schutz, "Imperialism," 231, 236.
12 "Fear of Catholics in colonial Pennsylvania, 1755–6," *American Catholic Historical Researches* 17, no. 2 (April 1900): 75–76.
13 "Pennsylvania Assembly: Appointment of Franklin as Agent to Go to England, and His acceptance, [28 January 1757–3 February 1757]," *Founders Online*, NARA.

CHAPTER 5: RAVINGS OF A MAD PROPHET: LONDON 1757–1773

1 "From Benjamin Franklin to Lord Kames, 3 January 1760," *Founders Online*, NARA.
2 "From Benjamin Franklin to Lord Kames, 3 January 1760," *Founders Online*, NARA.
3 "From Benjamin Franklin to William Franklin: Journal of Negotiations in London, 22 March 1775," *Founders Online*, NARA.
4 Pierre-Georges Roy, ed., *Voltaire, Mme de Pompadour et quelques arpents de neige* (Pierre-Georges Roy, 1898), 17–18, 19–20, 25–26.
5 Pierre Calmettes, ed., *Choiseul et Voltaire, d'après les lettres inédites du duc de Choiseul à Voltaire* (Plon-Nourrit, 1902), 163.
6 Étienne François de Choiseul, *Mémoire historique sur la negotiation de la France et de l'Angleterre depuis le 26 mars 1761 jusqu'au 26 septembre de la même année* (Wilson, Becket & De Hondt, 1769), 4–5.

7 P. J. Marshall, "William Burke and Guadeloupe," in *Edmund Burke and the British Empire in the West Indies: Wealth, Power, and Slavery* (Oxford University Press, 2019), 28, 30.
8 Michel Brunet, *Les Canadiens après la conquête* (Fides, 1969), 26–27.
9 Lionel Adolphe Groulx, *Lendmains de conquête* (Bibliothèque de l'Action française, 1920), 35, 39, 43.
10 "Except of a letter from Egremont to Amherst, 12 December 1761," Series B, vol. 37, *Canada History Online*, National Archives of Canada, 10–12.
11 "His Majesty's Most Gracious Speech to both Houses of Parliament, on Tuesday, the Eighteenth Day of November 1760" (Thomas Baskett, 1760).
12 Choiseul, *Mémoire*, 23, 25–26, 34.
13 Calmettes, *Choiseul et Voltaire*, 176.
14 "From Benjamin Franklin to Richard Jackson, 8 March 1763," *Founders Online*, NARA.
15 R. A. Humphreys, "Lord Shelburne and the Proclamation of 1763," *English Historical Review* 49, no. 194 (April 1934): 241, 244, 245.
16 Adam Shortt and Arthur G. Doughty, eds., *Documents relating to the constitutional history of Canada, 1759–1791*, 2nd and revised ed. (J. De L. Taché, 1918), 128–29, 132–34, 137–38.
17 "From Benjamin Franklin to Richard Jackson, 1 May 1764" and "To Benjamin Franklin from Baynton and Wharton, 3 November 1764," *Founders Online*, NARA.
18 "From Henry Bouquet (II), Fort Loudoun 22d. August 1764," *Franklin Papers*, franklinpapers.org.
19 Clarence Walworth Alvord and Clarence Edwin Carter, eds., *The Critical Period, 1763–1765*, British Series, vol. 1 (Illinois State Historical Library, 1915), 134–61.
20 "From Benjamin Franklin to Peter Collinson, 19 December 1763," *Founders Online*, NARA.
21 "To the Freeholders and Electors of the Province of Pennsylvania," *Pennsylvania Journal; and Weekly Advertiser*, September 27, 1764, quoted in "Papers from the Election Campaign, [September 1764]," *Founders Online*, NARA.
22 "From Benjamin Franklin to Richard Jackson, 11 October 1764," *Founders Online*, NARA.
23 "To Henry Bouquet, Philada. Augt. 16. 1764" and "From Henry Bouquet (I), Fort Loudoun 22d. August 1764," *Franklin Papers*, franklinpapers.org.

24 "William Smith: An Answer to Mr. Franklin's Remarks, [7 December 1764]," *Founders Online*, NARA; and Esmond Wright, *Franklin of Philadelphia* (Harvard University Press, 1986), 149.
25 "From Benjamin Franklin to Sarah Franklin, 8 November 1764," *Founders Online*, NARA.

CHAPTER 6: A NEW PAPIST ARMY: LONDON 1774–1775

1 Jared Sparks, ed., *The Works of Benjamin Franklin*, vol. 5 (Townsend Mac Coun., 1882), 21.
2 Scott C. Miller, "Ten Facts About the American Economy in the 18th Century," George Washington's Mount Vernon, online resource, mountvernon.org; and A. Rabushka, *Taxation in Colonial America* (Princeton University Press, 2008), 721.
3 Arthur Young, *Political Essays Concerning the Present State of the British Empire* (Research Reports, 1970), 20.
4 Arthur Meier Schlesinger, "The Significance of Immigration in American History," *American Journal of Sociology* 27, no. 1 (July 1921): 73–74.
5 Jack P. Greene, *Evaluating Empire and Confronting Colonialism in Eighteenth-Century Britain* (Cambridge University Press, 2013), 50.
6 Prince Hoare, *Memoirs of Granville Sharp, Esq.* (Henry Colburn, 1820), 100.
7 William Kingsford, *A History of Canada*, vol. 5, *1763–1775* (Roswell & Hutchison, 1892), n. 341.
8 Verner W. Crane, ed., *Benjamin Franklin's Letters to the Press, 1758–1775* (University of North Carolina Press, 1950), 239–40.
9 Lucy S. Sutherland, ed., *The Correspondence of Edmund Burke*, vol. 2 (University of Chicago Press, 1958), 523.
10 Smyth, *Writings*, vol. 6, 186.
11 Henry Cavendish, ed., *Debates of the House of Commons in the Year 1774 on the Bill for Making More Effectual Provision for the Government of the Province of Quebec* (Ridgway, 1839), 103.
12 Donald Fyson, "The Conquered and the Conqueror," in *Revisiting 1759: The Conquest of Canada in Historical Perspective*, ed. Phillip A. Buckner and John G. Reid (University of Toronto Press, 2012), 196.
13 Donald Fyson, "The Quebec Act and French Canadians: The Myth of the Seminal Moment," in *Entangling the Quebec Act*, ed. François Furstenberg and Hubert Ollivier (McGill-Queen's, 2020), 77–78, 80–81, 196–97.
14 Sutherland, *Correspondence*, vol. 2, 538.
15 Cavendish, *Debates*, 43, 213, 228, 238, 289.

16 Cavendish, *Debates*, 10, 57, 132, 166, 247, 251, 274.
17 Cavendish, *Debates*, 123, 134, 143, 194.
18 Cavendish, *Debates*, 88, 103, 137, 143, 150, 160, 206, 247, 280–81, 288.
19 Cavendish, *Debates*, 54–57.
20 Cavendish, *Debates*, iii–iv; Robert Christie, *A history of the late province of Lower Canada* (T. Cary & Co., 1848–1855), nn. 6–8.
21 "From Benjamin Franklin to William Franklin: Journal of Negotiations in London, 22 March 1775," *Founders Online*, NARA.
22 "From Benjamin Franklin to William Franklin: Journal of Negotiations in London, 22 March 1775," *Founders Online*, NARA.
23 "Answers to Franklin's 'Hints', [before 4 February 1775]," *Founders Online*, NARA.
24 John Stockdale, ed., *The Parliamentary Register; Or, History of the Proceedings And Debates of the House of Commons* (T. Gillet, 1802), 131–32.
25 Stockdale, *Register*, 178–79, 307–8, 492.

CHAPTER 7: A NEIGHBOURLY INVASION: PHILADELPHIA 1775

1 "From Benjamin Franklin to Humphry Marshall, 23 May 1775," *Founders Online*, NARA.
2 "From Thomas Jefferson to Francis Eppes, 26 June 1775," *Founders Online*, NARA.
3 William Bradford Reed, ed., *Life and Correspondence of Joseph Reed* (Lindsay and Blakiston, 1847), 78–79.
4 Paul H. Smith, ed., *Letters of Delegates to Congress, 1774–1789* (Library of Congress, 1976–2000), 335, 349–50, 352, 409.
5 Edmund Cody Burnett, *The Continental Congress* (Macmillan, 1941), vii–viii, 23.
6 Worthington Chauncey Ford, *Journals of the Continental Congress, 1774–1789*, vol. 1 (Government Printing Office, 1904), 62, 80, 88, 101, 106–9, 111, 113, 122.
7 Shortt and Doughty, *Documents*, vol. 1, 280, 282.
8 Shortt and Doughty, *Documents*, vol. 2, 583–84.
9 Thomas Chapais, *Cours d'histoire du Canada (1760–1791)*, vol. 1 (J-P Garneau, 1919), 201.
10 Shortt and Doughty, *Documents*, vol. 2, 670.
11 Peter Force, ed., *American Archives, 4th Series: Containing a Documentary History of the English Colonies in North America, From the King's Message*

to Parliament, of March 7, 1774, to the Declaration of Independence by the United States, vol. 2 (Clarke and Force, 1837–1846), 555–60, 645–46.

12 Justin Harvey Smith, *Our Struggle for the Fourteenth Colony* (G. P. Putnam, 1907), 139.

13 "To James Madison from William Bradford, 2 June 1775" and "From James Madison to William Bradford, 19 June 1775," *Founders Online*, NARA.

14 "From Benjamin Franklin to William Strahan, 5 July 1775," *Founders Online*, NARA.

15 "From John Adams to James Warren, 7 June 1775," *Founders Online*, NARA.

16 "To John Adams from Unknown, 9 June 1775," *Founders Online*, NARA.

17 "From Benjamin Franklin to Jonathan Shipley, 7 July 1775," *Founders Online*, NARA.

18 David Ramsay, *History of the American Revolution* (Downing & Phillips, 1789), 277; and Trudel, *La revolution*, 91.

19 Force, *American Archives, 4th Series*, vol. 2, 1048, 1067–68, 1096.

20 Julian P. Boyd, ed., *The Papers of Thomas Jefferson*, vol. 1, *1760–1776* (Princeton University Press, 1950), 174.

21 Ford, *Journals*, vol. 2, 99, 109–110.

22 Smith, *Letters*, 554.

23 Force, *American Archives, 4th Series*, vol. 2, 1134.

24 "From Benjamin Franklin to [Joseph Priestley], 7 July 1775: Extract," *Founders Online*, NARA.

25 "Jefferson's Annotated Copy of Franklin's Proposed Articles of Confederation, [June–July 1775]," *Founders Online*, NARA.

26 "From John Adams to James Warren, 21 May 1775," *Founders Online*, NARA.

27 "From George Washington to Major General Philip Schuyler, 20 August 1775," *Founders Online*, NARA.

28 "To George Washington from Major General Philip Schuyler, 27 August 1775," *Founders Online*, NARA.

29 "By the King, a Proclamation, For suppressing Rebellion and Sedition," Massachusetts Historical Society, masshist.org.

30 Smith, *Letters*, vol. 3, 58.

31 Ford, *Journals*, vol. 2, 182.

32 Force, *American Archives, 4th Series*, vol. 2, 1117.

33 Kenneth Roberts, *March to Quebec: Journals of the Members of Arnold's Expedition* (Doubleday, Doran, 1938), 220.

34 Charles Carroll, *Journal: Charles Carroll of Carrollton, During his Visit to Canada in 1776* (Maryland Historical Society, 1876), 15–16.

35 Ford, *Journals*, vol. 3, 339–40.
36 Boyd, *Papers*, vol. 1, 268–69.
37 Ford, *Journals*, vol. 3, 391.
38 Reed, *Joseph Reed*, 136.
39 Stockdale, *Register*, 3, 30–33.

CHAPTER 8: A NEST OF HORNETS: MONTREAL 1776

1 "From Benjamin Franklin to Emma Thompson, 8 February 1777," *Founders Online*, NARA.
2 "From Benjamin Franklin to Josiah Quincy, Sr., 15 April 1776," *Founders Online*, NARA.
3 Reed, *Joseph Reed*, 146–47.
4 "From John Adams to James Warren, 18 February 1776," *Founders Online*, NARA.
5 Smith, *Letters*, vol. 3, 494–95.
6 Ford, *Journals*, vol. 4, 85–86.
7 Ford, *Journals*, vol. 4, 85, 148–49, 216–17.
8 "From Benjamin Franklin to John Hancock, 13 April 1776," *Founders Online*, NARA.
9 Boyd, *Papers*, vol. 1, 250–51.
10 Louise Livingston Hunt, *Biographical Notes Concerning General Richard Montgomery: Together with Hitherto Unpublished Letters* (News Book and Job Printing House, 1876), 11.
11 John F. Roche, "Quebec Under Siege, 1775–1776: The Memorandums of Jacob Danford," *Canadian Historical Review* 50, no. 1 (March 1969): 72–74.
12 Force, *American Archives*, vol. 4, 656, 670.
13 Mercy Otis Warren, *History of the Rise, Progress, and Termination of the American Revolution: Interspersed with biographical, political and moral observations*, vol. 1 (E. Larkin, 1805), 266–67.
14 Boyd, *Papers*, vol. 1, 433.
15 Force, *American Archives*, vol. 4, 670–71, 674.
16 Force, *American Archives*, vol. 4, 669.
17 Thomas O'Brien Hanley, ed., *The John Carroll Papers*, vol. 1, *1755–1791* (University of Notre Dame Press, 1976), 47.
18 Carroll, *Journal*, 93.
19 Smith, *Letters*, vol. 3, 611, 612, 639–40.
20 Boyd, *Papers*, vol. 1, 446–47.

21 Smith, *Letters*, vol. 3, 645–47.
22 Carroll, *Journal*, 30–33.
23 Yvan Lamonde, *Ni avec eux ni sans eux* (Nota Bene, 1996), 47; and Jean-Pierre Wallot, "La pensée révolutionnaire et réformiste dans le Bas-Canada, 1773–1815," in *Un Québec qui bougeait: Trame socio-politique du Québec au tournant de XIXe siècle* (Editions du Boréal Express, 1973), 80, 256–57.
24 Pierre Foretier, "Notes and Reminiscences," in *Report of the Department of Public Archives for the Year 1945*, Dominion of Canada (Edmond Cloutier, 1946), xxii–vi.
25 Shortt and Doughty, *Documents*, vol. 2, 675.
26 George Rawlyk, *Revolution Rejected: 1775–1776* (Prentice-Hall, 1968), 10.
27 "From Benjamin Franklin to Charles Carroll and Samuel Chase, 27 May 1776," *Founders Online*, NARA.
28 Smith, *Letters*, vol. 3, 650–51, 666.
29 Smith, *Letters*, vol. 4, 4–5.
30 Force, *American Archives, 4th Series*, vol. 6, 587.
31 Kingsford, *History*, vol. 6, 78.
32 Force, *American Archives, 4th Series*, vol. 6, 812.
33 Smith, *Letters*, vol. 4, 365–66.
34 Ford, *Journals*, vol. 2, 289.
35 "Jane Mecom to Catherine Greene: Extract, Philadelphia 1st June 1776," *Franklin Papers Online*, franklinpapers.org.
36 "From Benjamin Franklin to Emma Thompson, 8 February 1777," *Founders Online*, NARA.
37 "From Benjamin Franklin to John Jay, 2 June 1779," *Founders Online*, NARA.
38 Force, *American Archives, 4th series*, vol. 6, 588.
39 "Sketch of Propositions for a Peace, [after 26 September 1776 and before 25 October 1776]," *Founders Online*, NARA.

CHAPTER 9: THE FINAL ATTEMPT: PARIS 1776–1783

1 "From Benjamin Franklin to John Adams, 20 April 1782," *Founders Online*, NARA.
2 Charles Sumner, "Monograph from an Old Notebook; With a Postscript: Eripuit Coelo Fulmen, Septrumque Tyrannis," *The Atlantic*, November 1863, 651.
3 "From Benjamin Franklin to Jane Mecom, 8 December 1776," *Founders Online*, NARA.

4 Jacques Barbeu Dubourg, trans., *Oeuvres de M. Franklin* (Quilleau, 1773).
5 George H. Guttridge, ed., *The Correspondence of Edmund Burke*, vol. 3 (University of Chicago Press, 1961), 310.
6 Francis Wharton, *The Revolutionary Diplomatic Correspondence of the United States*, vol. 2 (Government Printing Office, 1889), 231–32, 247, 257.
7 "A Plan of Treaties as Adopted (With Instructions)," *Papers of John Adams*, vol. 4, Adams Papers Digital Edition.
8 Ramsay, *History*, vol. 2, 60–61.
9 Smith, *Letters*, vol. 3, 179.
10 Étienne Françoise de Choiseul, "Memoire de Choiseul remis au Roy en 1765," *Journal des Savants* (January 1881): 178–79.
11 "From Benjamin Franklin to William Franklin, 28 August 1767," *Founders Online*, NARA.
12 John J. Meng, "The Place of Canada in French Diplomacy of the American Revolution," *Bulletin des recherches historiques* XXXIX (1933): 667.
13 Henri Doniol, *Histoire de la participation de la France à l'établissement des États-Unis d'Amérique*, vol. 1 (Imprimerie Nationale, 1886), 273.
14 Doniol, *Histoire*, vol. 1, 273; and Samuel Flagg Bemis, *The Diplomacy of the American Revolution* (Indiana University Press, 1967), 19.
15 Doniol, *Histoire*, vol. 1, 243–44.
16 Henry Steele Commager and Richard B. Morris, eds., *The Spirit of 'Seventy-Six: The Story of the American Revolution as Told by Participants* (Harper & Row, 1967), 681–82.
17 Meng, "The Place," 683–84.
18 Jared Sparks, *Lord Stormont Correspondence, 1776–1778*, MS Sparks 61, vol. 1, Houghton Library, Harvard University.
19 "From Benjamin Franklin to Bethia Alexander, 24 June 1782," *Founders Online*, NARA.
20 Charles Sumner, "Monograph," 651.
21 "From Benjamin Franklin to Emma Thompson, 8 February 1777," *Founders Online*, NARA.
22 Louis Philippe de Ségur, *Mémoires ou souvenirs et anecdotes*, vol. 1 (A. Eymery, 1824–1826), 116–17.
23 Durand Echeverria, *Mirage in the West: A History of the French Image of American Society to 1815* (Octagon Books, 1966), 62, 64.
24 Benjamin Hoy, *A Line of Blood and Dirt: Creating the Canada-United States Border Across Indigenous Lands* (Oxford University Press, 2021), 333–35; Smith, *Letters*, vol. 3, n9, 323; Meng, "The Place," 671–72.

25 Sparks, *Stormont Correspondence*, 269.
26 "From Benjamin Franklin to James Hutton, 1 February 1778," *Founders Online*, NARA.
27 "From Benjamin Franklin to David Hartley, 12 February 1778," *Founders Online*, NARA.
28 "From Benjamin Franklin to David Hartley, 26 October 1778," *Founders Online*, NARA.
29 Murray G. Lawson, "Canada and the Articles of Confederation," *American Historical Review* 58, no. 1 (October 1952): 49; Ford, *Journals*, vol. 12, 1041–48.
30 "From George Washington to Henry Laurens, 14 November 1778," *Founders Online*, NARA.
31 Ford, *Journals*, vol. 13, 363–67.
32 Warren, *History*, vol. 2, 132–33.
33 Ford, *Journals*, vol. 14, 959–62.
34 Thomas Hodgins, "British and American Diplomacy Affecting Canada," *Canadian Magazine* 10, no. 5 (March 1898): 380.
35 "To Benjamin Franklin from the Earl of Shelburne, 6 April 1782," *Founders Online*, NARA.
36 John Bigelow, ed., *The Works of Benjamin Franklin, including the Private as well as the Official and Scientific Correspondence, together with the Unmutilated and Correct Version of the Autobiography*, vol. 3 (G. P. Putnam's Sons, 1904), 77–78, 80, 82.
37 "'Supplement to the Boston Independent Chronicle,' [before 22 April 1782]," *Founders Online*, NARA.
38 "Franklin: Journal of the Peace Negotiations, 9 May[–1 July 1782]," *Founders Online*, NARA.
39 Bigelow, *Works*, vol. 9, 375–76.
40 Bigelow, *Works*, vol. 8, 408.
41 Bigelow, *Works*, vol. 9, 423; Edmond George Fitzmaurice, *Life of William Earl of Shelburne*, vol. 2, *1776–1785* (Macmillan, 1912), 173–75.
42 Augustin Belloste, "Analysis of Belloste's Pills, and their Manner of operating in the Human Body, by the Author himself; with full Directions for Using of this Remedy," *Eighteenth Century Collections Online*, 12.
43 Fitzmaurice, *Shelburne*, vol. 2, 194.
44 Fitzmaurice, *Shelburne*, vol. 2, n1, 180.
45 Wharton, *Diplomatic Correspondence*, vol. 6, 82–84.
46 "Proposed Articles for the Definitive Peace Treaty, [ca. 10–13 December 1782]," *Founders Online*, NARA.

47 Wharton, *Diplomatic Correspondence*, vol. 6, 131–32.
48 Wharton, *Diplomatic Correspondence*, vol. 6, 107, 131–32, 140; and Hodgins, *Diplomacy*, 387.
49 William Corbett, ed., *The parliamentary history of England, from the earliest period to the year 1803: from which last-mentioned epoch it is continued downwards in the work entitled, "The parliamentary debates,"* vol. XXIII (T. C. Hansard, 1814), 381–84, 397, 409–11, 464–65.
50 Smith, *Letters*, vol. 20, xx–xxi, xxiii, 10, 16, 34–35.
51 "Notes on Debates, 12–15 March 1783," *Founders Online*, NARA.
52 Smith, *Letters*, vol. 19, 639.
53 Smith, *Letters*, vol. 20, 237.
54 Isaacson, *Franklin*, 433.
55 Edmund Cody Burnett, *Letters of Members of the Continental Congress*, vol. 8 (Carnegie Institution of Washington, 1936), 315.
56 Lisa Gensel, "The Medical World of Benjamin Franklin," *Journal of the Royal Society of Medicine* 98, no. 12 (December 2005): 537.
57 "From John Adams to William Cranch, 19 March 1812," *Founders Online*, NARA.
58 "John Adams to Thomas Jefferson, 28 June 1812," *Founders Online*, NARA.
59 William R. Manning, ed., *Diplomatic Correspondence of the United States: Canadian Relations, 1784–1860*, vol. 1, *1784–1820* (Carnegie Endowment for International Peace, 1940), 200–204, 206, 211, 213, 641–43.
60 "By this morning's mail, we have received the proclamation of Brigadier-General Hull, to the inhabitants of Canada, which is here presented to our readers in an extra sheet: By William Hull," *Western Intelligencer*, July 20, 1812.
61 "General Smyth: To the Soldiers of the Army of the Center," *The War* 1, no. 24 (December 5, 1812): 103.
62 Manning, *Diplomatic Correspondence*, vol. 1, 214–16, 221, 672.
63 "Thomas Jefferson to William Duane, 4 August 1812," *Founders Online*, NARA.
64 *The Debates and Proceedings in the Congress of the United States, Thirteenth Congress, First Session* (Gales and Seaton, 1854), 952–55.

EPILOGUE: LETTING THE LOSERS WRITE CANADA'S HISTORY

1 Paul Ricoeur, *Memory, History, Forgetting* (University of Chicago Press, 2004), 452.
2 "Robert James Hunter to the Post Office," May 27, 1976, RG Series C-2, Box 103, file 208-7-60-U4, Library and Archives Canada.

3 Institut canadien de Québec, *Annuaire de l'Institut canadien de Québec* no. 3 (1876): 7–11.

4 H. J. J. B. Chouinard, *Troisième centenaire de la foundation de Québec, berceau du Canada, par Champlain, 1608–1908* (Laflamme & Proulx, 1908).

5 Nicole Neatby, "'Leaving the Past Behind': From Old Quebec to 'La Belle Province,'" in *Settling and Unsettling Memories: Essays in Canadian Public History*, ed. Nicole Neatby and Peter Hodgins (University of Toronto Press, 2012), 504.

6 H. V. Nelles, *The Art of Nation-Building: Pageantry and Spectacle at Quebec's Tercentenary* (University of Toronto Press, 1999), 36, 46, 76–77, 89, 190–92.

7 Alan Gordon, "Fissured Heritage Elites," in *Making Public Pasts: The Contested Terrain of Montreal's Public Memories, 1891–1930* (McGill-Queen's University Press, 2001), 50–64.

8 Rev. Dr. Scadding, *Brief Memoir of the Old French Fort at Toronto* (Copp Clark, 1884), 1–7.

9 Konrad Yakabuski, "Quebec's new history museum proposes an ethnocentric vision of the province's past," *Globe and Mail*, May 10, 2024.

10 Ken Burns, "Ken Burns turns his lens on Benjamin Franklin and delivers a lesson for the present day," interview by Piya Chattopadhyay, *The Sunday Magazine with Piya Chattopadhyay*, CBC Radio, April 3, 2022.

11 Eric Hobsbawm and Terence Ranger, eds., *The Invention of Tradition* (Cambridge University Press, 2007), 4, 12–13, 263.

12 William Pulteney, *An Appeal to Reason and Justice in Behalf of the British Constitution* (W. Nicholl, 1778).

13 Ramsay Cook, *Canada and the French-Canadian Question* (Macmillan, 1966), 119, 121.

14 J. L. Granatstein, *Yankee Go Home?: Canadians and Anti-Americanism* (HarperCollins, 1996), 2.

15 Justin Trudeau, "Diversity Is Canada's Strength," Speech at Canada House, London, U.K., November 26, 2015.

16 Charles Foran, "The Canada Experiment: Is This the World's First 'Post National' Country?," *The Guardian*, January 4, 2017.

17 Petra Dolata, "A New Canada in the Arctic? Arctic Policies under Harper," *Études canadiennes/Canadian Studies* 78 (2015): 131–54.

18 Kristin Bartenstein, "'Use It or Lose It': An Appropriate and Wise Slogan?," *Policy Options* (July 1, 2010).

19 David Eric Jessup, "J.E. Bernier and the Assertion of Canadian Sovereignty in the Arctic," *American Review of Canadian Studies* 38, no. 4 (2008): 409–27.

20 "Agenda, Interdepartmental Meeting on Canadian Participation in U.S. Bicentennial Celebrations," July 26, 1973, RG Series C-2, Box 26, file 208-5-50-A16, Library and Archives Canada.
21 Brown, "Buster," 257–58; and Swanson, "National Security Threat," 9–16.
22 Jay Famiglietti, "Will We Have to Pump the Great Lakes to California to Feed the Nation?," *New York Times*, August 5, 2024.
23 Spencer Van Dyk, "Trump Making 'Joke' About Canada Becoming 51st State Is 'Reassuring': Ambassador Hillman," *CTV News*, December 4, 2024.

Selected Bibliography

Books

Anderson, Fred. *Crucible of War: The Seven Years' War and the Fate of Empire in British North America, 1754–1766*. Vintage Books, 2001.

Anderson, Mark R. *Invasion of Canada by the Americans, 1775–1776, as Told Through Jean-Baptiste Badeaux's Three Rivers Journal and New York Captain William Goforth's Letters*. SUNY Press, 2016.

Boyd, Julian P., ed. *The Papers of Thomas Jefferson*. 30 vols. Princeton University Press, 1950–present.

Brunet, Michel. *Les Canadiens après la conquête*. Fides, 1969.

Bunker, Nick. *An Empire on the Edge: How Britain Came to Fight America*. Vintage, 2015.

Burnett, Edmund Cody, ed. *Letters of Members of the Continental Congress*. 8 vols. Carnegie Institution of Washington, 1864–1949.

Carroll, Charles. *Journal: Charles Carroll of Carrollton, During his Visit to Canada in 1776*. Maryland Historical Society, 1876.

Cavendish, Henry, ed. *Debates of the House of Commons in the Year 1774 on the Bill for Making More Effectual Provision for the Government of the Province of Quebec*. Ridgway, 1839.

Colley, Linda. *Britons*. Yale University Press, 2005.

Commager, Henry Steele, and Richard B. Morris, eds. *The Spirit of 'Seventy-Six: The Story of the American Revolution as Told by Participants*. Harper & Row, 1967.

Corbett, William, ed. *Parliamentary history of England, from the earliest period to the year 1803: from which last-mentioned epoch it is continued downwards in the work entitled, "The parliamentary debates."* 36 vols. T. C. Hansard, 1812–1820.

de Choiseul, Étienne Françoise. "Mémoire de Choiseul remis au Roy en 1765." *Journal des Savants* (January 1881).

———. *Mémoire historique sur la negotiation de la France et de l'Angleterre depuis le 26 mars 1761 jusqu'au 26 septembre de la même année*. Wilson, Becket & De Hondt, 1761.

Doniol, Henri. *Histoire de la participation de la France à l'établissement des États-Unis d'Amérique*. 5 vols. and supplement. Imprimerie Nationale, 1886–1900.

Echeverria, Durand. *Mirage in the West: A History of the French Image of American Society to 1815*. Octagon Books, 1966.

Fitzmaurice, Edmond George. *Life of William Earl of Shelburne*. Vol. 2, *1776–1785*. Macmillan, 1912.

Force, Peter, ed. *American Archives, Fourth Series and Fifth Series*. 9 vols. Clarke and Force, 1837–1853.

Ford, Worthington Chauncey, ed. *Journals of the Continental Congress, 1774–1789*. 34 vols. Government Printing Office, 1904–1937.

Franklin, Benjamin. *Benjamin Franklin's Letters to the Press, 1758–1775*. Edited by Verner W. Crane. University of North Carolina Press, 1950.

———. *Benjamin Franklin's Memoirs*. Edited by Max Farrand. University of California Press, 1949.

———. *Observations Concerning the Increase of Mankind, Peopling of Countries, &c*. S. Kneeland, 1755.

———. *The Papers of Benjamin Franklin*. Digital Edition. American Philosophical Society and Yale University, n.d.

———. *The Works of Benjamin Franklin*. Edited by Jared Sparks. 10 vols. Townsend Mac Coun., 1882.

———. *The Works of Benjamin Franklin, including the Private as well as the Official and Scientific Correspondence, together with the Unmutilated and Correct Version of the Autobiography*. Edited by John Bigelow. 12 vols. G. P. Putnam's Sons, 1904.

———. *The Writings of Benjamin Franklin*. Edited by Albert Henry Smyth. 10 vols. Macmillan, 1906. 10 vols.

Gabriel, Michael P., ed. *Quebec During the American Invasion, 1775–1776: The Journal of François Baby, Gabriel Taschereau, and Jenkin Williams*. Michigan University Press, 2005.

Garneau, François-Xavier. *Histoire du Canada: Depuis sa decouverte jusqu'à nos jours*. 4 vols. Imprimerie de Fréchette et Frère, 1845–1848.

Greene, Jack P. *Evaluating Empire and Confronting Colonialism in Eighteenth-Century Britain*. Cambridge University Press, 2013.

Groulx, Lionel Adolphe. *Lendmains de conquête*. Bibliothèque de l'Action française, 1920.

Hale, Edward E., and Edward E. Hale Jr. *Franklin in France; from original documents, most of which are now published for the first time*. 2 vols. Roberts Brothers, 1888.

Hobsbawm, Eric, and Terence Ranger, eds. *The Invention of Tradition*. Cambridge University Press, 2007.

Institut canadien de Québec. *Annuaire de l'Institut canadien de Québec*, no. 3 (1876).

Isaacson, Walter. *Benjamin Franklin: An American Life*. Simon & Schuster, 2004.

Kingsford, William. *A History of Canada*. 10 vols. Roswell & Hutchison, 1887–1898.

Lamonde, Yvan. *Ni avec eux ni sans eux*. Nota Bene, 1996.

Lanctôt, Gustave. *Canada and the American Revolution, 1774–1783*. Translated by Margaret M. Cameron. George G. Harrap, 1967.

Lemay, J. A. Leo. *The Life of Benjamin Franklin*. 3 vols. University of Pennsylvanian Press, 2005–2008.

Lennox, Jeffers. *North of America: Loyalists, Indigenous Nations, and the Borders of the Long American Revolution*. Yale University Press, 2022.

Manning, William R., ed. *Diplomatic Correspondence of the United States: Canadian Relations, 1784–1860*. Carnegie Endowment for International Peace, 1940.

Mulford, Carla J. *Benjamin Franklin and the Ends of Empire*. Oxford University Press, 2015.

Nelles, H. V. *The Art of Nation-Building: Pageantry and Spectacle at Quebec's Tercentenary*. University of Toronto Press, 1999.

O'Callaghan, E. B., ed. *Documents Relative to the Colonial History of the State of New York*. 15 vols. Weed, Parsons, 1853–1887.

Ouellet, Richard, and Jean-Pierre Therrien, eds. *L'invasion du Canada par les Bastonnois: Journal de M. Sanguinet*. Ministère des Affaires culturelles, 1975.

Parkman, Francis. *Half-Century of Conflict: France and England in North America*. 2 vols. Little, Brown, 1907.

Ramsay, David. *History of the American Revolution*. 2 vols. Downing and Phillips, 1789, 1815.

Roberts, Kenneth. *March to Quebec: Journals of the Members of Arnold's Expedition*. Doubleday, Doran, 1938.

Roy, Pierre-Georges, ed. *Voltaire, Mme de Pompadour et quelques arpents de neige*. Pierre-Georges Roy, 1898.

Shortt, Adam, and Arthur G. Doughty, eds. *Documents relating to the constitutional history of Canada, 1759–1791*. 2nd and revised ed. J. de L. Taché, 1918.

Shovlin, John. *Trading with the Enemy*. Yale University Press, 2021.

Silhouette, Étienne. *Mémoires des commissaires du roi et de ceux de Sa Majesté britannique sur les possessions & les droits respectifs des deux couronnes en Amérique — avec les actes publics & pièces justificatives*. 4 vols. l'Imprimerie royale, 1755–1757.

Smith, Paul H., ed. *Letters of Delegates to Congress, 1774–1789*. 26 vols. Library of Congress, 1976–2000.

Sparks, Jared. *The Life of Benjamin Franklin*. Blakeman and Mason, 1859.

Stockdale, John, ed. *Parliamentary Register; Or, History of the Proceedings And Debates of the House of Commons: Containing an Account of the Most Interesting Speeches And Motions, Accurate Copies of the Most Remarkable Letters And Papers, of the Most Material Evidence, Petitions, &c. Laid Before And Offered to the House*. 17 vols. T. Gillet, 1802.

Stourzh, Gerald. *Benjamin Franklin and American Foreign Policy*. 2nd ed. University of Chicago Press, 1969.

Trudel, Marcel. *La revolution américaine: Pourquoi la France refuse le Canada: 1775–1783*. Éditions de Boréal Express, 1976.

Van Doren, Carl. *Benjamin Franklin*. Penguin Books, 1991.

Verreau, H. A. *Invasion du Canada par les Américans: Collection de mémoires*. Eusébe Senégal, 1873.

Warren, Mercy Otis. *History of the Rise, Progress, and Termination of the American Revolution: Interspersed with biographical, political and moral observations*. 3 vols. E. Larkin, 1805.

Wharton, Francis. *The Revolutionary Diplomatic Correspondence of the United States*. 6 vols. Government Printing Office, 1889.

White, Richard. *The Middle Ground*. Cambridge University Press, 2011.

Wood, Gordon S. *The Americanization of Benjamin Franklin*. Penguin, 2004.

Book Chapters

Caron, Ivanhoë. "Les Canadiens Français et l'invasion américaine de 1774–1775." In *Mémoires et comptes rendus de la Société royale du Canada*, vol. 23, Third Series, First Section, May 1929.

Fyson, Donald. "The Conquered and the Conqueror." In *Revisiting 1759: The Conquest of Canada in Historical Perspective*, edited by Phillip A. Buckner and John G. Reid. University of Toronto Press, 2012.

———. "The Quebec Act and French Canadians: The Myth of the Seminal Moment." In *Entangling the Quebec Act*, edited by François Furstenberg and Hubert Ollivier. McGill-Queen's, 2020.

Lennox, Jeffers. "Revolution Expected: The Invasion of Quebec and American Independence." In *Violence, Order, and Unrest: A History of British North America, 1749—1876*, edited by Elizabeth Manke, Jerry Bannister, and Denis McKim. University of Toronto Press, 2019.

Marshall, P. J. "William Burke and Guadeloupe." In *Edmund Burke and the British Empire in the West Indies: Wealth, Power, and Slavery*. Oxford University Press, 2019.

Neatby, Nicole. "'Leaving the Past Behind': From Old Quebec to 'La Belle Province.'" In *Settling and Unsettling Memories: Essays in Canadian Public History*, edited by Nicole Neatby and Peter Hodgins. University of Toronto Press, 2012.

Wallot, Jean-Pierre. "La pensée révolutionnaire et réformiste dans le Bas-Canada, 1773–1815." In *Un Québec qui bougeait: Trame socio-politique du Québec au tournant de XIXe siècle*. Editions du Boréal Express, 1973.

Articles

Curtis, Thomas D. "Riches, Real Estate, and Resistance: How Land Speculation, Debt, and Trade Monopolies Led to the American Revolution." *American Journal of Economics and Sociology* 73, no. 3 (July 2014): 474–626.

Dewar, Helen. "Canada or Guadeloupe? French and British Perceptions of Empire, 1760–1763." *Canadian Historical Review* 91, no. 4 (December 2010): 637–60.

Edney, Matthew H. "John Mitchell's Map of North America (1755): A Study of the Use and Publication of Official Maps in Eighteenth-Century Britain." *Imago Mundi* 60, no. 1 (2008): 63–85.

Ellison, Amy Noel. "Montgomery's Misfortune." *Early American Studies: An Interdisciplinary Journal* 15, no. 3 (Summer 2017): 591–616.

Griffith, Sally F. "'Order, Discipline, and a Few Cannon': Benjamin Franklin, the Association, and the Rhetoric and Practice of Boosterism." *Pennsylvania Magazine of History and Biography* 116, no. 2 (April 1992): 131–55.

James, Alfred P. "Benjamin Franklin's Ohio Valley Lands." *Proceedings of the American Philosophical Society* 98, no. 4 (August 16, 1954): 255–65.

Lena, Alberto. "Benjamin Franklin's 'Canada Pamphlet' or 'The Ravings of a Mad Prophet': Nationalism, Ethnicity and Imperialism." *European Journal of American Culture* 20, no. 1 (April 2001): 36–49.

Leyland, Herbert T. "The Ohio Company: A Colonial Corporation." *Quarterly Publication of the Historical and Philosophical Society of Ohio* 16, no. 1 (January–June 1921): 1–20.

Meng, John J. "The Place of Canada in French Diplomacy of the American Revolution." *Bulletin des recherches historiques* XXXIX (1933): 666–87.

Riddell, William Renwick. "Benjamin Franklin and Canada." *Pennsylvania Magazine of History and Biography* 48, no. 2 (1924): 111–58.

Trudel, Marcel. "The Jumonville Affair." *Quarterly Journal of the Pennsylvania Historical and Museum Commission* XXI, no. 4 (October 1954): 351–81.

Map Credits

Page 10: A French View of North America, 1708

Based on two 1708 maps by French cartographer Guillaume de l'Isle, *L'Amerique septentrionale: dressée sur les observations de Mrs. de l'Academie Royale des Sciences & quelques autres, & sur les memoires les plus recens* and *Carte du Canada ou de la Nouvelle France et des decouvertes que y ont ete faites. Dressee sur plusieurs observations et sur un grand nombre de relations imprimees ou manuscrites.* Sources: David Rumsey Map Collection and New York Public Library Digital Collections.

Page 16: Major Indigenous Peoples in Eastern North America, 1763

Based on a segment of the map *Indian Groups, Regions, and Topography of the North American Interior*, from Fred Anderson, *Crucible of War* (Vintage Books, 2000).

Page 30: A British View of North America, 1733

Based on a segment of the 1733 map by British cartographer Henry Popple, *A map of the British Empire in America with the French and Spanish settlements adjacent thereto.* Sources: Library of Congress and Barry Lawrence Ruderman Antique Maps.

Page 44: A French View of Eastern North America, 1755

Based on a 1755 map by French cartographer Jacques-Nicolas Bellin, *Partie Orientale de la Nouvelle France ou du Canada.* Source: Bibliothèque nationale de France, département Cartes et plans, GE C-10919.

Page 62: A British View of North America, 1755

Based on a 1755 map by British cartographer John Mitchell, *A map of the British and French dominions in North America, with the roads, distances, limits, and extent of the settlements, humbly inscribed to the Right Honourable the Earl of Halifax, and the other Right Honourable the Lords Commissioners for Trade & Plantations.* Source: Library of Congress.

Page 63: A French View of North America, 1755

Based on a segment of the 1755 map by French cartographer Jacques-Nicolas Bellin, *Carte de l'Amérique septentrionale depuis le 28 degré de latitude jusqu'au 72e.* Source: Bibliothèque nationale de France, département Cartes et plans, GE DD-2987 (8534 B).

Page 84: A British View of North America After the 1763 Royal Proclamation

Based on a 1763 map by British cartographer John Gibson, *The British Governments in North America, Laid Down Agreeable to the Proclamation of Oct. 7, 1763.* Source: Tennessee Virtual Archive.

Page 108: A British View of North America After the 1774 Quebec Act

Based on the 1777 map by British cartographers William Faden and Thomas Jefferys, *The North American atlas, selected from the most authentic maps, charts, plans, &c. hitherto published*, with the 1763 proclamation line taken from the 1763 map by British cartographer John Gibson, *The British Governments in North America, Laid Down Agreeable to the Proclamation of Oct. 7, 1763*. Source: Library of Congress.

Page 122: Major Land Speculation Proposals, 1763–1775

Based on the map *Proposed Western Colonies, 1763–1775*, in *The American Nation: A History*, vol. 8, edited by Albert Bushnell Hart (Harper and Brothers, 1905).

Page 134: American Invasion Routes, 1775

Based on a 1777 map by British cartographer William Faden and French cartographer Claude Joseph Sauthier, *A map of the inhabited part of Canada from the French surveys, with the frontiers of New York and New England*; with further details from *A view of the rivers Kenebec and Chaudiere, with Colonel Arnold's route to Quebec*, unattributed; a 1755 map by British cartographer John Mitchell, *Mr. Jay's Map: Extract from a Map of the British and French Dominions in North America*; and a 1795 map depicting the New England states, marked with the route of Benedict Arnold's expedition to Quebec City in September 1775. Sources: Library of Congress, New York Public Library Digital Collections, and Geographicus Rare Antique Maps.

Page 160: Plan of the Town of Montreal, 1758

Based on a 1764 map by French cartographer Jacques-Nicolas Bellin, *L'isle de Montréal et ses environs*, and on a 1758 map by British cartographer Thomas Jefferys, *Plan of the Town and Fortifications of Montreal or Ville Marie in Canada*, which appeared in the November 1759 edition of the *Universal*

Magazine. Sources: Bibliothèque nationale de France, département Cartes et plans, GE DD-2987 (8685); and Barry Lawrence Ruderman Antique Maps.

Page 184: The Borders of Canada and the United States, 1783

Based on a 1783 map by British cartographer John Wallis, *The United States of America As Laid Down from the Best Authorities, Agreeable to the Peace of 1783*. Source: Library of Congress.

Index

Note: Page numbers in italics refer to images, and numbers with an *m* refer to maps

About the Author

Madelaine Drohan is an award-winning author and former foreign correspondent who covered business and politics in Canada, Europe, and Africa. She was Canada correspondent for *The Economist* from 2006 to 2020 and European correspondent for *The Globe and Mail* from 1991 to 1999. Her book *Making a Killing: How and Why Corporations Use Armed Force to Do Business* won the Ottawa Book Award and was short-listed for the National Business Book of the Year Award in 2004. She has held research fellowships with the Public Policy Forum (2015–2016), the Chumir Foundation for Ethics in Leadership (2004–2005), and the Thomson Reuters Foundation at the University of Oxford (1998–1999). She is a senior fellow at the Graduate School of Public and International Affairs at the University of Ottawa.